White Voters in 21st Century America

I0121798

The United States is experiencing remarkable demographic changes that are having an important impact on the American electorate. As the minority share of the voting-eligible population continues to grow, the political clout of non-Hispanic whites will further decline. The 2012 election demonstrated that the Democratic Party can secure an Electoral College victory even when it loses badly, in the aggregate, among non-Hispanic whites. This does not mean that white voters are unimportant, however. The political behavior of whites in the decades ahead will largely determine the direction of American politics.

This book examines the political behavior of non-Hispanic whites. It considers the trends within the white vote, how white voters differ geographically, and the primary fault lines among white voters. It also examines how white political behavior changes in response to diversity. It considers whether or not the day is approaching when whites consolidate into a largely homogeneous voting bloc, or whether whites will remain politically heterogeneous in the decades ahead.

Whereas other books have examined the political behavior of specific social classes within the non-Hispanic white community (working-class whites, for example), this is the first book to examine whites as a whole and to provide a useful summary of recent trends within this group and thoughtful speculation about its future.

George Hawley is Assistant Professor of Political Science at the University of Alabama. His research interests include demography, electoral behavior, political parties, immigration policy, and the U.S. Congress.

Routledge Research in American Politics and Governance

White Voters in 21st Century America

George Hawley

Routledge
Taylor & Francis Group

NEW YORK AND LONDON

First published 2015
by Routledge
711 Third Avenue, New York, NY 10017, USA

and by Routledge
2 Park Square, Milton Park, Abingdon, Oxfordshire OX14 4RN

First issued in paperback 2017

Routledge is an imprint of the Taylor & Francis Group, an informa business

Library of Congress Cataloging-in-Publication Data
Hawley, George (Political scientist)
    White voters in 21st century America / George Hawley.
        pages cm — (Routledge research in american politics and governance)
    1. Voting—United States.   2. Elections—United States.   3. Whites—United States—Politics and government.   4. Whites—Race identity—United States.   5. Whites—United States—Social conditions.   I. Title.
    JK1967.H38   2014
    324.973'093208909—dc23
    2014015940

ISBN 13: 978-1-138-06624-3 (pbk)
ISBN 13: 978-1-138-01774-0 (hbk)

Typeset in Sabon
by Apex CoVantage, LLC

For Henry

Contents

Figures

Tables

Acknowledgments

While it deals with a decidedly different topic, this book was a natural extension of my doctoral dissertation and my previous book, *Voting and Migration Patterns in the U.S.* While working on that project, it became apparent that in many ways the migratory patterns—and the political consequences of those migratory patterns—of non-Hispanic whites were decidedly different from other groups within the American electorate. This increased my curiosity about white voter behavior, and while preparing my previous book manuscript I began to think of new questions. While I initially planned to write a series of discrete articles on similar subjects, it soon became apparent that each of my new questions fit within a single theme and therefore should be considered in a single volume.

Because this work immediately followed my previous book, I wish to thank many of the same people. Members of my dissertation committee, which included Richard Murray, Jeronimo Cortina, and Jennifer Clark of the University of Houston, and James Gimpel of the University of Maryland, have all been vital to my development as a scholar. I also thank my former colleagues at the University of Houston Honors College, Jacqueline Hunsicker and Jeremy Bailey.

I am also grateful to new colleagues who have been tremendously helpful. I am thankful to Richard Fording, chair of the Political Science Department at the University of Alabama, for negotiating my summer research funding in 2013.

I am grateful to Rick and Leslie Whiston for their generosity during the summer of 2013. Without their kindness and support, this book would have taken considerably longer to complete. I am also grateful to Arlene DiPietro, who exhibited incredible patience and generosity during a very difficult time for our family. Stan Evans was also a major source of encouragement. My parents have also been an important source of support throughout my intellectual development.

Unless I am actually in the classroom, I prefer not to talk about politics. This ceases to be true if I am near a campfire in the North Cascades. I am grateful to my non-academic friends for putting up with my annual rants. I am more grateful to them for serving as my unpaid focus group, giving me insights into how Americans not ensconced in academia feel about trends in national politics. I give special thanks to Adam Baldridge, Ryan Byers, Ryan Cavanaugh, Andy Erikson, Brady Kornelis, Zach Marquess, Stephen Martuscelli, Phil Melson, Steve Vanko, Joe Willis, and Anthony Wilson.

I am thankful to the editorial staff at Routledge, especially Darcy Bullock and Natalja Mortensen, for helping me through this process. I am similarly grateful to the anonymous reviewers for catching several major mistakes and offering suggestions that greatly improved this work.

As always, I am grateful to my wife, Kristen, for her support and encouragement, and for her patience with me as I worked bizarre hours in order to finish this manuscript. Kristen is my most diligent editor and my best sounding board. My son Henry also provided a great incentive to complete this project in a timely manner; I am thankful that he decided to adopt a more regular sleep schedule at a crucial time. I apologize to Jasper for taking him on fewer neighborhood walks in recent months and for moving to a city without a dog park.

If this book makes any contribution to the field of political science, credit must be shared with all of the preceding people. Any mistakes that appear in this work belong to me alone.

Introduction
Thinking about White Voters

To a meaningful extent, this book's existence is a sign of the profound demographic changes that have occurred in the United States in the last 50 years.[1] In the early 1960s, discussing "white voters" in the United States would have been redundant. It would have been sufficient to title this book, *Voters*. Outside of the South, Indian reservations, and many urban areas, most of the United States was overwhelmingly white. The South had the largest minority population, and in this region African Americans were largely prohibited from voting. Thus, the Venn diagram of all voters and white voters would have almost perfectly overlapped. As a result of the Voting Rights Act and large-scale, consistent immigration from Latin America, Asia, and Africa, that is no longer the case. As this century progresses, whites will continue to shrink as an overall percentage of the electorate.

In 2011, the number of minority births (minority defined as anyone who is not racially white or who ethnically identifies as Latino) outnumbered the number of white births for the first time in U.S. history.[2] Non-Hispanic whites are expected to be a minority of the U.S. population by the middle of the 21st century. As a result, pundits, political activists, and political scientists have taken a justified interest in the voting patterns of minority voters, as their political clout will continue to grow in the decades ahead.

The decline of whites as the dominant force in the electorate is further exacerbated by the decline in white voter turnout in comparison to other racial groups. Whereas the turnout rate of whites was once far higher than the turnout rate of most other racial groups, this is no longer necessarily true. In 2012, the voter turnout rate for African Americans was not just higher than the turnout rate for other minority groups; some evidence suggests it was higher than the turnout rate for whites.[3] Whether white turnout rates will remain comparatively low in the future remains to be seen, but this trend can only hasten the decline of white political influence.

In recent years, there has been a noticeable change in public discourse regarding race and vote choice. Indeed, judging by the tone of recent commentary, whites transitioned from being so overwhelmingly dominant that they did not need to be discussed as a unique voting group to being all but irrelevant, seemingly overnight. It is frequently noted that the Republican

Party's failure to lure a greater share of the non-white vote will doom the party to irrelevancy. The Republican Party is now derided as "male, pale, and stale,"[4] as though winning by large margins among a large group in the electorate is a source of weakness. The fact that the Democratic Party, which has long failed to win a majority of white voters, has experienced a slow decline in its share of the white vote in presidential elections is not treated as a similarly interesting development by most commentators.

It is not just liberal pundits and mainstream journalists who deride the Republican Party's status as the "white party." Following Mitt Romney's loss in the 2012 presidential election, the Republican National Committee (RNC) released a memo detailing the party's mistakes and ways it can improve its electoral fortunes in the future.[5] What immediately stands out is that the memo focused almost entirely on minorities in the electorate. It called for immediate Republican support for immigration reform, which presumably means a pathway to citizenship for undocumented immigrants. It suggested the party must reach out to minority groups such as the National Association for the Advancement of Colored People and the National Council of La Raza. It also suggested the party must embrace more liberal positions on gay rights.

Reports on the demise of whites as an important segment of the electorate may be premature. The above-mentioned memo and other comments made by Republican and conservative leaders imply a number of assumptions on their part. First of all, these comments suggest that the Republican Party has reached a ceiling in its support from whites. This may not be true. A neglected result of the 2012 presidential election was that Romney performed worse among whites in a few critical swing states than he performed among whites nationwide. In Ohio and Pennsylvania, states in which whites remain the overwhelming majority of the electorate and will remain the majority of voters for many election cycles to come, exit polls show that Romney won 57 percent of white voters. In Wisconsin, he won 51 percent of the white vote. In Iowa and New Hampshire, he won only 47 percent of all votes cast by whites. Nationwide, Romney won 59 percent of the white vote. Had Romney performed as well among whites in these battleground states as he performed among whites in the nation overall, he would have won the election. One can easily imagine the Republican Party boosting its share of the white vote in these critical states in future presidential elections, securing an Electoral College victory even if the party fails to make significant gains in its share of the minority vote.

Another assumption that Republican leaders and conservative pundits apparently make when making prescriptions for further minority outreach is that the party can make significant inroads among Latinos, Asian Americans, African Americans, and members of the LGBT community of all races and ethnicities by making few, if any, changes to their policy platform. They may be mistaken. Suggestions in the RNC memo regarding African American voters were entirely focused on engaging with members of that community, rather than making any particular policy changes—as though public policies have nothing to do with African American support for the Democratic Party.

To improve the party's position among Latinos, the memo focused almost exclusively on immigration reform. While Latinos are more in favor of liberalizing immigration reforms than other segments of the electorate, it is not true that immigration is the only policy issue that, on average, separates Latinos from non-Hispanic whites. According to a report published by the Pew Hispanic Center, immigration was not the leading issue for Latino voters; it followed education, jobs, health care, and the budget as top priorities.[6] Latinos are also more likely to describe themselves as liberals than whites and more likely to prefer a larger government.[7] There is little reason to believe this will change even if the GOP changes its immigration policies.

Finally, it seems taken for granted that the GOP could make all of these efforts to increase its share of the minority vote without alienating its current demographic base. The reality may be that whites support the Republican Party for the same reasons that minorities, on average, oppose it. That is, the conservative policies on issues such as welfare, immigration, and affirmative action that alienate many minority voters may be the very policies that attract many white voters. To change its policy platform to reach out to minorities may encourage whites, the largest traditional source of Republican voters, to stay home on Election Day. If that is the case, effective efforts to increase the party's share of minority votes may actually do the party more harm than good.

Not all pundits are focused primarily on the Republican efforts to expand its support from non-whites. Sean Trende, a political analyst at *RealClearPolitics*, conducted a significant amount of research on white voters in recent election cycles. He argued, as will be argued in Chapter 2 of this volume, that the decline in white voter turnout in 2012 was one of the most interesting and important developments of that year.[8] He also noted, as will be noted in forthcoming chapters of this volume, that whites have been trending Republican for years, which is why the GOP remains highly competitive in spite of demographic trends and may remain competitive for many election cycles to come.[9] Some prominent commentators have challenged Trende's conclusions, and their objections to his analysis will also be considered in the pages ahead.

At this point in time, there has been relatively little examination of the political behavior of contemporary whites *as* whites. When whites are discussed, they are usually broken up into sub-categories: blue-collar workers, women, college educated, Evangelicals, Southerners, etc. This is less frequent in discussions of minority groups, who are often discussed in popular media as coherent elements of the Democratic Party's electoral coalition. There are good reasons for this. Compared to African Americans, Latinos, and Asian Americans, whites are more heterogeneous in their voting patterns, both geographically and in terms of their individual demographic attributes. This is not to say that all non-whites vote as a unified bloc—they do not. However, compared to minority voters, the sole knowledge that a voter is white provides relatively little predictive power in terms of vote choice unless other attributes are also known. In the face of the rapidly changing demographic makeup of the United States, this may also change.

As whites continue to decrease as a percentage of the total U.S. population, the day is approaching when whites are just one more minority group among many. When that occurs, will whites begin to view themselves as possessing collective interests and organize politically to advance those interests? This is clearly already the case in some parts of the South, a region that has always possessed a great deal of racial diversity. Throughout American history, whites have been divided when it comes to vote choice— if this had not been so, there would have been little political diversity at all in U.S. politics until relatively recently. Whether this political heterogeneity among whites will continue in the face of changing demographics is an open question.

To a meaningful degree, the future of American politics depends on the future behavior of white voters. Due to their approaching minority status, will whites coalesce into a single voting bloc? If so, will elections become little more than racial head counts? If whites remain equally split between the two parties in the years ahead, and non-whites continue to vote so disproportionately for Democrats, will the United States become, for all intents and purposes, a one-party nation? Both scenarios are potentially problematic for the future of American democracy. For this reason, a study of white voters is timely.

Discussions of race are challenging, as one always runs into problems of definition. In contrast to earlier periods in intellectual history, the social sciences today treat race purely as a social construct, rather than as a biological category. This book does not challenge that understanding. However, regardless of whether or not race has any biological meaning, it has considerable predictive power when studying a wide variety of issues, even when controlling for a plethora of other individual characteristics. This is particularly true in political science. One would be hard pressed to create a quantitative model of vote choice in which race was not a significant variable, regardless of how many additional variables were included.

That being said, it is not always easy to categorize individuals according to race. When this book discusses "whites" in the context of aggregate data, it uses the same definition as the U.S. Census Bureau, which follows the guidelines developed by the U.S. Office of Management and Budget (OMB). The OMB requires the use of at least five racial categories: White, Black or African American, American Indian or Alaska Native, Asian, and Native Hawaiian or Other Pacific Islander. The only ethnicity that is regularly recorded by the Census Bureau is whether or not a person identifies as Hispanic or Latino. Frequently when social scientists discuss whites, they specify that they mean "non-Hispanic whites." To avoid the awkwardness

of that lengthy phrase, when this book discusses whites as a group, it specifically refers to whites who do not identify as Hispanic.

One potential problem with the race categories provided by the Census
Bureau is that they lump several groups into the white category that do
not necessarily identify as white. Arabs, for example, are typically classified as white, though they do not necessarily identify themselves as such.
Any scholar who has conducted survey research among a diverse population has likely experienced an indignant response from respondents who do
not believe they fit within any of the five categories. Respondents may take
offense when they feel forced to describe themselves as "Other." Usually
when survey respondents identify as "Other," they are given an opportunity
to provide their own racial category. These responses are often interesting.
In the author's own experience, respondents frequently name their family's
country of origin as their race (Mexican, Lebanese, and even Irish). In some
cases, students refuse to provide any response at all and give a reason for
doing so ("the only race that matters is THE HUMAN RACE!"; "race is a
social construct with no meaning"). For the purposes of this study, the only
people considered white are those who self-identify as white and do not consider themselves Latino. No effort was made to determine the actual race of
individuals who chose not to self-identify.

Another problem with this simplistic definition of race is that it may
mask important heterogeneity within racial and ethnic groups. This is
well documented with regard to other racial and ethnic categories. We
know that Latinos vary in their political behavior according to their—or
their ancestors'—country of origin. Cuban Americans are more likely to
be Republicans than are Mexican Americans.[10] The same trend is present
among Asians. Vietnamese Americans are, on average, much more Republican than Bangladeshi Americans.[11] There is also variation among whites
according to ethnic background, though this is less pronounced and less
commented on in contemporary social science. Chapter 3 of this volume
will examine this issue in greater detail.

This book draws relatively little from the field of "whiteness studies,"
which examines the social construction of white identity. As a result, it
should not be classified as a part of that literature.[12] Also, just as this book
will not delve into the origins of race as a means of categorizing human
beings, this book will provide only a minimal examination of the origins
and meaning of racism and prejudice. While these are important subjects,
they are beyond the scope of what is being considered here. There is a rich
literature on all of these subjects, and the relevant research will be cited
when appropriate.

Elements of this book draw heavily on the work of historians who explain
contemporary political trends as a result of past history. For example, white
Americans who are predominantly descended from East Anglian Puritans
behave differently today, on average, from white Americans descended from
Scots-Irish settlers in Appalachia. This has been thoroughly documented by

historians such as David Hackett Fischer and Colin Woodard. This book does not begin from the simplistic assumption that all white Americans have lost their ancestral differences in the American "melting pot." However, there is some validity to melting-pot arguments, at least when it comes to whites. Americans who identify entirely as white are likely to be a mix of different European groups, and many may have no knowledge of their own genealogy whatsoever. Nonetheless, it would be a mistake to assume that whites' family histories have zero importance to their contemporary political behavior. This book will consider the degree to which these historical differences remain relevant today and whether these differences will finally fade away in the decades ahead.

This book is not a guidebook for any political party or politician interested in maximizing the support of white voters, nor does this book make the case that white voters are any more or less "important" than other groups of voters. The fact that non-whites are excluded from most of the forthcoming analysis is not a statement on the degree to which non-whites are worthy of study. To the extent possible, this book will also refrain from making normative statements about white political behavior or moral judgments about the actions of political parties and candidates. This book will build on a wide variety of literature within the fields of sociology and political science. It seeks to shed new light on a portion of the electorate that, while shrinking in relative terms, will remain the absolute majority of voters for decades to come.

This book was motivated by several questions. Throughout most of American history, white voters probably did not identify with a party based on their race. After all, for most of this history, the American electorate was predominantly white, and this was not a personal trait that voters would have considered salient compared to other traits (such as specific ethnicity, religion, or socioeconomic status). However, much research indicates that, for as long as minority voters have been part of the American electorate, membership in a racial minority group has been a powerful influence on political attitudes and political behavior. As we approach a period in which whites are just one racial minority group among many, will "whiteness" start to matter in ways it did not matter before? Will whites merge into a largely homogeneous voting bloc in which white Democrats are increasingly rare? This book examines major trends in the white vote to see if this is beginning to occur.

This book is written for political scientists and other academics, and statistical models are employed in most chapters. Specifically, much of the analysis in this book relies on multiple regression. When attempting to isolate the effects of a specific characteristic on individual behaviors such as party identification and vote choice, researchers run into a potential problem: Many variables may be correlated with each other, making it difficult to discern precisely which variable influences political behavior. Multiple regression allows analysts to isolate the effects of one variable while controlling for many others in order to ensure that an apparent relationship is not spurious. The methods used in this book are not novel, and social scientists should have no problem deciphering the various tables and figures.

This book may also be of interest to non-academics who do not care to examine tables of coefficients. For this reason, all statistical models are provided at the end of chapters as appendices, though their interpretation appears in the main text. Where appropriate, the results of these models are presented as figures, also within the main text. Non-experts with no background in quantitative social science will be able to follow the arguments made in each chapter.

This book examines trends in the white vote in recent decades, keeping in mind the considerable variation in white voting patterns from region to region. It also examines white turnout in recent election cycles and considers why white voter turnout has declined in presidential elections since 2004. It examines how white voting behavior responds to changing demographics in different contexts. It looks at those demographic and geographic "gaps" that most divide white voters and shows where those gaps have been shrinking. It concludes with some informed speculation about the future of the white electorate and American politics.

NOTES

1. Some projections suggest non-Hispanic whites will be a minority within the United States by 2050. As recently as 1960, non-Hispanic whites were 85 percent of the total U.S. population. Jeffrey S. Passel and D'Vera Cohn. "U.S. Population Projections: 2005–2050," *Pew Research Center*, February 11, 2008, accessed October 13, 2013, http://pewsocialtrends.org/files/2010/10/85.pdf.
2. Sabrina Tavernise, "Whites Account for Under Half of Births in U.S.," *New York Times*, May 17, 2012, accessed April 4, 2013, www.nytimes.com/2012/05/17/us/whites-account-for-under-half-of-births-in-us.html?pagewanted=all&_r=0.
3. Hope Yen, "In a First, Black Voter Turnout Rate Surpasses Whites," *Associated Press*, April 28, 2013, accessed April 29, 2013, http://news.yahoo.com/first-black-voter-turnout-rate-passes-whites-115957314.html.
4. David Edwards, "Nation Editor: GOP is 'Male, Pale and Stale,'" *The Raw Story*, May 17, 2010, accessed March 3, 2013, www.rawstory.com/rs/2010/05/17/nation-editor-gop-male-pale-stale/.
5. Benjy Sarlin, 2013, "6 Big Takeaways from the RNC's Incredible 2012 Autopsy," *Talking Points Memo*, March 28, 2013, accessed April 4, 2013, http://tpmdc.talkingpointsmemo.com/2013/03/6-big-takeaways-from-the-rncs-incredible-election-autopsy.php.
6. Mark Hugo Lopez and Ana Gonzalez-Berrara, *Latino Voters Support Obama by 3–1 Ratio, but Are Less Certain About Voting* (Washington, DC: Pew Hispanic Center, 2012), 8.
7. Paul Taylor, Mark Hugo Lopez, Jessica Hamar Martinez, and Gabriel Velasco, *When Labels Don't Fit: Hispanics and their View of Identity* (Washington, DC: Pew Hispanic Center, 2013), 5.
8. Sean Trende, "The Case of the Missing White Voters, Revisited," *RealClear Politics*, June 21, 2013, accessed July 27, 2013, www.realclearpolitics.com/

articles/2013/06/21/the_case_of_the_missing_white_voters_revisited_118 893.html.

9. Sean Trende, "Does GOP Have to Pass Immigration Reform?" *RealClear Politics*, June 25, 2013, accessed July 27, 2013, www.realclearpolitics.com/articles/ 2013/06/25/does_the_gop_have_to_pass_immigration_reform_118952-2.html.

10. Antonio Gonzalez and Steven Ochoa, "The Latino Vote in 2008: Trends and Characteristics," William C. Velasquez Institute, November 2008, accessed October 13, 2013, www.wcvi.org/data/election/wcvi_nov2008nationalanalysis_ 121808.pdf.

11. Asian American Legal Defense Fund, "New Findings: Asian American Vote in 2012 Varied by Ethnic Group and Geographic Location," January 17, 2013, accessed October 13, 2013, http://aaldef.org/press-releases/press-release/new-findings-Asian-American-vote-in-2012-varied-widely-by-ethnic-group-and-geo graphic-location.html.

12. Whiteness studies largely examine the historical development of whiteness as a social construction. For readers interested in this subject, David R. Roediger's books *The Wages of Whiteness: Race and the American Working Class* (New York: Verso, 1991) and *Working Toward Whiteness: How America's Immigrants Became White* (New York: Basic Books, 2005) and Mathew Frye Jacobson's *Whiteness of a Different Color: European Immigrants and the Alchemy of Race* (Cambridge, MA: Harvard University Press, 1998), would be valuable starting points.

1 Is There a "White Vote"?

INTRODUCTION

When considering the issue of white voters, the first question worth asking is whether or not it even makes sense to lump this massive percentage of the electorate together. Can we speak of the "white vote" in a manner analogous to the "African American vote"? The knowledge that a voter is black provides a tremendous amount of predictive power in terms of that person's vote choice—in the overwhelming majority of cases, such a voter will support Democrats all the way down the ballot. Latinos and Asians are also quite likely to support Democratic candidates in most circumstances, though in the case of these other minority groups, the support for Democrats is less universal and there is meaningful variation depending on their country of origin—Cuban Americans and Vietnamese Americans are more likely to support Republicans than other Latino and Asian groups, for example.[1] Looking nationwide, is there any evidence of racial bloc voting among whites? If not, are there reasons to expect such behavior in the future?

This chapter will examine broad trends in white voter behavior, examining changes in the white vote over time. Beyond vote choice, this chapter will also look at policy preferences among whites, considering whether there are any policy issues on which whites in all states and regions broadly agree. Finally, it will briefly consider those policy issues where whites are clearly distinct from racial and ethnic minorities in their opinions.

Of all the empirical chapters in this book, this is the least methodologically sophisticated. This chapter looks at whites as a group, making no effort to examine sub-categories within that racial group, beyond state-by-state differences. It reveals that whites remain highly divided in terms of party identification, policy preferences, and voting behavior.

TRENDS IN WHITE PRESIDENTIAL VOTING

It is neither novel nor controversial to say that whites are the demographic base of the Republican Party. While not all whites are Republicans, and in some states a majority of whites consistently vote for Democratic candidates, the overwhelming majority of votes cast for Republican candidates come from whites. However, white support for the GOP has not been equally strong in all recent elections. Since the 1970s, whites have given different levels of support to Republican presidential candidates.

When we examine aggregate vote choice in presidential elections over the last 30 years,[2] we see that white support for the Republican candidate dropped below 50 percent only twice in this period (1992 and 1996). In both cases, the white Republican vote was split by the presence of Reform Party candidate Ross Perot on the ticket. White support for Republicans reached a peak in the 1980s, and two thirds of white voters supported Ronald Reagan in his landslide reelection victory in 1984. George H. W. Bush performed almost as well in 1988.

The strong Republican showing among whites in the 1980s is not surprising, given the GOP's political fortunes in presidential elections during that period. Ronald Reagan won landslide victories in 1980 and 1984, and George H. W. Bush's electoral performance in 1988 was equally impressive. The strong performance of Republican candidates among whites in the most recent elections is much more interesting. According to exit polls, Mitt Romney won 59 percent of the white vote in 2012, yet failed to win the presidency. This is only one percentage point less than the share of the white vote earned by George H. W. Bush in his 40-state victory over Michael Dukakis. Not only did Romney perform better than McCain among white voters, but he performed better than George W. Bush in either 2000 or 2004.

We should be cautious before inferring too much from this finding. Although Romney performed quite well among whites who voted, this does not necessarily mean that Romney was more popular among whites in 2012 than Bush was in 2004. Many whites who showed up at the polls for Bush may have stayed home for Romney—the relatively low voter turnout among whites in 2012 indicates this is a strong possibility. Despite that caveat, exit polls do show that much of the GOP's message continues to resonate with its demographic base. Indeed, had Gerald Ford or George H. W. Bush performed as well as Mitt Romney among white voters, they would have won their reelection bids. With that much support from whites, Bob Dole would have defeated Bill Clinton. Unfortunately for the GOP, strong support from whites is no longer enough to win the presidency because white voters are no longer the overwhelming majority of the electorate that they were in 1976 or even 1996.

Although the GOP has benefited from its slowly increasing share of the white vote, it has increased its support from whites at a rate too slow to overcome the growing minority electorate, which consistently votes heavily for Democrats.

THE WHITE PRESIDENTIAL VOTE BY STATE

Examining the overall percentage of white votes earned by the two parties nationwide can be an informative exercise, but its value is limited when we consider the enormous state-by-state variation in white voting preferences. Presidential elections are not determined by popular vote, but by states via the Electoral College. Thus white vote choice in presidential elections should also be considered at the state level.

One source of vote choice data by racial group at the state level can be obtained from CNN's exit poll database.[3] As is always the case when considering exit polls, a degree of caution should be exercised when interpreting results. There are well-publicized cases in which exit polls were initially mistaken about an election outcome—in Florida in 2000 and Ohio in 2004, for example. Given the limited sample size, we become less certain about exit polls' results when considering smaller subgroups within the sample—in this case, non-Hispanic whites. Nonetheless, exit polls are useful tools for political scientists, and we can be reasonably certain in most cases that the true result was within a few percentage points of the estimated results.[4] Furthermore, we are presently more interested in broad trends than in perfectly predicting the election outcome in a particular state.

One finding that immediately stands out is the huge variability in the "white vote" as we look across the nation. Nationwide, these exit polls indicate that 59 percent of whites supported Romney; however, the standard deviation when we consider white vote at the state level was an impressive 11.45 percentage points. In Mississippi, it would be only a slight exaggeration to say that presidential elections could be conducted by the Census Bureau, sparing individual voters the trouble of turning out to vote. A huge majority (96 percent) of African Americans in the state voted for Obama, and 89 percent of white Mississippians voted for Romney. On the other hand, 66 percent of white Vermonters voted for Obama. Indeed, even if the franchise in Vermont was restricted exclusively to white men, as was the case in early American history, Obama would have still won almost 60 percent of the vote. There are a handful of other states in which this is true. Obama also won a majority of white men in Washington State, Oregon, Maine, and Massachusetts. Obama almost certainly also won a majority of all major white groups in Hawaii, but there are no available exit poll data for that state.

Not every state is included in the CNN exit poll database every year. However, a sufficient number of states have been included since 2000 to see the direction of trends among white voters. It is worth comparing the 2000 and 2012 presidential elections. In both elections, the Democratic candidate narrowly won a victory in the popular vote—though the margin of victory obviously was larger in the latter election. As noted above, however, Al Gore performed better among white voters nationwide than Barack Obama. Of the 26 states with available exit poll data broken down by racial groups in both 2000 and 2012, the mean change in the white vote was 3.57 more percentage points for the Republican candidate in the latter election. The decrease in the Democratic share of the vote was not uniform across the nation, however. Figure 1.1 shows the change in the state-level white vote for which there were available data.

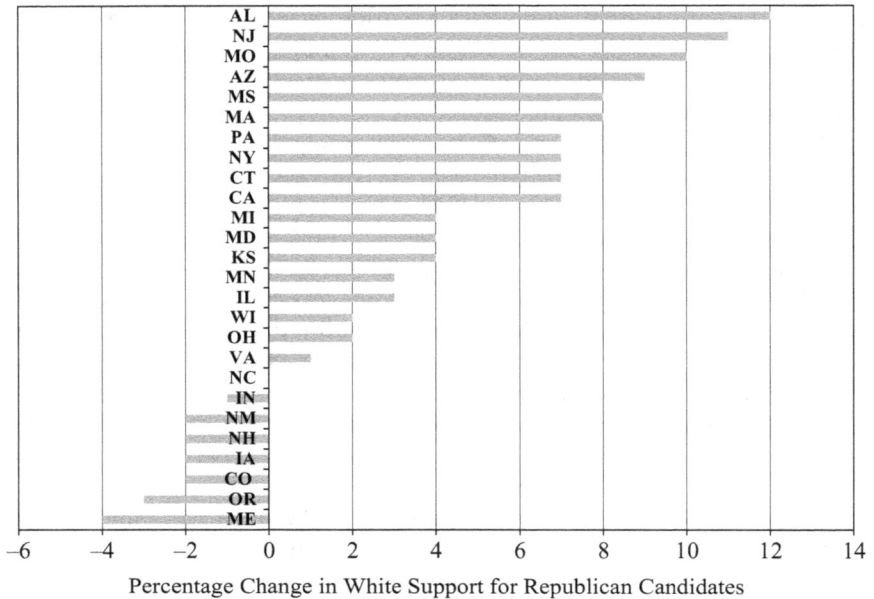

Figure 1.1 Change in White Vote for GOP Candidates in Presidential Elections, 2000–2012 Percentage Change

We see that most states witnessed an increase in the Republican share of the white vote in presidential elections. This was most dramatic in Alabama, where Romney won a remarkable 84 percent of the white vote in 2012, compared to the 72 percent won by Bush in 2000. We see a number of states in which support for Republicans among whites dropped. In Maine, white support for the Republican candidate dropped by four percentage points between the two elections, and in Oregon the drop was three percentage points.

It is interesting how little the states in which whites became more Republican apparently have in common. The two states with the most dramatic change in favor of the GOP among whites were Alabama and New Jersey. Two of the states where whites became less Republican between the two elections were in New England (New Hampshire and Maine) as were two of the states that became more Republican (Connecticut and Massachusetts). The large swing for Massachusetts can surely be attributed to the fact that Mitt Romney was the former governor of that state and Bush performed exceptionally poorly there in 2000. In spite of that impressive improvement among whites in Massachusetts between the two elections, Romney nonetheless lost Massachusetts by a large margin in 2012.

What could explain these changes? With the exception of New Mexico, one attribute that all states in which whites became less Republican have in common is demographic: They are overwhelmingly white. We also see that many of the states in which whites became more Republican were less white than the national average. Indeed, the Pearson's r correlation coefficient[5] for the state-level change in the white vote for Republicans and the percentage of the state-level population that was white as of the 2000 census was a moderate -0.46. That is, the whiter a state was at the start of the 21st century, the smaller the shift within whites in that state toward the Republican Party. In states that were less white in the aggregate, whites, on average, became more Republican. The potential relationship between demographic change and white vote choice will be explored in greater detail in Chapter 7 in this volume.

An equally interesting question is whether white voters are becoming more homogeneous nationwide in terms of vote choice or whether geographic differences remain as important as ever. Of the 26 states for which there were exit poll data in both 2000 and 2012, we see little evidence that geographic differences among white voters are decreasing. According to these exit polls, in 2000 only 34 percent of Massachusetts whites voted for Bush, but 81 percent did so in Mississippi—thus the gap in the white vote between the least and the most Republican states was 47 percentage points. In 2012, only 40 percent of whites in Maine voted for Romney, but 89 percent of whites in Mississippi did so—a gap of 49 percentage points. The standard deviation for these states in 2000 was 10.15 percentage points, but was 11.45 percentage points in 2012. Thus, although the trend nationwide has been toward higher levels of Republican voting among whites, this trend has not been uniform, and voting differences between whites in different states remain large and have even grown. Although the gap remains just as large between the most Democratic state and the most Republican state, the minimum white support for the GOP and the maximum white support for the GOP have both noticeably increased.

WHITE POLICY PREFERENCES AND POLITICAL ATTITUDES ACROSS THE STATES

There are limits to what we can infer about political attitudes from vote choice alone. After all, the United States does not have two major parties. Instead, there are 50 Republican parties and 50 Democratic parties at the state level, each with their own platforms and candidates. We should not overstate this, as partisan polarization has led to greater homogeneity within the Republican and Democratic Parties, both at the elite level and at the mass level.[6] In addition to vote choice, an examination of public policy preferences across the nation may shed light on which issues most divide white voters.

Before examining polarization of the electorate, a critical first step is defining what polarization actually means. How polarization is defined will largely determine the degree to which it can be found among voters.

Generally speaking, when we speak of a "polarized" America, we mean that the country is largely divided into two competing camps that disagree with each other on fundamental issues, that the ideological distance between these groups is large, and that within each camp most people agree with each other on a plethora of issues. In a polarized country, few people are moderates and there are few incentives or opportunities to compromise. When thinking about polarization in geographic terms, we typically mean that some geographic units overwhelmingly vote for one party, and other geographic units overwhelmingly vote for the other. Because this book focuses exclusively on white voters, this section will consider whether, within the white electorate, there is any immediately apparent issue polarization across states.

While it is true that whites are shrinking as a proportion of the electorate, they remain a majority of all voters. Thus, previous studies that considered issue polarization of the entire electorate can tell us a great deal about issue polarization among whites. Although the hypothesis that the electorate is more polarized than ever remains a consistent theme in public discourse about American politics, there is a considerable body of literature arguing that polarization of the electorate is a myth.

Some of the most important studies challenging the polarization hypothesis were conducted by Morris Fiorina.[7] Fiorina and his coauthors have argued that polarization is predominantly a phenomenon among elites and that, when we look at the electorate as a whole, we see that most people are moderates and pragmatic. This is true even of those ostensibly polarizing issues related to the "culture war": issues such as gun control and abortion.

For political scientists, this is not a novel view. Philip Converse argued in 1964 that most voters actually have relatively few ideological constraints and only a small percentage of a population will develop a consistent and coherent ideology.[8] But, there are many political scientists who disagree with Fiorina's conclusions, and it would be a mistake to consider his work to be the final word on the issue.[9]

Fiorina argued that when we use survey data to consider political preferences in "Red" (Republican) and "Blue" (Democratic) states, we do not see dramatic differences in terms of political opinions.[10] In much of his analysis he relied on the American National Election Study (ANES) conducted in 2004, and divided respondents between those living in states that supported George W. Bush and states that supported John Kerry in the 2004 presidential election. In terms of party identification, ideology, support for immigration, and favorable attitudes toward different groups, he found relatively modest gaps between Red States and Blue States.

One might suspect that the trend toward polarization is different depending on whether you are considering different racial groups or viewing the electorate as a whole. Perhaps whites are more geographically polarized along Red State, Blue State lines than other demographic groups. This is not implausible when we consider the degree to which African Americans are, on average, consistently Democratic nationwide regardless of the state context. Perhaps geographic polarization is predominantly a white phenomenon.

One way to consider this question is to recreate Fiorina's 2004 study of "feeling thermometers" of different groups, but to compare his findings to data restricted exclusively to whites. Specifically, Fiorina used the ANES questions in which respondents were asked to rate different groups on a 0–100 scale, with higher "temperatures" corresponding to a greater favorability for that group. The groups he used were the Democratic Party, the Republican Party, Liberals, Conservatives, Christian Fundamentalists, Jews, Catholics, Muslims, and Gays and Lesbians.[11] In all cases, Fiorina found that the differences in the average scores for Red States and Blue States were relatively small. When the data were restricted to whites only, this finding remained consistent for most groups listed by the ANES.

However, there was greater evidence of polarization in attitudes toward the separate parties when the results were restricted to whites. The difference was notable in regard to feelings toward Republicans. Fiorina found that the mean favorability score for the Republican Party in Red States was 56; in Blue States it was 51. When the data were restricted to white voters, there was a slightly larger gap between the two state groups: The mean score in Red States was 60 and the mean score in Blue States was 52—a difference of eight degrees. While this is not a huge gap in either case, and the difference between the two findings was only three degrees, this does suggest that what little geographic partisan polarization in attitudes toward parties we see is predominantly driven by whites.

Even when exclusively examining whites, using Fiorina's method provides little evidence that white Americans are polarized into Red States and Blue States. Nonetheless, it may be worth considering whether this limited polarization is higher now than it was in the past. When this method is applied to earlier election cycles, we see different results. The year 1978 was the first one in which the ANES feeling thermometer question was asked about the Republican Party. In that year, the mean favorability for the Republican Party among whites in Red States (defined as states that supported the Republican Party in the 1976 presidential election) was 60.7. For whites residing in Blue States, the mean favorability rating for the Republican Party was 60.8. The margin was not just extraordinarily close, but the mean favorability for the GOP was actually *higher* in states that voted against the party in the previous presidential election. Thus, while it may be a stretch to say that whites are polarized in their attitudes toward the parties along Red State–Blue State lines, they certainly exhibit more evidence of partisan polarization now than in the past. Furthermore, when we look at the Red State–Blue State divide on attitudes toward the Republican Party among whites in 2008, we see that it continued to grow—it was a difference of a little more than nine degrees. In 2012, it dropped back down to a difference of about seven degrees.

One potential problem with these findings, and with other findings presented by Fiorina and his coauthors, is that they are the result of lumping all Red and Blue states together, perhaps neglecting important differences between the states. While the number of "swing states" is not large, combining states that went strongly for one party with those states that were a virtual tie will mask a great deal of state-by-state variation. If the data are disaggregated into individual states, rather than into the dichotomous categories based on Electoral College vote, we may see greater variation. Unfortunately, there are limits to how much disaggregation can be done using the ANES, as this dataset relied on a relatively small number of observations (in 2004, there were 1,212 observations).

One study that records a much larger number of observations is the National Annenberg Election Survey (NAES). This survey, which was conducted over the phone and online, asked 57,967 Americans during the 2008 election cycle questions regarding their demographic attributes, political behavior, and political beliefs. Of these respondents, 45,541 were white. This is a sufficient number to make reasonable estimates about differences of opinion across the states. Even with this large number of total observations, one should note that in some states there were only a few hundred respondents. Thus, one should not use these estimates to infer precise estimates of white public opinion in individual states. To make such inferences, it would be appropriate to rely on more sophisticated methods, such as multilevel regression with poststratification.[12] In this case, however, we are less interested in determining policy attitudes in each state with absolute precision than in determining in more general terms if there is a high level of variation in white opinion across the states. For this more modest goal, simple disaggregation by state is sufficient.

The 2008 NAES did not ask feeling thermometer questions analogous to those asked in the ANES, but it did ask a number of questions related to policy. Results for different white opinions across the states can be found in Table 1.1. When considering individual states, rather than the relatively crude Red State vs. Blue state distinction, we see greater evidence of geographic polarization across the electorate. The smallest gap between public opinion across the states was in regard to cutting taxes. Even here, the gap between the state with the most liberal attitude and the state with the most conservative attitude was 21.9 percentage points. The policy questions with the largest gaps across the states were gay marriage and the Iraq War. In this case, the difference between the most liberal and the most conservative state was 41.9 and 44.5 percentage points, respectively.

These numbers suggest that whites exhibit high levels of geographic polarization in terms of policy. This finding is not necessarily at odds with Fiorina's argument, as he was largely making the case that it makes little sense to divide the nation between Red States and Blue States. However, it apparently makes a great deal of sense to distinguish whites in Alabama from whites in Massachusetts. Knowing where a white American lives is a meaningful predictor for what that white person believes about policy.

Table 1.1   State-by-State Differences in White Opinion on Policy

	Mean	Standard Deviation	Minimum	Maximum	Difference Min to Max
% Favor Cutting Taxes	38.0	4.9	25.5	47.4	21.9
% Favor Environmental Protection Over Economic Growth	34.4	6.9	21.2	50.0	28.8
% Favor Free Trade Agreements	43.3	6.6	28.5	58.8	30.3
% Favor Border Fence	60.9	6.4	40.0	75.0	35.0
% Favor Government Health Insurance	45.1	7.0	29.0	64.7	35.7
% Opposed to All Abortion Restrictions	31.1	10.2	12.0	50.8	38.7
% Support Gay Marriage	28.1	10.2	9.9	51.8	41.9
% Believe Iraq War "Worth It"	38.9	9.7	17.0	61.5	44.5

Source: 2008 National Annenberg Election Study

These findings also demonstrate that, if a party is attempting to pursue a policy agenda that maximizes the "white vote," it will be relatively difficult to develop a platform that pleases large majorities of all whites. On some policies, majorities of whites in most states favored the conservative position; on other policies they favored liberal positions. It is interesting to note, however, that one issue the Republican Party has chosen to emphasize in recent years is an issue on which a majority of whites oppose the GOP position in all states: tax cuts. According to these data there was not a single state in which a majority of whites favored new tax cuts in 2008. Nor do a majority of whites favor further free trade agreements in most states. The Republican Party's message on cultural issues and immigration, however, apparently has higher levels of favorability among whites in most states. Strong majorities in most states favored a border fence, favored at least some restrictions on abortion, and opposed full marriage rights for gay Americans. There are other issues on which strong majorities of whites are in agreement, though not many. This can be verified by turning to the 2012 ANES.

ARE THERE ISSUES OF WIDESPREAD AGREEMENT AMONG WHITES AND BETWEEN WHITES AND NON-WHITES? EVIDENCE FROM 2012

The above findings indicate that, when we look across the states, there is considerable variation in white opinion when it comes to policy. This finding, combined with the finding that there is remarkable voting hetero-geneity in voting behavior among whites across the different states, may be encouraging for those concerned that whites are coalescing into a single coherent voting bloc. It is worth investigating whether there are policy areas on which whites overwhelmingly agree. To investigate this, a return to the ANES data will be useful, this time analyzing the 2012 survey. Table 1.2 shows the percentage of whites who agree with specific policies. To show how whites differ from other demographic categories in the electorate, this table also shows the mean support for each policy by non-whites. The fact

Table 1.2   Percent of Whites and Non-Whites Favoring Specific Policies

	White	Non-White	Difference
Favor Unrestricted Access to Abortion	44.1	45.1	0.9
Favor Increasing Taxes on Millionaires	76.6	75.1	1.5
Favor Allowing Gays to Serve Openly in the Military	86.6	84.8	1.8
Favor Laws Protecting Gays from Job Discrimination	75.2	77.0	1.8
Favor Additional Federal Spending on Science and Technology	46.3	48.5	2.2
Favor Complete Prohibition of Abortion	11.6	13.9	2.3
Favors Full Marriage Rights for Homosexuals	41.9	39.0	2.8
Favor Increasing Corporate Taxes to Reduce Deficit	56.9	60.2	3.3
Favor Increasing Immigration	12.8	16.5	3.7
Favor Additional Federal Spending on Crime	48.1	59.3	11.3
Favor Additional Federal Spending on Social Security	45.0	56.6	11.6
Favor Decreasing Immigration	48.4	34.7	13.7
Favor Additional Federal Spending on Welfare	9.7	23.5	13.8
Favor Increased Federal Spending on the Environment	36.7	51.2	14.5
Favor New Gun Control	41.9	56.7	14.8
Favor Additional Federal Spending on Schools	58.7	73.7	15.0
Favor the Death Penalty	77.8	62.5	15.4
Favor Additional Federal Spending on Childcare	28.8	46.9	18.2
Favor Additional Federal Spending on the Poor	29.6	52.4	22.8
Favor Affirmative Action	11.3	38.3	27.0

Source: 2012 ANES

that all non-whites are lumped into a single category is potentially problematic given the heterogeneity of the non-white U.S. population. There is furthermore no a priori reason to expect African Americans will have similar attitudes toward non-racial policy issues as Asian Americans or Latinos. However, such an analysis can indicate whether there is a substantial white vs. non-white gap on any policy issues and let us know if there is evidence of policy polarization along these racial lines.

Here we see that there are indeed policies either supported or opposed by enormous percentages of whites, though we also see that some policies supported by large majorities of whites are predominantly advocated by the Democratic Party and others are generally advocated by the Republican Party. Whites overwhelmingly opposed increasing spending on welfare. A large majority also were opposed to Affirmative Action in hiring. Very few favored increasing the number of immigrants, and a near majority favored decreasing current levels of immigration.

A substantial number of whites believed there should be no restrictions on abortion. Of those who believed there should be some restriction on abortion, they were split on what kinds of restrictions should be in place, a finding noted by other scholars.[13] We should also remember, from Table 1.1, that there were dramatic differences in attitudes toward this question across the states. Interestingly, a huge majority favored allowing gays in the military and laws that protected gays from discrimination—though, as noted in the preceding table, they were more ambivalent on the question of full marriage rights for gay Americans. Whites were relatively split on important questions such as Social Security and federal spending on crime—though it is interesting to note that almost a majority of whites continue to favor additional spending on crime, despite the fact that violent crime has decreased dramatically in recent decades.[14]

Turning to the average differences between whites and non-whites, we see a number of issues where these two racial categories differ dramatically, and several issues on which they are virtually indistinguishable. On social issues such as gays in the military, gay marriage, and abortion, whites and non-whites differ very little.

When it comes to immigration, the percentage of both whites and non-whites in favor of increasing immigration was small (12.8 percent and 16.5 percent, respectively). However, among those who did not want to see immigration increase, whites and non-whites differed substantially. Whereas only about one-third of non-whites wanted immigration to decrease, about one-half of whites wanted to see immigration rates decline. A greater percentage of non-whites than whites were comfortable with the immigration rate remaining unchanged.

Some of the biggest differences between whites and non-whites were on issues of social spending. Non-whites tended to be much more favorable toward increases in federal spending on things like schools and the poor. There was also a substantial gap on the issue of gun control and Affirmative

Action—the latter difference is not surprising, as this issue, perhaps more than any other, can be reasonably viewed as a "zero sum" racial policy that specifically benefits one part of American society. The question about Affirmative Action may have had an even greater gap had it been worded differently. The ANES only specifically asked respondents about their support for Affirmative Action for African Americans and did not mention other minority groups.

The finding that relatively few white Americans favor increased welfare spending at a time of widespread economic distress may seem surprising. However, it has been suggested that there is a racial element to white attitudes toward welfare. In his book, *Why Americans Hate Welfare,* Martin Gilens argued that white Americans are particularly averse to welfare policies because they believe these policies predominantly favor blacks.[15] Gilens noted that white Americans often mistakenly believe that African Americans represent a majority of welfare recipients. White Americans thus oppose welfare spending because they view it as a form of redistribution from whites to blacks.[16] This hypothesis helps explain why Americans are less in favor of generous welfare policies than Western Europeans, who live in nations with far fewer racial and ethnic minorities. The possibility that local demographic context influences attitudes on policies such as economic redistribution will be considered in greater detail in Chapter 6 in this volume.

From these findings, it would appear that policies that are most alienating to whites are those that predominantly favor non-whites (Affirmative Action, increased immigration, perhaps welfare) and those that discriminate against gays—though many whites remain skeptical of full marriage equality. These findings also indicate that the difference in aggregate vote choice between whites and non-whites is at least partially due to differences in policy preferences. On every question about spending, a greater percentage of non-whites compared to whites wanted to see spending increased.

CONCLUSION

From this cursory examination of white voting behavior and policy preferences, we can begin to answer the question of whether or not there is such a thing as the "white vote." At this point in time, the answer is no. While there has been a recent uptick in the percentage of whites supporting the Republican Party in presidential elections, this varies dramatically across the states. While white Americans may not be polarized along the Red State–Blue State divide, the difference in their political behaviors and policy attitudes in different states is dramatic. This important heterogeneity is not inexplicable, and it will be explored in greater detail in chapters ahead.

When we look at the policy preferences of white America, we see that whites remain almost evenly split on many crucial issues. However, there are issues on which overwhelming percentages agree. Only a tiny percentage of whites favor increases in immigration. Whites are also strongly opposed to Affirmative Action. On the other hand, whites appear strongly in favor of certain gay rights, such as allowing gays in the military and using laws to protect gays from discrimination—though they remain less enthusiastic about full marriage equality for homosexuals.

When it comes to economics, on average, whites are actually somewhat populist. Most white Americans do not support Tea Party, libertarian economics. Three-quarters favored higher taxes on the wealthiest Americans, and almost 60 percent favored additional taxes on corporations in order to reduce the budget deficit. However, white Americans are also generally opposed to straightforward economic redistribution; less than 10 percent favored additional spending on welfare, and less than 30 percent favored additional spending on the poor.

It is an open question as to which, if any, of these issues determines vote choice among whites.[17] While very few whites support Affirmative Action, it is unlikely that many whites are single-issue voters on Affirmative Action. On the other hand, it is not inconceivable that many whites are turned off by the Republican Party specifically because of the party's apparent hostility to gay and lesbian Americans. If these sexuality issues were off the political table, might pro-gay members of the white electorate begin voting on other issues? It is worth noting that, of those whites who favored gays in the military, only 12.10 percent also favored Affirmative Action—a number only slightly higher than whites overall. Similarly, only 10.56 percent of this group favored higher spending on welfare, which is virtually indistinguishable from the number of whites overall who favored this policy.

The arrival of a post-gay marriage era in American politics, should it ever arrive, may actually be beneficial to the Republican Party's standing among whites, particularly when we consider that many of the other issues that apparently unite large numbers of whites are issues where whites tend to be in agreement with the GOP's platform. This is especially true of issues that are intertwined with issues of race, such as Affirmative Action, welfare, and immigration. None of this is definitive, of course, as attitudes of whites toward these racial subjects are not set in stone and may also evolve. The rapid change in attitudes toward homosexuality in recent decades is a powerful example of this. Furthermore, even if policy questions related to homosexuality are removed from the political arena, those who favored liberal policies on this issue may continue to reward the Democratic Party for many election cycles to come as a result of their leadership on this subject.

This chapter also demonstrates a number of points on which whites differ from non-whites when it comes to public policies. On a number of issues, it does not appear that race is particularly important. Large majorities of whites and non-whites favor higher taxes on the wealthy and on corporations, for example. We do, however, see many issues where the racial gap is large and there are opposing majorities. In all such cases, whites are more conservative than non-whites. This indicates that the GOP's poor performance among non-whites is based on policies, rather than a simple failure of the Republican Party to engage in sufficient rhetorical outreach to minority communities.

The most important finding of this chapter is that whites are not monolithic in their political attitudes and voting behavior, and it may not be an exaggeration to say white voters are polarized geographically, at least on some policy issues. Understanding why whites vote the way they do in different contexts is an important subject. The third chapter of this book considers this issue, examining whether ethnicity and regional history continue to influence white voters. The next chapter, however, attempts to uncover which whites chose to stay home in 2012, despite voting in large numbers in the previous two elections.

NOTES

1. Benjamin Bishin and Casey A. Klofstad. "The Political Incorporation of Cuban Americans: Why Won't Little Havana Turn Blue?" *Political Research Quarterly* 65(2012): 586; Paul Taylor, *The Rise of Asian Americans*, Washington, DC: Pew Research Center, 2006, 17.
2. Data on vote choice by racial group for each racial category can be found at the Roper Center Public Opinion Archive, accessed March 24, 2013, www.ropercenter.uconn.edu/.
3. CNN presidential election polls, accessed March 27, 2012, www.cnn.com/election/2012/results/race/president.
4. For a good overview of the debate about the discrepancy between exit poll results and actual vote tallies, see Mark Lindeman and Rick Brady, "Behind the Controversy: A Primer on U.S. Presidential Election Polls." *Public Opinion Pros* January 2006, accessed March 28, 2013, www.publicopinionpros.norc.org/from_field/2006/jan/lindeman_ii.asp
5. Pearson's *r* is a measure of linear correlation between two variables, taking values between 1 (perfect positive correlation), 0 (no correlation), and –1 (perfect negative correlation). The large negative value for this coefficient in the text indicates a strong negative correlation.
6. For a thorough analysis of the increasing polarization of American politics at the congressional level, see Nolan McCarty, Keith T. Poole, and Howard Rosenthal, *Polarized America: The Dance of Ideology and Unequal Riches* (Cambridge, MA: MIT Press, 2006). For a study of how the two parties became more ideologically homogeneous at the level of the electorate in recent decades, I recommend Matthew Levendusky, *The Partisan Sort: How Liberals Became Democrats and Conservatives Became Republicans* (Chicago: University of Chicago Press, 2009).
7. Morris Fiorina, Samuel J. Abrams, and Jeremy C. Pope, *Culture War? The Myth of a Polarized America* (New York: Pearson Longman, 2005).
8. Philip Converse, "The Nature of Belief Systems in Mass Publics." In *Ideology and Discontent,* ed. David Apter (New York: The Free Press, 1964), 206–264.
9. For a response to Fiorina and others who posit that polarization is a myth see Alan I. Abramowitz and Kyle L. Saunders, "Is Polarization a Myth?" *Journal of Politics* 70(2008): 542–555, or Gary C. Jacobson, "The Electoral Origins of Polarized Politics Evidence from the 2010 Cooperative Congressional Election Study," *American Behavioral Scientist* 56(2012): 1612–1630.

10. Fiorina et al., *Culture War*, Chapter 3.
11. Ibid, 48.
12. Jeffrey R. Lax and Justin H. Philips, "How Should We Estimate Public Opinion in the States?" *American Journal of Political Science* 53(2009): 107–121.
13. Fiorina et al., *Culture War*, Chapter 5.
14. Terry Frieden, "U.S. Violent Crime Down for Fifth Straight Year," *CNN Justice*, October 29 2012, accessed April 6, 2013, www.cnn.com/2012/10/29/justice/us-violent-crime.
15. Martin Gilens, *Why Americans Hate Welfare* (Chicago, University of Chicago Press, 1999).
16. Ibid, 68.
17. It is actually still debated within political science whether issues determine party identification and vote choice at all. Rather than being policy based, party identification may be predominantly driven by social identity. Vote choice may also be determined by retrospective or prospective economic evaluations, rather than specific policies. For a detailed explanation of this debate, as well as a compelling argument for the position that issues actually matter a great deal, see Stephen Anselobahere, Jonathan Rodden, and James R. Snyder Jr., "The Strength of Issues: Using Multiple Measures to Gauge Preference Stability, Ideological Constraint, and Issue Voting," *American Political Science Review* 102(2008): 215–232.

Appendix 1.1 Question Wording in the 2012 ANES and 2008 NAES

APPENDIX 1.1

This chapter, as well as most that follow, relies heavily on data from the 2012 American National Election Study (ANES) and the 2008 National Annenberg Election Study (NAES). Both studies are available for free online, though the latter study is only available to academics involved in academic research. The ANES data can be found at the following URL: www.election studies.org/. The NAES data are available at www.annenbergpublicpolicy center.org/political-communication/naes/.

These data come with codebooks explaining the survey methodology, as well as the question wording. The precise wording for the questions used in this chapter can be found below. This section also explains how multiple responses were combined into a single category if that was the case.

2012 ANES

Immigration

"Do you think the number of immigrants from foreign countries who are permitted to come to the United States to live should be decreased a lot, decreased a little, left the same as it is now, increased a little, or increased a lot?"

In the descriptive statistics in this chapter, those who wanted immigration increased a little and increased a lot were combined into a single category.

Corporate Taxes

"Would you favor, oppose, or neither favor nor oppose a plan to reduce the federal budget deficit if it included the following: Increase corporate taxes."

Taxes on Millionaires

"Do you favor, oppose, or neither favor nor oppose increasing income taxes on people making over one million dollars per year?"

Spending on Social Security

"Should federal spending on Social Security be increased, decreased, or kept the same?"

Spending on Public Schools

"Should federal spending on public schools be increased, decreased, or kept the same?"

Science and Technology

"Should federal spending on science and technology be increased, decreased, or kept the same?"

Crime

"Should federal spending on crime be increased, decreased, or kept the same?"

Welfare

"Should federal spending on welfare be increased, decreased, or kept the same?"

Childcare

"Should federal spending on childcare be increased, decreased, or kept the same?"

The Poor

"Should federal spending on the aid to the poor be increased, decreased, or kept the same?"

The Environment

"Should federal spending on protecting the environment be increased, decreased, or kept the same?"

Abortion

"There has been some discussion about abortion during recent years. Which one of the opinions on this page best agrees with your view? You can just tell me the number of the opinion you choose. 1. By law, abortion should never be permitted. 2. The law should permit abortion only in case of rape, incest, or when the woman's life is in danger. 3. The law should permit abortion for reasons other than rape, incest, or danger to the woman. 4. By law, a woman should always be able to obtain an abortion as a matter of personal choice."

Gun Control

"Do you think the federal government should make it more difficult for people to buy a gun than it is now, make it easier for people to buy a gun, or keep these rules about the same as they are now?"

Death Penalty

"Do you favor or oppose the death penalty for persons convicted of murder?"

Protections of Gays Against Discrimination

"Do you favor or oppose laws to protect gays and lesbians against job discrimination?"

Gays in the Military

"Do you think homosexuals should be allowed to serve in the United States Armed Forces or don't you think so?"

Same-Sex Marriage

"Which comes closest to your view? 1. Gay and lesbian couples should be allowed to legally marry. 2. Gay and lesbian couples should be allowed to form civil unions but not legally marry. 3. There should be no legal recognition of a gay or lesbian couple's relationship."

Affirmative Action:

"What about your opinion—are you for or against preferential hiring and promotion of blacks?"

2008 NAES

Taxes

"Which of the following options comes closest to your view on what we should be doing about federal income taxes? Taxes should be cut. Taxes should be kept pretty much as they are. Taxes should be raised if necessary in order to maintain current federal programs and services."

Free Trade

"Do you favor or oppose the federal government in Washington negotiating more free trade agreements like NAFTA?"

Government Health Insurance

"Which do you think would be better for the country: having one health insurance program covering all Americans that would be administered by the government and paid for by taxpayers, or keeping the current system where many people get their insurance from private employers and some have no insurance?"

Border Fence

"I'm going to read you a proposal some have made regarding immigration. Please tell me whether you strongly favor, somewhat favor, somewhat oppose, or strongly oppose it: increase border security by building a fence along part of the US border with Mexico."

Environmental Protection

"I am going to read you a pair of statements. Please tell me which of the two statements comes closest to your opinion: Protecting the environment should be a top priority, even if that means higher consumer prices. Protecting the environment is important, but it is more important to keep the economy growing."

Gay Marriage

"There has been much talk recently about whether gays and lesbians should have the legal right to marry someone of the same sex. Which of the following options comes closest to your position on this issue? I support full marriage rights for gay and lesbian couples. I support civil unions or domestic partnerships, but not gay marriage. I do not support any form of legal recognition of the relationships of gay and lesbian couples."

Iraq War

"All in all, do you think the situation in Iraq was worth going to war over, or not?

2 The "Missing" White Votes of 2012

INTRODUCTION

The previous chapter noted that, in 2012, Mitt Romney performed better among white voters than any Republican presidential candidate since 1988, winning 59 percent of all white voters, according to exit polls. This is five percentage points more than the Republican candidate earned in 2008. This fact is important because it demonstrates the declining clout of whites as a group within the electorate. Had George H. W. Bush or Bob Dole earned such a large share of the white vote, they would almost certainly have won in 1992 and 1996, respectively. This demonstrates that winning a majority, even a substantial majority, of white votes is no longer sufficient to earn a victory in presidential elections. As whites continue to decline as a percentage of the electorate, even lopsided victories among whites for the GOP will be insufficient to win presidential elections without a substantial increase in the party's share of votes from Latinos, African Americans, and Asians.

There is more to this story, however. One of the less publicized aspects of the 2012 election was the decline in the percentage of the white voting age population that turned out to vote compared to the previous two elections. According to the Current Population Survey conducted by the U.S. Census Bureau, 64.1 percent of whites over the age of 18 voted in 2012, compared to 66.1 percent in 2008 and 67.2 percent in 2004.[1] That is, although the minority share of the vote increased because of the nation's demographic changes and a surge in turnout from African Americans, there was also a meaningful decrease in white turnout. Had white turnout been substantially higher in 2012, then the election may have been much closer.

This is not to say that, had a slightly larger number of whites showed up at the polls, Romney would have won the presidential election. That is not the case. President Obama defeated Governor Romney by about five million votes.[2] If white voter turnout had been as high in 2012 as it had been in 2004, there would have been an additional 4.7 million votes cast—thus, even if Romney had won every one of these additional votes, he would still have failed to win the popular vote.[3] Furthermore, there is no way to know for sure if whites who stayed home in 2012 would have voted in greater numbers for Romney than Obama; the fact that Romney won a greater share of the white vote in 2012 than McCain won in 2008 suggests that many of the white voters who chose not to vote in the latter election were former Obama voters who likely would have voted for Obama again had they voted.

This chapter will consider recent trends in white voter turnout. It will examine which geographic and demographic elements of the white electorate failed to turn out in 2012. The results of this inquiry have important implications. If we can surmise that a majority of the voters who stayed home in 2012 would have voted for Romney, we might also be able to say with some plausibility that the clout of white Republican voters was artificially weak in 2012. If there is a higher turnout rate among whites in future elections, the GOP may again secure the presidency even if it fails to substantially boost its share among non-white voters—though this will be difficult if minority turnout remains high in the future. On the other hand, if it appears that white non-voters in 2012 were less likely to vote Republican than those who did vote, then Romney's impressive victory among whites could be largely attributed to apathy among white Democrats. If that is the case, the GOP will do even worse in future elections if the Democratic Party is able to again mobilize this portion of the electorate.

This chapter will not be able to answer these questions definitively. From aggregate turnout data, it is not possible to be certain how non-voting whites would have voted. Thus, all of the forthcoming analysis should be interpreted with some caution. Nonetheless, this survey of the turnout results from the two most recent elections can allow us to draw meaningful inferences about the trends in white turnout.

EXPLANATIONS FOR VOTER TURNOUT

Voter turnout is one of the most studied subjects within political science. Voting is perhaps the most important form of political participation most Americans will engage in, and major demographic gaps in voter turnout raise concerns about the degree to which a group in the electorate is politically incorporated and represented in the policy process. If a group fails to participate politically by voting, government will presumably be less responsive to that group's needs. There is further concern that, if a large percentage of eligible voters fail to turn out, the legitimacy of the elected government will be in doubt.

It is well established that Americans vote at lower rates, on average, than voters in most other democratic countries—though the trend in voter turnout has been downward in most developed democracies.[4] There are a number of plausible explanations for this trend in the United States. For one, voting is more difficult in the United States than in other democracies. Registering is a time-consuming process, and the state takes little active role in registering potential voters. Unlike citizens of several other developed democracies, Americans are not required to register and certainly not required to vote. Americans furthermore must re-register every time they move, which is problematic given the frequency with which Americans change residences.

It is also argued that the nature of the electoral system of the United States discourages higher levels of voter participation. Whereas most developed democracies have some form of proportional representation, and hence multiple political parties, the winner-take-all districts in the United States virtually assure a two-party system. Given these narrow choices, many Americans may feel that neither major party accurately reflects their policy preferences, but they also recognize that a vote for a third party candidate would be a "wasted" vote.[5] In contrast, in proportional representation systems, even parties with relatively little support overall can be represented in the national legislature.

The United States furthermore has a much larger undocumented immigrant population than any other nation, as well as a large number of felons who are ineligible to vote. When these groups are excluded from the denominator used to calculate voter turnout, the voter turnout rate in the United States does not appear quite so unusual. Michael P. McDonald and Samuel L. Popkin argued that voting has not actually declined substantially in the United States, but the ineligible population has dramatically increased.[6]

While we may be rightfully concerned when voter turnout is low, in some sense it is remarkable that voter turnout is consistently as high as it is. After all, if the issue is considered from a rational choice framework, one should only vote if the costs of voting are lower than the difference an election outcome will make to a person's individual utility multiplied by the probability that this person will cast the deciding vote—that is, you have to expect to get more out of voting than you put into it. In a presidential election, the probability that any one person will break a perfect tie is virtually zero.[7] Thus, if there are any costs associated with voting (costs such as learning about the candidates, the time it takes to register, and the time it takes to show up to cast a ballot), then voting in a presidential election is an irrational act, even if one cares a great deal about who will win a given election. Scholars can only get around this problem by ascribing some additional benefits to voting, such as a feeling of personal satisfaction in response to fulfilling one's civic duty. On the other hand, John Adrich has argued that the problem voter turnout poses for rational choice theories has been overstated. Although the benefits of voting are surely small for most people, the costs of voting are also quite small for most people most of the time.[8]

As racial minorities and the economically disadvantaged have traditionally voted at lower rates than whites and the economically advantaged, it is commonly asserted that higher turnout rates will lead to more victories by progressive candidates and more redistributive policies. This argument was made by Arend Lijphart,[9] who suggested that compulsory voting would be the best solution to this issue. The fact that it is usually Republicans who favor new barriers to voting, such as greater identification requirements, lends plausibility to the argument that more voters means more Democratic voters.

A number of prominent political scientists have challenged the assumption that higher turnout necessarily benefits Democrats and that the comparatively low turnout rate in the United States leads to less progressive policies than we would otherwise see. James DeNardo argued that peripheral voters—those who vote infrequently—are fickle in their vote choice, and on average a higher turnout of this group tends to benefit the minority party—whichever party that happens to be.[10] If that was true in 2012, then a higher voter turnout would have benefited Mitt Romney. Citrin, Schickler, and Sides considered whether recent senate elections would have turned out differently if turnout was higher. They found that, although non-voters are typically more Democratic than voters, there are exceptions to this. They further found that, given that most House and Senate elections are not even remotely competitive, any partisan difference between voters and non-voters would be insufficient to cause a different outcome, even in conditions of universal turnout.[11]

All of the prominent research on the electoral consequences of turnout was written at a time when a greater percentage of whites voted than blacks; that is, the most important literature on the subject was written prior to 2008. Thus, most of this literature suggests it is plausible to infer that higher turnout will benefit the Democratic Party. But this may have changed in recent presidential elections. The long-present gap between white and black Americans in presidential voting has actually reversed, with African Americans voting at least as frequently as white Americans in presidential elections—though Latinos continue to vote at lower rates than non-Hispanic whites.

Given these recent developments, one might plausibly hypothesize that, in the latest presidential election, non-voters were actually more Republican, on average, than voters. Again, this is not to say that Romney would have won the election had white voter turnout been substantially higher. Most states were not close in 2012, and a slight increase in white turnout would have been insufficient to change most states from Blue to Red, even if we could demonstrate that most of the non-voting whites would have voted for Romney.

Although there is little reason to expect that the decline in white voter turnout made the key difference in the 2012 presidential election, it is worth examining the changes in turnout for whites with different demographic characteristics between the two most recent elections nationwide. Again, one of the interesting aspects of the 2012 presidential election was the fact that, while a greater percentage of white voters than in any presidential election since 1988 preferred the Republican candidate, a smaller percentage of whites turned out to vote than was the case in other recent elections.

Had white turnout remained high, would Romney have performed so well among whites? That is, were the "missing" white voters disenchanted former Obama voters or were they potential Republican voters who were unimpressed by Mitt Romney? The answer to this question can help us predict the future of the white electorate.

This book is not the first serious study of recent trends in white turnout. Sean Trende at *RealClearPolitics* analyzed white turnout data. He found that white voter turnout dropped most precipitously among poorer whites in the North who were not Evangelicals. Trende further noted that this portion of the electorate was also the base of the support for Ross Perot in 1992. If this profile of the "missing" white voters is correct, it is not difficult to see why they chose to stay home in 2012. As Trende put it, "Given the overall demographic and political orientation of these voters, one can see why they would stay home rather than vote for an urban liberal like President Obama or a severely pro-business venture capitalist like Mitt Romney."[12]

Other analysts have challenged Trende's conclusions. Ruy Teixeira and Alan Abramowitz argued that there really were not any "missing" white voters in 2012—or, to put it another way, there were plenty of missing non-whites as well.[13] Trende responded to this critique by noting that he never claimed that whites were the only group that stayed home in 2012, but the data he analyzed clearly indicated that white turnout decreased substantially more than turnout for other demographic groups.[14] Trende further reiterated that he never argued a higher white turnout would have necessarily led to a Romney victory.

Other prominent commentators weighed in on this discussion. Nate Cohn of *The New Republic* examined aggregate vote change from 2000 to 2012 at the county level and concluded that Obama really only had a problem with white southerners, but did reasonably well with whites elsewhere.[15] The GOP's improvement among whites only served to make Red States more red, but did little to improve the party's performance elsewhere. Cohn further argued that to make a major breakthrough among non-southern whites, the Republican Party will need to downplay cultural issues that repel whites in places like Colorado and Washington. Unfortunately for the GOP, the major gains the party enjoyed among whites occurred in places where major gains were unnecessary. Increasing the party's share of the white vote by 12 percentage points in Alabama since 2000 did nothing to improve the party's fortunes overall—the GOP easily won that state in all recent election cycles.

POSSIBLE CAUSES OF WHITE TURNOUT DECLINE

Before fully exploring the data, it is worth considering a number of possible explanations for the decline in white turnout in the most recent presidential election. Recent political trends provide several plausible hypotheses.

One could suspect that whites of all political and ideological affiliations have become politically demoralized and are dropping out of the political process. One could also argue that either the Republican or the Democratic Party (or both) have failed to motivate parts of their base.

There are a number of reasons why voters of all political persuasions may be presently turned off from political participation. A key determinant of political participation is interest in politics.[16] To be interested in partisan politics, one must believe that the two parties are genuinely different on major issues. Perhaps some voters feel, to quote the segregationist presidential candidate George Wallace, that there is not a "dime's worth of difference" between the two parties. These kinds of attitudes are not exclusive to Americans on the extreme right. This sentiment was also expressed by other third-party candidates such as Ross Perot and Ralph Nader.

In spite of the argument that there is tremendous political polarization in the United States, critics who claim the two major parties do not offer voters a genuine choice may have a point. The hyperbole of strong partisans notwithstanding, a case can be made that the two major candidates in 2012 differed primarily at the margins. The signature achievement of the Obama Administration's first term was a health care bill that was largely modeled on legislation that was implemented in Massachusetts when Mitt Romney was governor of that state—the individual mandate, which is one of the cornerstones of both Romney and Obama's health care policies, was previously promoted by the conservative Heritage Foundation.[17]

To the frustration of many American progressives, there was furthermore a great deal of continuity in terms of foreign policy between the Bush and Obama Administrations. For example, Obama did not keep his campaign promise to shut down Guantanamo Bay. This continuity would likely have continued in a Romney Administration. One could thus reasonably hypothesize that ideologues on both sides of the political divide were demoralized by the relatively small differences between the two candidates in terms of policy, and they chose to stay home.

On the other hand, we could also argue that there were important differences between the two parties, and the electorate recognized these differences, but one or both of those parties failed to appeal to some segment of the white population that had previously offered it support. During the Republican primaries, there was speculation that Romney's status as a Mormon would turn off Evangelical Christians, and they would simply stay home on Election Day. Romney's history as a moderate governor of a heavily Democratic state may have also discouraged Tea Party Republicans who would have turned out for a more doctrinaire conservative—though the inclusion of Paul Ryan, a strong fiscal conservative, on the ticket should have made this unlikely.

Thinking in terms of personality, one can imagine voters who found John McCain very appealing but were less enamored with Romney. While both Republican candidates had previously nurtured reputations as moderates,

McCain's status as a veteran and war hero was undoubtedly appealing to a large number of whites who may have been unimpressed by Romney's privileged background. Romney's status as an Ivy League graduate and cofounder and CEO of Bain Capital probably did not help him build a personal appeal among working-class whites. He may have also hamstrung himself with his politically tone-deaf comments about 47 percent of Americans being dependent on government and therefore being unlikely to vote for him.[18] If this is the case, then Romney's problem was not that he failed to energize Tea Party conservatives, but that his economic conservatism and perceived elitism were actually a turnoff to those working-class whites once described as "Reagan Democrats." The political characteristics of this group will be examined in greater detail in a forthcoming chapter.

There are also reasons that we might expect that some whites who supported Obama in 2008 chose to stay home in the subsequent election. There was a tremendous amount of enthusiasm surrounding Obama in 2008, and that energy surely brought many new voters to the polls. Barack Obama's status as a young, eloquent speaker promising "hope" and "change" at a time of economic distress, foreign policy quagmires, and a hugely unpopular incumbent president mobilized a large percentage of Americans. This phenomenon was most notable among African Americans, who voted in record numbers in both 2008 and 2012. After the election ended, however, and President Obama had to begin the actual business of governing, some disillusionment was inevitable. Although Obama kept many campaign promises—such as the passage of health care legislation and the end of combat operations in Iraq—others remained unfulfilled as of November 2012. For example, there was no meaningful immigration reform passed during Obama's first term. Furthermore, while a recession that began prior to the 2008 election came to an end during Obama's watch, economic growth remained sluggish through his first term, and unemployment remains high throughout the nation at the time of this writing.

Conservative commentator Michael Medved argued that the nasty tone of the 2012 presidential campaign, particularly the negative advertising of the Obama campaign, discouraged many people from voting and that most of those who failed to show up to the polls would have voted for Romney:

> I visited Ohio the week before the election for a Cleveland town-hall meeting to generate enthusiasm for the Romney-Ryan ticket. The universal complaint from people on the ground in that crucial and advertising-saturated swing state involved thoroughgoing disgust, even rage, at the way nasty attack ads had taken over all the networks and cable outlets. The negativity couldn't discourage the conservative activists who came out by the thousands to participate in our event, but it's easy to see how the nasty tone might lead others to turn off the tube altogether and to tune out a political season that had turned unspeakably petty and bitter.[19]

It is important not to discount the possibility that Obama's race played a role in declining white voter turnout. On the one hand, the election of the first African American may have demoralized racist whites and convinced them that engagement with the electoral process was a waste of time. On the other hand, we should not discount the possibility that many whites sincerely believed the election of the first African American president would genuinely usher in a new "post-racial" America, and when the reality failed to live up this expectation, they turned on Obama.

There were a few minor racial scandals during Obama's first term that may have spurred racial anxieties among some whites who would otherwise have voted for the Democratic candidate in 2012. There was suspicion that the Justice Department dismissed, for racial reasons, allegations that the New Black Panther Party engaged in voter intimidation in Philadelphia.[20] Attorney General Eric Holder further opened himself up to criticism from conservatives when, while explaining the controversy, he described African Americans as "my people"; this left leaders of the Justice Department, and by extension the entire Obama Administration, more vulnerable to the criticism that they were more concerned with African Americans and their interests than the interests of other demographic groups.[21] Obama also faced a minor uproar following the arrest of Professor Henry Louis Gates, an African American, by police sergeant James Crowley, who is white, for disorderly conduct outside Gates' home in 2009. Obama found himself part of the controversy when he asserted that Crowley "acted stupidly" by arresting Gates.[22] Obama also chose to weigh in on the fatal shooting of Trayvon Martin, a young African American, by George Zimmerman, a Latino, noting that if he had a son of his own, "he would look like Trayvon."[23] This shooting and the subsequent trial proved to be one of the most racially polarizing events in recent American history.

None of these events have proven politically consequential, and they hardly build a compelling case that the Obama Administration is openly hostile to white Americans. Nonetheless, from 2008 to 2012, some whites who previously supported Obama may have become sufficiently suspicious of him on racial grounds to stay home during the latter election.

DID WHITES REALLY BECOME MORE REPUBLICAN BETWEEN 2008 AND 2012?

As noted above, exit polls indicate that whites in 2012 were more Republican in their voting patterns than in any election since the 1980s. On its face this would suggest that whites became more Republican in terms of party identification. However, the difference between 2008 and 2012 may have been driven by differences in turnout, rather than any change in either partisanship or ideology.

To consider this possibility, it will be helpful to consult the General Social Survey (GSS). The GSS, conducted by the National Opinion Research Center, has surveyed Americans since 1972. Like the ANES, the GSS takes special care to ensure that respondents are randomly selected; thus we have can be sufficiently confident that estimates provided by the GSS reflect opinions of the nation at large. The GSS is also useful for a study of opinion change over time because many of its core questions have remained unchanged since it was first conducted.

The GSS asks respondents both the party with which they identify and their ideological inclinations. Thus, these data can be used to test whether there was a major shift in white political affiliations between 2008 and 2012. Party identification was presented as a seven-point scale (strong Democrat, not strong Democrat, independent leaning toward Democrat, independent, independent leaning toward Republican, not strong Republican, and strong Republican). Respondents were also given the option of stating that they preferred another party. Ideology was a seven-point scale (extremely liberal, liberal, slightly liberal, moderate, slightly conservative, conservative, and extremely conservative).

Unsurprisingly, there was relatively little change among whites in those two different years. For most people, party identification and ideology are relatively stable,[24] and we should not expect massive swings among any portion of the public without some important exogenous shock. What we do find conspicuously absent from the 2012 GSS is any strong evidence that whites became more Republican or more conservative since 2008. In fact, while the difference was within the margin of error in most cases, all the evidence indicates that whites became slightly *less* Republican and *less* conservative. In 2008, 41.7 percent of whites identified as a strong or weak Republican or as an independent who leaned Republican. In 2008, only 38.9 percent of whites identified as any type of Republican. This is not a dramatic difference, but it is useful to note that there was virtually no difference between the percentages of whites who identified as Democrats in the two years. The percentage of true independents (that is, independents who did not admit to leaning toward either of the major parties) increased by about 2 percent between the two elections (from 15 percent to 17 percent).[25]

Perhaps ideology is a better measure than party identification. It may be the case that many Republican voters actually do not admit to affiliating with the Republican Party. It is possible that the rise in Republican voting among whites is driven by the increasing number of whites who identify themselves as pure independents to pollsters, despite their exclusive support for the GOP. Given the degree to which members of the Tea Party assert their allegiance to their ideas rather than their political party, this is not completely implausible. For this reason, it may be useful to look at trends in ideology among whites to see if whites are increasingly likely to identify as conservatives.

At least according to the GSS, the trend in ideology is congruent with the trend in party identification. The number of whites who identified as liberal of any sort between the two years increased from 24 percent to 27 percent. The number who identified as conservative of any sort declined from 39.2 percent to 36.5 percent. It is interesting to note that this decline was only present among the "conservative" and the "slightly conservative" categories. The percentage of respondents who identified as "strong conservatives" actually increased slightly, as did the percentage that identified as "strong liberals"—thus, we could make the argument that whites became more ideologically polarized between 2008 and 2012.

What about the ideological inclinations of white independents—did they become more or less conservative during this period? Whether we are considering pure independents alone, or pure independents as well as those independents who admit to leaning toward a specific party, the results are largely the same. The GSS does not indicate that independents became more conservative or more liberal. There was virtually no change in the mean ideology of white independents during this period.

Although there was modest evidence of an ideological shift to the left among some whites between 2008 and 2012, whites are still more likely to identify as conservative than as liberal. The important thing to note is that, according to the GSS, whites did not, on average, become more conservative or likely to identify as Republican between these two election years. The lack of evidence for a major change in white ideological inclinations or party identification within this short period does not change the fact that whites have, on average, slowly become more Republican and conservative over the past several decades. Rather, it simply indicates that there was not enough of a change in any direction to account for the change in aggregate white vote choice between 2008 and 2012. This finding suggests that the explanation for the comparatively strong Republican showing in 2012 among whites can be attributed to changes in white turnout, though a more in-depth look at turnout trends in recent years is necessary.

EXTERNAL EFFICACY AND RACIAL RESENTMENT

When considering white voter behavior in recent presidential elections, President Obama's race should not be discounted as a potential influence. We might surmise that, if whites felt increasingly threatened racially in recent years, they would turn out to vote in record numbers. This is clearly not what has occurred, as voter turnout among whites was lower in 2008 and 2012 than it was in 2004. Relatedly, we might expect that whites with anti-black attitudes became completely turned off by politics following the election of the first African American president. In other words, Obama's election may have undermined the sense of political efficacy of those whites with less progressive attitudes on race, leading them to withdraw from the electorate.

Before turning to the question of efficacy and race, it is worth considering whether or not there have been any meaningful changes in white racial attitudes since Obama's election. The ANES can provide a useful starting point. There are a number of questions related to racial attitudes that are consistently asked on the survey.

Discerning Americans' true racial attitudes from public opinion surveys is a challenge. As public, openly racist comments are considered taboo throughout most of America, even the most racist white American may feel uncomfortable sharing his or her true racial feelings with a pollster. One kind of racial attitude that remains generally acceptable to many white Americans is a form of racial resentment. As Kinder and Sanders put it,

> A new form of prejudice has come to prominence. . . . At its center are the contentions that blacks do not try hard enough to overcome the difficulties they face and they take what they have not earned. Today, we say, prejudice is expressed in the language of American individualism.[26]

According to Kinder and Sanders, blatant racial prejudice has declined, but feelings of racial resentment remain strong among whites, and these feelings have profound political consequences. This line of research has led to the development of a new series of common questions designed to tap racial resentment.[27]

There are four questions on the 2012 ANES that can effectively measure white feelings of racial resentment.[28] Respondents were asked the degree to which they agree or disagree with the following statements: "It's really a matter of some people not trying hard enough; if blacks would only try harder they could be just as well off as whites"; "Over the past few years, blacks have gotten less than they deserve"; "Generations of slavery and discrimination have created conditions that make it difficult for blacks to work their way out of the lower class"; "Irish, Italians, Jewish and many other minorities overcame prejudice and worked their way up. Blacks should do the same without any special favors." Responses to these questions were highly correlated,[29] making it possible to generate a scale, with lower values being associated with lower levels of racial resentment and higher values associated with higher levels of racial resentment. This scale was then normalized to take a value between 0 and 1.[30]

Some literature indicates that President Obama's election should have led to lower levels of prejudice among whites. Zoltan Hajnal examined how white racial attitudes were influenced by living in a community governed by an African American mayor. He found that, at least among white Democrats and independents, living in a municipality with an African American mayor was associated with less racial tension and greater sympathy for African Americans.[31] Examining the relationship between generational membership and racial attitudes in the 2010 Cooperative Congressional Election Study, Nteta and Greenlee concluded that the Obama's election did lead white Americans, particularly the youngest white Americans, to hold more liberal racial attitudes.[32]

In contrast to Nteta and Greenlee's findings, the present author's examination of the ANES surveys in 2008 and 2012 found little indication that the election of President Obama assuaged feelings of racial resentment among whites. Among white respondents to the 2008 ANES, the mean racial resentment score was 0.65; in 2012, the mean score was 0.67. That is, these data indicate that racial resentment actually *increased* slightly among whites over this period.[33] Furthermore, the largest increase in racial resentment over these four years actually occurred among the *youngest* whites. Whereas the mean racial resentment score for whites under 30 was 0.59 in 2008, in 2012 it was 0.64. There was a generational gap in racial resentment in both surveys—the oldest whites exhibited more racial resentment than the youngest whites—but that white generation gap in racial resentment was cut in half over the course of four years.

Returning to the question of turnout, it is worth investigating whether the relationship between racial attitudes and voting was the same in 2008 and 2012. If they were a substantive predictor, and predicted a lower probability of turnout in the latter year but not the former, we could infer that those with higher levels of racial resentment failed to turn out in 2012. The results of this model can be found in Appendix 2.1. In this model, self-reported voter turnout is the dependent variable. Given the dichotomous nature of the dependent variable, a logit model was appropriate.[34] The key independent variable was the respondent's racial resentment score, though a large number of additional independent variables were also included. Coefficients in a logit model can be difficult to interpret, and for this reason odds ratios were presented in the table.

This model indicates that racial resentment was both a substantively and statistically significant variable in 2012, but not in 2008.[35] Specifically, compared to whites with the lowest level of racial resentment, whites with the highest possible racial resentment score were only 0.49 times as likely to vote, on average and controlling for all other variables. This is important because it suggests that one of the effects of the Obama presidency was the political disengagement of whites with strong anti-black feelings. This may help explain why white voter turnout declined between the 2008 and 2012 elections—though it does little to explain why Romney won a greater share of the white vote.[36]

There is a problem with examining separate models to consider how the effects of this and other variables differed between these two elections. While we can say that, based on these separate analyses, a variable was statistically or substantively significant in one period but not in another, we cannot determine whether the coefficients in the two models were significantly different from each other. In order to determine this, the data must be combined into a single model, and an interaction term must be added. The author combined these two datasets and created such a model including this interaction. While the results of this model were substantively congruent with the results of the two separate models, the interaction between year and racial resentment was not statistically significant. That is, we cannot say with any confidence that racial resentment played a greater role in white turnout in 2012 than in 2008.

In spite of this caveat about comparing the coefficients in two models, it is worth noting that we see a number of additional interesting findings when we compare the results from both years. In 2008, we see that age mattered very little in terms of voter turnout. There was no statistically discernible difference between whites in the youngest age cohort and whites in the middle age cohorts (those between 30 and 65). In other words, in 2008 the age gap in white voter turnout all but disappeared. The age gap returned for whites in 2012, however, and all other age cohorts reported voting at higher rates than the youngest cohort, controlling for other variables, in the latter election.

Why might racial resentment have possibly played a role in white voter turnout in 2012 and perhaps in 2008? As suggested at the start of this section, one possible answer is that the election of President Obama decreased feelings of political efficacy among whites with high levels of racial resentment. Political efficacy is defined as

> the feeling that individual political action does have, or can have, an impact upon the political process, i.e., that it is worthwhile to perform one's civic duties. It is the feeling that political and social change is possible, and that the individual citizen can play a part in bringing about this change.[37]

Efficacy is usually distinguished between internal efficacy—the belief an individual has about her competency to engage in politics—and external efficacy—an individual's belief about the degree to which an individual can actually influence politics and policy. A lack of efficacy may lead to a lower level of interest in politics and ultimately a withdrawal from political participation.

Political efficacy is related to the issue of political alienation—that is, a negative view of the political system. Franz Neuman explained that alienation is a "conscious rejection of the whole political system which expresses itself in apathy."[38] Those who are politically alienated are more likely to feel that they have no power to influence politics and, as a result, tend to withdraw from political activity.

Have white feelings of efficacy changed in recent years? There are reasons to expect they might have changed, for at least some whites. There was evidence that African Americans experienced an increase in political efficacy in 2008, and the fact that Barack Obama provided them descriptive representation is one compelling explanation for this finding.[39] This finding was congruent with other research indicating that descriptive representation

increases minority feelings of empowerment and minority political participation.[40] Descriptive representation is when an elected representative not
only advances a group's preferences but also shares that group's attributes—
be it gender, region, religion, or race. If gaining descriptive representation
in the nation's highest elected office increased the feelings of efficacy among
African Americans, it is similarly possible that the loss of descriptive representation decreased these feelings among whites. The ANES asked a number
of questions that tap into feelings of efficacy in 2008 and 2012 that allow
us to consider this issue.

One question asked in both 2008 and 2012 was whether or not individuals agreed or disagreed with the following statement: "Public officials don't
care much what people like me think." Respondents were specifically asked
to place themselves on a five-point scale ranging from "agree strongly" to
"disagree strongly." In 2008, 60 percent of whites either agreed or strongly
agreed with this statement. In 2012, this percentage increased. In the latter
year, almost 68 percent of whites either agreed or strongly agreed with this
statement. While the change is not enormous, these are substantial differences and indicate that there was a meaningful drop in the degree to which
whites felt a sense of efficacy in regard to political activity.

Is there a relationship between feelings of racial resentment and political efficacy among whites? A look at the descriptive statistics from 2012
suggests that there is. Among whites with a racial resentment score one
standard deviation above the mean, the mean political efficacy score was 1.2
(on a scale of 0 to 4). Among whites with a racial resentment score one standard deviation below the mean, the mean political efficacy score was 2.3. It
appears that whites with higher levels of racial resentment had lower levels
of political efficacy. In 2008, those whites with the highest racial resentment
scores had a mean political efficacy score of 1.6 and those whites with the
lowest racial resentment scores had a mean political efficacy score of 2.6.
This suggests that both groups experienced a decline in feelings of external
efficacy, but the decline was slightly larger for those at the high end of the
racial resentment scale.

The relationship between efficacy and racial resentment may be spurious,
however, if another variable correlated with racial resentment is actually
driving feelings of efficacy. For example, if white Republicans are generally
less trustful of government, and they tend to have higher levels of racial
resentment, then racial resentment may actually not have any direct influence
on feelings of efficacy. A least-squares regression model can tell us if this is
the case. In the model in Appendix 2.2, the dependent variable was based on
the question regarding external efficacy mentioned in the preceding paragraph,
in which lower values indicate a lower level of external efficacy. This model
contains the same control variables as appeared in the preceding models.

The most interesting thing to note about this model is that very few variables predicted white feelings of efficacy. Education, age, and income had no

statistically discernible effect. Party identification, however, had an effect. Both self-identified Democrats and Republicans were more likely to claim a higher level of efficacy than independents, and in both cases this was statistically significant. We should be careful before inferring the direction of the causal arrow in this case. It may not be that identifying with one of the major parties rather than as an independent causes an individual to have higher feelings of efficacy. It is equally (or perhaps more) plausible that those with low levels of external efficacy choose not to identify with a party.

We see some compelling evidence that racial resentment leads to a lower sense of political efficacy. Compared to those whites with the lowest levels of racial resentment, those with the highest levels of racial resentment placed themselves, on average and controlling for all other variables, 0.68 points lower on the external efficacy scale.

The results of these models suggest that one effect of Obama's candidacy and presidency was a decline in voter turnout among whites with higher levels of racial resentment—though the percentage of whites who expressed such feelings changed little between these two elections. While there are a number of reasons this might have been the case, it appears that feelings of external political efficacy were lower among whites who had higher levels of racial resentment, and lower levels of efficacy are associated with lower turnout.

We might expect that white Republicans have, on average, higher levels of racial resentment than white Democrats. If this is the case, then the preceding findings should indicate that the decline of voter turnout among racially resentful whites has hurt the GOP more than the Democrats. This is also a question we can examine using the ANES. The mean racial resentment score among all whites was 0.66. Among whites with a resentment score above the mean, 45 percent identified as Republican. Among whites with a resentment score below the mean, only about 20 percent identified as Republican. Compared to 2008, white Republicans in 2012 had a slightly higher mean racial resentment score, and the mean score for white Democrats was slightly lower—suggesting that the correlation between racial attitudes and vote choice is increasing among whites. These results indicate that the decline in voting among more racist whites hurt the GOP far more than the Democrats.

We cannot necessarily infer that the election of the first African American president was the cause (or the sole cause) of declining political engagement among the more racist elements of the white electorate. Other trends may explain this. For example, in 2011, for the first time in U.S. history, the number of non-white births exceeded the number of white births, and the coming minority status of whites became more apparent to a greater percentage of the American population. This demographic trend may also have proven demoralizing to racially resentful whites, and this event was in no way related to Obama's presidency.

DID ROMNEY'S MORMONISM TURN OFF WHITE REPUBLICAN VOTERS?

During Mitt Romney's bids for the Republican Party's presidential nomination in 2008 and 2012, some suspected that Romney's religious affiliation would prove to be a stumbling block. Many Evangelical Christians have negative attitudes toward the Church of Jesus Christ of Latter-Day Saints, and some prominent Evangelicals have even Mormonism as a "false religion."[41] In the years leading up to Romney's first presidential bid, some commentators suggested his religion would damage his viability as a candidate in Republican primaries. Back in 2005, Amy Sullivan wrote the following in *The Washington Monthly*:

> [Romney's] obstacle is the evangelical base—a voting bloc that now makes up 30 percent of the Republican electorate and that wields particular influence in primary states like South Carolina and Virginia. Just as it is hard to overestimate the importance of evangelicalism in the modern Republican Party, it is nearly impossible to overemphasize the problem evangelicals have with Mormonism. Evangelicals don't have the same vague anti-LDS prejudice that some Americans do. For them it's a doctrinal thing, based on very specific theological disputes that can't be overcome by personality or charm or even shared positions on social issues. Romney's journalistic boosters either don't understand these doctrinal issues or try to sidestep them. But ignoring them won't make them go away. To evangelicals, Mormonism isn't just another religion. It's a cult.[42]

Romney's religious affiliation proved less problematic for Republican voters than many anticipated. It is true that, in the Republican primaries, Romney performed poorly in many states with the highest number of Evangelical Christians—most states in the Deep South and lower Midwest gave their support to Newt Gingrich or Rick Santorum in the Republican primaries. However, once Romney secured the nomination, it appeared that most Evangelical Republicans offered their support to Romney. Early polling showed that large majorities of white Evangelicals supported Romney over Obama, even those who did not believe Mormons were actually Christian.[43]

The broad support that Evangelicals apparently offered Romney does not necessarily indicate, however, that Romney's religion played no role in voter turnout in 2012. There may have been some Republicans who stayed home that year because of their hostility to the Mormon faith. On the other hand, if they were uncomfortable with a Mormon in the White House, religion may have actually motivated additional white Democrats to turn out to the polls.

The 2012 ANES is again a useful starting point for considering this question. As noted in the previous chapter, this survey asked respondents to provide a "feeling thermometer" regarding a number of groups and individuals. These scores can range between 0 (indicating a very low rating) and 100 (indicating a very high rating). Higher scores mean that an individual is more favorable toward a particular group. Using this score, it is possible to discern whether there was any relationship between white attitudes toward Mormons and white turnout, as well as whether this relationship varied according to partisanship. Among all whites, the mean feeling thermometer was 52 degrees—feeling neither close nor far away from this religious group. The mean may not tell us very much, as one might expect that feelings toward Mormons are polarized; half of whites may strongly dislike Mormons, and the other half may feel very close to Mormons. However, a look at the distribution of feelings indicates that this was not the case—the distribution was not bimodal. Most answers were somewhere around 50 degrees, although there was some variation according to partisan group. Among white Republicans, the mean thermometer score for Mormons was 57 degrees; among white Democrats it was 47 degrees; and among white Independents the mean was 52 degrees.

These data also indicate that there was a very small correlation between attitudes toward Mormons and voter turnout. The correlation coefficient for voter turnout and attitudes toward Mormons was positive (indicating that whites who had warm feelings toward Mormons were more likely to vote), but small (0.11). This differed according to partisan group, however. Among white Democrats, there was virtually no correlation between attitudes toward Mormons and voting (correlation coefficient of 0.01). It was higher, however, among Independents (0.11) and Republicans (0.14). Among white Republicans who described themselves as "born again" Christians, the correlation was 0.16. Among born-again Christians who described themselves as Independent, the correlation was 0.2. This indicates that, to the extent that there was a relationship between attitudes toward Mormons and voter turnout, it was strongest among Republicans and Independents, particularly among white Republicans and Independents who were also born-again Christians. Such Republicans and Independents who had negative attitudes toward Mormons were slightly less likely to vote, though the small size of this effect indicates that this was not sufficient to explain the aggregate drop in white voter turnout.

To determine whether there was a significant relationship between feelings toward Mormons and voter turnout among whites after controlling for a myriad of other variables, the author re-created the logit model for voter turnout in 2012 found in Appendix 2.1, but included feelings toward Mormons as an independent variable. This model also included an interaction between the Mormon feeling thermometer and party identification. The model demonstrates that the relationship between feelings toward Mormons and voter turnout was not spurious. Independents and Republicans with strong positive feelings toward Mormons were more likely to vote; Democrats with strong positive feelings toward Mormons were less likely to vote.

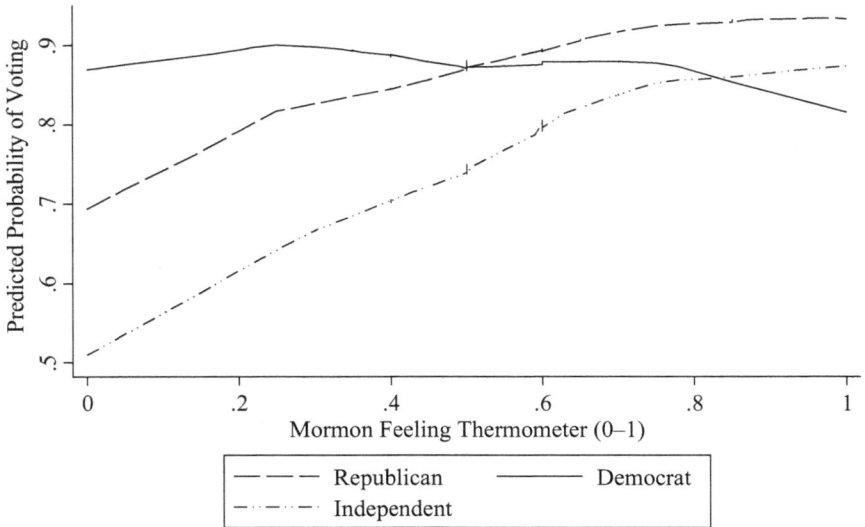

Figure 2.1   Feelings toward Mormons and Probability of Voting in 2012

After creating the model, the author generated the predicted probability of voting for each respondent and then plotted the relationship between that probability and feelings toward Mormons; this figure relied on locally weighted scatterplot smoothing (LOWESS)[44]. The results can be found in Figure 2.1. This figure shows that the relationship between voting and feelings toward Mormons was strongest among Independents. The relationship was weaker among Republicans, but in the same direction. There was only a small relationship between these variables for white Democrats.

Unfortunately, the ANES did not ask respondents for their attitude toward Mormons in 2008. We may reasonably suspect that feelings toward Mormons had an influence on voter turnout in 2012 because of Mitt Romney's presence on the Republican ticket, but not in previous years in which this would not have been an issue. We cannot know this for sure, however.

A CLOSER LOOK AT WHITE TURNOUT

The Current Population Survey (CPS), which is administered by the U.S. Census Bureau, conducts a voter turnout survey the November of each election year. The CPS Voting and Registration Supplement is one of the most valuable tools for political scientists who study American voter turnout, as it surveys a substantial percentage of the population and collects a large amount of additional demographic, geographic, and economic data for each respondent.

Overall, whites voted at lower rates in 2012 than in 2008. The decrease was not consistent nationwide, however, and in some states white turnout actually increased. Some of the most dramatic changes can be explained by the characteristics of a presidential or vice presidential candidate in one of the two elections. The state that exhibited the greatest drop in white turnout was Alaska (a drop of 7.3 percentage points), which can probably be attributed to the fact that former Alaska governor Sarah Palin was on the ballot in 2008 but not in 2012. Utah experienced the most substantial increase in white turnout (an increase of 5.4 percentage points). The presence of Mitt Romney at the top of the Republican ticket surely played some role in this increase.

Looking at other states, however, an initial glance at the changes in white voter turnout at the state level between 2008 and 2012 does not strongly suggest a relationship between changes in aggregate white vote choice and changes in white turnout. The correlation between white turnout change and aggregate white vote choice change (as measured via exit polls) between the two elections was negligible. Of the ten states that saw the greatest decline in white voter turnout between the two elections, seven gave their electoral votes to Romney. Of the ten states that saw the greatest increase in white voter turnout, five voted for Romney. The states that saw the greatest change in aggregate white vote choice did not always experience a substantive change in white turnout. Among whites in Michigan, there was an eight percentage point increase in the share of the white vote that went to the Republican candidate between 2008 and 2012, but there was virtually no change in the white turnout rate. Therefore, this increase in the Republican share of the white vote in Michigan cannot be solely attributed to changes in turnout.

Interestingly, there were some cases where neighboring states with similar political cultures nonetheless exhibited dramatically different changes in terms of white turnout. From 2008 to 2012, white turnout increased by 1.5 percentage points in Kansas, but declined by 5.6 percentage points in neighboring Nebraska. White voter turnout increased by 3.4 percentage points in Mississippi but declined by 7.2 percentage points in Louisiana.

The decline in white turnout was not consistent across the white electorate. Some groups of white voters changed relatively little between the two elections, whereas the turnout of others dropped substantially. Table 2.1 shows the percentage point change in voter turnout between the two election years. See Appendix 2.3 for the full turnout results for all groups within the white electorate in both years.

We see clearly that there was a linear relationship between education levels and the degree to which whites' voter turnout declined between the two elections. Whites with higher education levels were much more likely to vote in both elections, and there was little change between the two elections. Some caution should be exercised here, as it is established that Americans with higher levels of education are more likely than Americans with less

Table 2.1   Percentage Change in White Voter Turnout, 2008–2012

	All	Married	Unmarried	No HS Diploma	HS Diploma	Some College	College Degree
All	−2.02	−0.41	−1.18	−2.68	−2.36	−3.7	−2.35
Men	−1.63	−0.41	−1.45	−2.98	−2.06	−2.53	−1.93
Women	−2.31	−0.39	−1.75	−2.36	−2.55	−4.69	−2.77

	Advanced Degree	Age 18–29	Age 30–44	Age 45–64	Age 65+	HS Diploma or Less, Under 30
All	−1.92	−6.09	−2.94	−1.75	0.75	−8.43
Men	−2.5	−5.16	−3.4	−1.26	0.8	−7.3
Women	−1.35	−7.08	−2.46	−2.19	0.66	−11.19

Source: CPS November Voting and Registration Supplement, 2008 & 2012

education to tell pollsters that they voted when they actually did not, and the CPS does not subsequently verify whether respondents actually voted. That being said, there is little reason to expect that highly educated whites were *more* likely to over-report voting in 2012 than in 2008, so we can trust that this group changed relatively little between the two elections.

There was similarly a linear relationship between age and changes in voter turnout. In fact, the oldest cohort of whites actually turned out in greater numbers in 2012 than in 2008. We also see that there was a more modest decline for married whites than for unmarried whites. Men declined less than women, though in both election years the turnout rate for women was actually higher than the turnout rate for men.

The most dramatic change in white turnout occurred among the youngest whites, and this was particularly true for whites with lower levels of education. For whites with a high school education or less, there was a decline of 8.4 percentage points between the two elections. This is a significant decline, especially when one considers that the turnout rate for this group was relatively low to begin with—only about 35 percent of this group voted in 2008. This suggests that young, working-class whites were particularly alienated from electoral politics in 2012 compared to other whites.

It is important to note that the whites who experienced the most substantial decline in turnout between the two elections were those who had a relatively high probability of voting for Obama in 2008—the unmarried and the young. This indicates that the strong showing of Romney among white voters in 2012 was largely because the Democrats failed to mobilize their white former supporters, rather than because a large number of whites defected between the two elections.

It would be incorrect to infer that the entire change in aggregate white voting patterns could be entirely ascribed to different turnout rates, however.

Although there was a 1.6 percentage point decrease in voter turnout for white men between 2008 and 2012, Obama's share among white men dropped by six percentage points between the two elections (from 41 percent to 35 percent), according to exit polls. Voter turnout among whites ages 18–29 declined by 6.1 percentage points, but Obama's support from this group declined by 10 percentage points (from 54 percent to 44 percent).[45]

This table seems to indicate that the white voters in 2008 who failed to turn out in 2012 were members of groups that were more likely to support Democrats than other groups within the white electorate. Such a conclusion may be mistaken, however. We saw that the whites who experienced the largest decline in turnout were whites under 30 with lower levels of education. While we might infer that this was one of the more Democratic groups within the white electorate, it is important to remember that whites with a college degree actually voted in greater numbers for Obama than whites without a degree. Whites with a college degree narrowly gave a majority of their votes to McCain (51 percent), whereas a larger majority of whites without a college degree voted for McCain (58 percent).

Among young whites, the education gap in vote choice was equally substantial. Young whites (under the age of 30) who earned, at most, a high school diploma, voted almost evenly for the two candidates—about 48 percent of them voted for John McCain, according to exit polls. On the other hand, only 40 percent of whites in that age category with a college degree voted for McCain. In other words, young whites with lower levels of education were in the category of under-30 whites that was *most likely* to support McCain. This was also the group that experienced the most dramatic change in turnout between the two elections.

CONCLUSION

Based on what we have seen thus far, there is not conclusive evidence indicating that the decline in white voting between 2008 and 2012 occurred predominantly among former Republican or former Democratic voters. Racial resentment was associated with lower levels of voter turnout in 2012. White Republicans tend to score higher on the racial resentment scale than white Democrats, which suggests that much of the decline in white voting was beneficial to the Democratic Party. However, we do not have decisive evidence suggesting that the effect of this variable was substantively different in 2008.

It also appears that much of the decline in white voter turnout occurred among whites quite likely to support the Democratic Party. This is congruent with the finding that white voters were more likely to support the Republican candidate in 2012 than in previous elections, despite the fact that there was little survey evidence suggesting that whites became, as a group, more Republican or conservative during this short period. We saw that the age gap among whites when it came to voter turnout virtually disappeared in

2008 but returned in 2012. Given the strength of Obama's support among young whites in 2008, this decline in turnout among young whites surely benefited the GOP.

It would be easy to discern which party benefited from the decline in white voter turnout if there was an obvious linear relationship between the percentage of each group within the white electorate that supported one of the major candidates in 2008 and the change in voter turnout within that group in the latter election. If we found that the whites most supportive of Obama were also the whites who neglected to show up in the latter election, we could say that Romney's strong showing among white voters was due to a failure on the Democrats' part to mobilize their previous white voters. Instead, we see that the groups that were most likely to support Democrats (those with the highest levels of education) continued to turn out in large numbers, as did the portions of the white electorate that are most likely to support Republicans (the married, those in the oldest age cohort).

We should not discount the possibility that a significant percentage of whites who turned out for Romney voted for Obama in 2008 or would have had they been old enough. Although there was a seven percentage point drop in voter turnout among white men under the age of 30, there was an eleven percentage point drop in the support that white men in that age category gave to Obama. This difference in aggregate vote choice probably cannot be entirely explained by a decline in turnout from the previous election.[46] We can say with some confidence that the increase in white support for the Republican candidate between the two elections was driven by more than just a decline in turnout among white Democrats—though, again, we should remember that it does not appear that a large percentage of whites changed their party identification during this four-year period.

It is increasingly clear that the Democratic Party has developed a problem among young whites with lower levels of education. Exit polls indicate that Democratic voting within this group declined by 13 percentage points between 2008 and 2012.[47] This is problematic for the Democratic Party even if this change was due entirely to a drop in voter turnout. At a time of widespread economic difficulty for young Americans, the party in favor of economic redistribution should presumably experience relatively high levels of support from portions of the electorate that are more economically vulnerable. At the time of the 2012 presidential election, the unemployment rate for those under 30 was a staggering 11.8 percent.[48] While whites in this age category were in a better situation than Americans in this category overall, their rates of unemployment were nonetheless also quite high. The cause of this apparent widespread disenchantment with the Democratic Party is not immediately clear, though we should not discount rising racial anxiety among less educated whites as a potential cause—the fact that there was not a corresponding drop in Democratic support from young non-whites suggests this is not an implausible hypothesis.

Some may also be concerned by the lack of a substantial generation gap among whites when it comes to racial resentment. Among all whites, the mean racial resentment score was 0.67. Among the youngest cohort of whites (those under 30), the mean racial resentment score was 0.64—only slightly lower than whites overall. The relationship between racial resentment and party identification was also slightly higher among young whites than other whites—about 48 percent of young whites with above-average resentment scores reported identifying with the Republican Party, compared to 44 percent of whites over 30 with above-average resentment scores. Thus, feelings of racial resentment among whites do not appear to be dissipating, and the political consequences of those feelings appear to be increasing. This subject will be further explored in Chapter 7 in this volume.

The Democratic Party's weakness among younger whites could potentially represent a new source of votes for the GOP—though they clearly failed to make a major breakthrough in 2012, as indicated by the low turn-out rate of young whites. Had turnout been considerably higher among younger whites, and if those potential voters had given as much support to Romney as those who actually voted in 2012, Obama's margin of victory would have been much more narrow.

NOTES

1. Detailed tables can be accessed at the following URL: www.census.gov/hhes/www/socdemo/voting/publications/historical/index.html (accessed May 27, 2012).
2. Ed Kilgore, "Final 2012 Results," *Washington Monthly*, January 4, 2013, accessed October 14, 2013, www.washingtonmonthly.com/political-animal-a/2013_01/final_2012_results042198.php.
3. Steven A. Camorata, *Who Voted in 2012: Results from the Census Bureau's November Voting and Registration Supplement*, Washington, DC: The Center for Immigration Studies, 2012.
4. Andres Blais, "Turnout in Elections," in *The Oxford Handbook of Political Behavior*, eds. Russell J. Dalton and Hans-Dieter Klingemann (New York: Oxford University Press, 2007), 624.
5. Teixeira, Ruy, *Why Americans Don't Vote: Turnout Decline in the United States, 1960–1984*, Westport, CT: Greenwood Press, 1987, p. 7–8.
6. Michael P. McDonald and Samuel Popkin, "The Myth of the Vanishing Voter," *American Political Science Review*, 95(2001): 968.
7. Indeed, in a presidential election, such a close race would certainly be decided by the courts or congress, thus the probability that any single individual will cast the deciding vote in such an election is actually zero.
8. John H. Aldrich, "Rational Choice and Turnout," *American Journal of Political Science*, 37(1993), 271.
9. Arend Lijphart, "Unequal Participation: Democracy's Unresolved Dilemma," *American Political Science Review*, 91(1997), 8–10.
10. James DeNardo, "Turnout and the Vote: The Joke's on the Democrats," *American Political Science Review*, 74(1980), 418.

11. Jack Citrin, Eric Schickler, and John Sides, "What if Everyone Voted? Simulating the Impact of Increased Turnout in Senate Elections." *American Journal of Political Science*, 47(2003), 88.
12. Sean Trende, "The Case of the Missing White Voters, Revisited," *Real Clear Politics*, June 21, 2013, accessed June 21, 2013, www.realclearpolitics.com/articles/2013/06/21/the_case_of_the_missing_white_voters_revisited_118893.html.
13. Ruy Teixeira and Alan Abramowitz, "No, Republicans, 'Missing White' Voters won't Save You," *ThinkProgress*, July 9, 2013, accessed August 5, 2013, http://thinkprogress.org/election/2013/07/09/2266841/trende-republicans-white-voters-missing/?mobile=nc.
14. Sean Trende, "Yes, the Missing Whites Matter," *Real Clear Politics*, July 12, 2013, accessed August 5, 2013, www.realclearpolitics.com/articles/2013/07/12/yes_the_missing_whites_matter_119170.html.
15. Nate Cohn, "Winning More White Voters won't Save the GOP," *The New Republic,* July 9, 2013, accessed October 14, 2013, www.newrepublic.com/article/113782/immigration-reform-2013-white-voters-wont-save-gop.
16. Sidney Verba, Kay Lehman Schlozman, and Henry E. Brady, *Voice and Equality: Civic Volunteerism in American Politics* (Cambridge, MA: Harvard University Press, 1995), 361.
17. Avik Roy, "How the Heritage Foundation, a Conservative Think Tank, Promoted the Individual Mandate," *Forbes*, October 20, 2011, accessed July 29, 2013, www.forbes.com/sites/aroy/2011/10/20/how-a-conservative-think-tank-invented-the-individual-mandate/.
18. Philip Rucker, "Romney's '47 percent' Comments aren't Going Away, and they're Taking a Toll," *The Washington Post*, October 1, 2012, accessed June 6, 2013. www.washingtonpost.com/politics/decision2012/romneys-47-percent-comments-arent-going-away/2012/10/01/17604654–0be5–11e2-a310–2363842b7057_story.html.
19. Michael Medved, "Obama's Dirty Little Secret to Winning the 2012 Presidential Election," *The Daily Beast*, November 12, 2012, accessed October 14, 2013, www.thedailybeast.com/articles/2012/11/12/obama-s-dirty-little-secret-to-winning-the-2012-presidential-election.html.
20. Jerry Markon, "Report: Justice Dept. Tried Hiding Officials' Roles in Panther Lawsuit Dismissal," *The Washington Post*, October 29, 2010, accessed June 6, 2013, www.washingtonpost.com/wp-dyn/content/article/2010/10/28/AR2010102807129.html.
21. James Taranto was one conservative columnist who immediately attacked Eric Holder for this statement. Taranto specifically states, "If he approaches the job with the attitude that any group smaller than all Americans is 'my people,' he is the wrong man for the position." James Taranto, "Eric Holder's People," *The Wall Street Journal*, March 2, 2011, accessed June 6, 2013, http://online.wsj.com/article/SB10001424052748703559604576176381487078812.html.
22. Ben Feller, "Beer Summit Begins: Obama Sits Down with Crowley, Gates," *The Huffington Post*, September 30, 2009, accessed June 6, 2013, www.huffingtonpost.com/2009/07/30/beer-summit-begins-obama-_n_248254.html.
23. Matt Williams, "Obama: Trayvon Martin Death a Tragedy that Must be Investigated," *The Guardian*, March 23, 2012, accessed June 6, 2013, www.guardian.co.uk/world/2012/mar/23/obama-trayvon-martin-tragedy.
24. Erik Schickler and Donald Philip Green, "The Stability of Party Identification in Western Democracies: Results from Eight Panel Surveys," *Comparative Political Studies*, 30(1997), 451–452.
25. The author also examined the 2008 and 2012 ANES to see if there was a meaningful difference in Republican identification. The results of those polls were substantively identical to those of the GSS.

26. Donald R. Kinder and Lynn M. Sanders, *Divided by Color: Racial Politics and Democratic Ideals* (Chicago: University of Chicago Press, 1996), 105–106.
27. It is worth noting that some commentators question the validity of racial resentment as a measure of racism. Writing in *The American Spectator*, Robert VerBruggen argued that the statements used to generate the racial resentment scale are simply conservative statements with a racial element unnecessarily inserted: "Mainstream conservatives believe that people of all races can improve their lot in life through hard work, and further that most poverty is the result of behavior. (These are not crazy beliefs: Those who finish high school, work full-time, and marry before having children rarely end up in poverty and usually end up in the middle class.) When presented with a statement that racializes that sentiment, should conservatives decline to agree? Maybe, but liberals—who believe that structural barriers, more than behavior, affect people's outcomes in life—face no such tradeoff, so any gap between liberals and conservatives could represent mere differences in political beliefs." Robert VerBruggen, "Diagnosing Racism," *The American Spectator*, April 27, 2010, accessed November 12, 2013, http://spectator.org/articles/39675/looking-drawing. While these is a valid criticism, it is worth noting that racial resentment is commonly used by political scientists. Furthermore, if racial resentment was simply a measure of conservatism, then racial resentment should cease to be a statistically- or substantively significant variable after a measure of ideology is included; this is not what we find.
28. The ANES first began including questions on racial resentment in 1986. The questions asked then and in 2012 were similar.
29. The reliability coefficient of this scale was 0.79.
30. The scale was generated using the same methods used by Kinder and Saunders.
31. Zoltan L. Hajnal, "White Residents, Black Incumbents, and a Declining Racial Divide," *The American Political Science Review*, 95(2001): 603–617.
32. Tatishe M. Nteta and Jill S. Greenlee, "A Change is Gonna Come: Generational Membership and White Racial Attitudes in the 21st Century," *Political Psychology*, Forthcoming.
33. It is worth noting that on this point there is some disagreement between the ANES and the General Social Survey, which also asks a number of questions that can be used to measure racial resentment. While the GSS also showed little change among whites on this variable between 2008 and 2012, the change was slightly more substantive, and what little change there was indicated that whites became slightly less prejudiced over this period. There was evidence suggesting that fewer white Americans supported "special treatment" for African Americans in 2012 than in 2008, however.
34. Any introductory statistics textbook will provide a useful introduction to logistic regression and the interpretation of odds ratios. For readers interested in online resources, I recommend the Institute for Digital Research and Education at UCLA. For this subject in particular, see "FAQ: How Do I Interpret Odds Ratios in Logistic Regression," UCLA: Statistical Consulting Group, accessed April 29, 2013, www.ats.ucla.edu/stat/mult_pkg/faq/general/odds_ratio.htm.
35. As the text notes, because these are completely separate regression models, we cannot necessarily compare the two coefficients in the different models. Furthermore, the smaller standard errors in the latter election are also a function of the larger sample size. That being said, even in 2008 there were more than 1,000 white respondents in the model, which should be more than sufficient for discovering whether or not racial resentment played any role in voter turnout in that year. The fact that the coefficient was much smaller in the former year (though in the same direction), and nowhere near statistically significant, provides evidence that racial resentment played a role in 2012 but not in 2008.

36. In case racial resentment was a more powerful predictor for white turnout in the more distant past, these models were also created using 1992 data, though this model is not presented in the table. The results were congruent with those from 2008. That is, in 1992 there was no statistically-significant evidence that whites with higher levels of racial resentment were less likely to vote.

37. Angus Campbell, Gerald Gurin, Warren E. Miller, Sylvia Eberhart, Robert O. McWilliams, *The Voter Decides* (Evanston, IL: Row, Peterson, 1954), 187.

38. Neuman, Franz, *The Democratic and the Authoritarian State: Essays in Political and Legal Theory* (New York: Free Press, 1957), 290.

39. Jennifer L. Merolla, Abbylin H. Sellers, Derek J. Fowler, "Descriptive Representation, Political Efficacy, and African Americans in the 2008 Presidential Election," *Political Psychology*, forthcoming.

40. Susan A. Banducci, Todd Donovan, and Jeffrey A. Karp, "Minority Representation, Empowerment, and Participation," *The Journal of Politics*, 66(2004): 534–556; Adrian Pantoja and Gary Segura, "Does Ethnicity Matter? Descriptive Representation in Legislatures and Political Alienation Among Latinos," *Social Science Quarterly*, 84(2003): 441–460.

41. David S. Reynolds, "Why Evangelicals Don't Like Mormons." *The New York Times,* January 25, 2012, accessed October 14, 2013, http://campaignstops. blogs.nytimes.com/2012/01/25/why-evangelicals-dont-like-mormons/?_r=0.

42. Amy Sullivan, "Mitt Romney's Evangelical Problem," *The Washington Monthly*, September 2005, accessed October 14, 2013, www.washington monthly.com/features/2005/0509.sullivan1.html.

43. Napp Nazworth, "Poll: White Evangelicals Who Say Mormons Not Christian Strongly Back Romney," *The Christian Post*, May 10, 2012, accessed October, 14, 2013, www.christianpost.com/news/poll-white-evangelicals-who-say-mormons-not-christian-strongly-back-romney-74727/.

44. LOWESS uses locally weighted regression to smooth data. This method is "local" in the sense that each value is determined by neighboring points.

45. See CNN exit polls for breakdowns of demographic voting patterns in both years. 2008: www.cnn.com/ELECTION/2008/results/polls/#val=USP00p1 (accessed November 7, 2013); 2012: www.cnn.com/election/2012/results/race/president (accessed November 7, 2013).

46. Pew Research Center, "Young Voters Supported Obama Less, But May Have Mattered More," November 26, 2012, accessed June 6, 2012, www.people-press.org/2012/11/26/young-voters-supported-obama-less-but-may-have-mattered-more/.

47. Ibid.

48. Dave Boyer, "Under-30 Unemployment Rate at 11.8 Percent," *The Washington Times,* October 5, 2012, accessed June 6, 2013, www.washingtontimes.com/blog/inside-politics/2012/oct/5/under-30-unemployment-rate-118-percent/.

Appendix 2.1 Logit Models for White Voter Turnout, 2008 and 2012

	2008		2012	
	Odds Ratio	Robust Std. Err.	Odds Ratio	Robust Std. Err.
Republican	4.02	(1.13)*	2.38	(0.42)*
Democrat	1.92	(0.48)*	2.70	(0.52)*
Conservative (0–6)	0.96	(0.09)	1.13	(0.07)
Female	1.40	(0.27)	1.12	(0.15)
College Degree	3.35	(0.91)*	3.91	(0.69)*
Married	1.33	(0.30)	1.46	(0.22)*
Age 30–44	0.84	(0.25)	2.65	(0.52)*
Age 45–64	1.41	(0.40)	4.75	(0.87)*
Age 65 Plus	2.48	(0.81)*	11.93	(2.68)*
Born Again	1.04	(0.23)	1.10	(0.17)
Income 2nd Quartile	1.20	(0.30)	1.25	(0.24)
Income 3rd Quartile	1.54	(0.45)	1.73	(0.34)*
Income 4th Quartile	1.89	(0.81)	1.83	(0.42)*
Income Unknown	3.05	(1.51)*	1.23	(0.37)
Racial Resentment (Standardized 0–1)	0.74	(0.31)	0.49	(0.16)*
Constant	0.96	(0.43)	0.31	(0.10)*
Observations	1003		3029	

* $p < 0.05$

Appendix 2.2 OLS Regression Model of External Efficacy

	Coef.	Robust Std. Err.
Republican	0.20	(0.08)*
Democrat	0.32	(0.09)*
Conservative (0–6)	0.00	(0.03)
Female	−0.06	(0.07)
College Degree	0.09	(0.07)
Married	−0.20	(0.07)*
Age 30–44	0.02	(0.11)
Age 45–64	0.07	(0.09)
Age 65 Plus	0.09	(0.11)
Born Again	0.02	(0.08)
Income 2nd Quartile	−0.08	(0.11)
Income 3rd Quartile	−0.01	(0.11)
Income 4th Quartile	0.11	(0.17)
Income Unknown	0.12	(0.17)
Racial Resentment (Standardized 0–1)	−0.68	(0.17)*
Constant	1.63	(0.18)
Observations	1521	
R-Squared	0.07	

* $p < 0.05$

Appendix 2.3 Turnout Rates of Different White Groups, 2008 and 2012

			2008			
	All	Married	Unmarried	No HS Diploma	HS Diploma	Some College	College Degree
All	66.12	71.32	55.5	37.74	56.41	69.38	79.05
Men	64.19	71.11	51.27	36.35	53.34	67.2	78.18
Women	67.93	71.52	59.94	39.18	59.31	71.24	79.89

	Advanced Degree	18–29	30–44	45–64	65+	HS Diploma or Less, Under 30
All	85.22	52.16	64.14	71.22	72.65	34.97
Men	85.23	48.6	61.5	69.23	74.81	32.86
Women	85.2	55.77	66.71	73.1	70.94	37.73

			2012			
	All	Married	Unmarried	No HS Diploma	HS Diploma	Some College	College Degree
All	64.1	70.91	54.32	35.06	54.05	65.68	76.7
Men	62.56	70.7	49.82	33.37	51.28	64.67	76.25
Women	65.62	71.13	58.19	36.82	56.76	66.55	77.12

	Advanced Degree	18–29	30–44	45–64	65+	HS Diploma or Less, Under 30
All	83.3	46.07	61.2	69.47	73.4	26.54
Men	82.73	43.44	58.1	67.97	75.61	25.56
Women	83.85	48.69	64.25	70.91	71.6	26.54

Source: CPS November Voting and Registration Supplement, 2008 & 2012

3 The Enduring Influence of Ethnicity and History

INTRODUCTION

For many observers, it is axiomatic that white Americans have been absorbed into a single culture due to the American "melting pot." The melting pot myth is a cornerstone of the American historical narrative. This narrative suggests that, wherever immigrants came from, once in the United States they were eventually incorporated into an Anglo-Protestant culture that values, according to the late Samuel Huntington,

> the English language; Christianity; religious commitment; English concepts of the rule of law, including the responsibility of rulers and the rights of individuals; and dissenting Protestant values of individualism, the work ethic, and the belief that humans have the ability and the duty to try to create a heaven on earth, a "city on a hill."[1]

When political surveys ask respondents to name their genealogical background, if an individual identifies as white and non-Hispanic, there is not typically a follow-up question to determine whether they predominantly identify as English, German, Swedish, Polish, or any other European nationality. There is sound logic to this practice. Nonetheless, the tendency to discount ethnic and other historical differences between white Americans may mask some important lingering political differences among white ethnic groups. This chapter will consider whether the melting pot narrative is true for whites, at least with regard to political behavior.

Beyond ethnic differences, this chapter will also consider regional differences between whites when it comes to politics—though the two issues are interrelated. When we consider how whites are divided along regional lines, the dominant trend in political science is to divide whites into a dichotomous variable: Southern vs. non-Southern. There are strong historical reasons to do so. However, there are other geographic divides that may be of comparable importance, based on divergent histories and migration patterns. This chapter will also consider whether recent talk of multiple "American Nations"[2] is justified when we examine survey data.

This question is relevant because it speaks to the question of whether or not whites are beginning to coalesce into a major voting bloc. For white voters, is "whiteness" per se a politically relevant characteristic, or are other characteristics, such as specific ethnicity, more important? Have ethnic and geographic differences between whites become less politically important in recent years, or do they still explain a great deal of white voter behavior?

This chapter will begin with a survey of the literature arguing that whites really have melted into a single coherent group, no longer divided by ethnicity and history. It will then consider literature suggesting that ethnicity and regional history continue to divide white Americans. It will also examine empirically whether ethnicity and geography remain important determinants of white party identification.

WHY ETHNIC DIFFERENCES BETWEEN WHITES?

The political differences between black and white Americans can be easily explained by the history of race relations in the United States. The long history of racism toward blacks in America is well known and does not require a lengthy discussion here. African Americans first suffered under slavery and later Jim Crow laws, and continue to be a disadvantaged group in the United States. It is not difficult to understand why African Americans developed cultural and political attributes distinct from the white American population. Similarly, the relationship between Native Americans and the U.S. government is equally well known, and enormous economic disparities between Native Americans and whites remain.

In comparison, a cursory examination of the United States today suggests that the differences between white ethnic groups are relatively superficial—indeed, they may amount to little more than different levels of enthusiasm for holidays like St. Patrick's Day and Columbus Day. The historical experiences of different white ethnic groups are less well remembered or remarked on by contemporary commentators, but they nonetheless were once quite important and may remain relevant today.

One of the key points on which white ethnic groups diverged, particularly in earlier periods of American history, was religion. While Maryland was initially founded as a refuge for English Catholics, the overwhelming majority of the original European settlers in what is now the United States were Protestants—Maryland itself became majority Protestant in a relatively short period of time. Colonial America was not monolithically English, as there was a substantial German or Dutch population in many colonies, but the overwhelming majority of non-English whites were also Protestant during the colonial era and the first decades following the American Revolution. While we should not discount the religious differences between the colonies—New England was overwhelmingly made up of Calvinist Puritans, Pennsylvania and the surrounding areas had a large contingent of Quakers,

and Virginia and other Southern colonies were predominantly Anglican—
the early United States was, broadly conceived, an almost monolithically
Protestant nation.

Waves of immigration changed the religious landscape of the United
States. In the middle part of the 19th century, the United States experienced a massive in-migration of Irish immigrants, largely motivated by fam-
ine in that country. While these immigrants of course spoke English, they
were overwhelmingly Catholic. A large number of the German immigrants
during this period were also Catholic. This important religious difference
spurred hostility on the part of native-born white Americans. The anti-
immigrant "Know Nothing" movement of the 1850s was largely driven by
anti-Catholic sentiment.[3] Catholics were particularly suspect because they
were believed to harbor anti-republican views and there was widespread
suspicion that they were controlled by the Pope. New immigrants from
Italy and Eastern Europe later in the century, who were also predominantly
Catholic or Jewish, caused similar concerns. The Ku Klux Klan later incorporated anti-Catholic and anti-Jewish rhetoric into its message. In 1928,
Democratic presidential candidate Al Smith likely suffered at the ballot box
because of his Catholicism. As recently as 1960, John F. Kennedy had to
reassure voters that his Catholicism would not affect his decision making.

Religion was not the only source of tension between native-born whites
and white immigrants who arrived later in the 19th century and into the
20th century. Because many arrived impoverished, they also suffered economic exploitation and had to work the least desirable jobs. The long-time
residents of these communities furthermore resented these newcomers who
appeared to be displacing them. This mutual hostility would further reinforce ethnic solidarity for both the new ethnic groups and those whites who
could trace their origins to the colonial period.[4] Beyond these obvious religious and economic differences, more recent European immigrants tended
to settle in ethnic enclaves that reinforced their sense of unity. This community segregation delayed a common sense of "whiteness" among Europeans
of different ancestries.

Throughout the 19th century, ethnicity and immigration status were clear
dividing lines in American politics. The Democrats cultivated their reputa-
tion as the pro-immigrant party early on, and Irish Catholics were heavily
Democratic for many decades. Support for the Whig and later the Republican Party came predominantly from English Protestants. The Republican
Party also enjoyed some success with German and Scandinavian immigrants
in its early years.[5]

Clearly, ethnic identity was an important determinant of white vote
choice well into the 20th century. However, when thinking about ethnicity
and political identity and behavior, we should consider the possibility that
the causal arrow points in the other direction. That is, perhaps politics rein-
forces ethnic ties and delays assimilation. At the peak of their power, political machines in urban areas emphasized ethnicity as part of their political

strategies. Some government jobs may have only been available to members of specific white ethnic groups, for example. The fact that only members of specific ethnic groups had a high probability of receiving specific benefits likely increased the degree to which individuals identified with their ethnicity and allowed their ethnic backgrounds to inform their politics.

There are reasons to expect a delay between a group's entrance into the United States and that group's foray into politics as a cohesive, organized force. Ethnic consciousness is obviously the most important ingredient of ethnic politics. However, ethnic consciousness will not have political consequences without a meaningful way for that consciousness to be expressed. That is, unless there are politicians and political parties interested and capable of mobilizing that ethnic consciousness, it will not be politically relevant. For this reason, white ethnic politics may have been unlikely for first-generation ethnic groups, as many of these groups' members may have been predominantly illiterate, poor, and unable to speak English.[6] At the time of their arrival, these groups had no powerful political champions of their own, and the existing power structure may have made little effort to activate them politically.[7] In other words, in order for ethnic politics to develop, there first had to be some assimilation and upward economic mobility.

THE CASE FOR THE MELTING POT

The study of white ethnicity and how it shapes vote choice and other political behaviors is no longer common in political science. This is understandable. Compared to immigration from Latin America, Asia, and Africa, the number of white immigrants from Europe in recent decades has been small. Only 46 percent of second-generation immigrants and 20 percent of first-generation immigrants identify as white.[8] Thus, a majority of white Americans have few direct familial ties to Europe. Most white Americans do not have a parent who was not born in the United States.

While there was once a great deal of ethnic segregation within large cities and surrounding communities—Irish neighborhoods, Italian neighborhoods, etc.—these communities are increasingly rare, though they do still exist. The *Chicago Tribune*, for example, recently reported on the decline of Irish neighborhoods in Chicago and the shrinking distinction between European ethnic groups.[9]

The United States has long experienced high levels of internal migrations, and while many communities and neighborhoods were once dominated by a single white ethnic group, most geographic units now contain a mixture of different white groups. Most white Americans are furthermore a mixture of multiple European ethnicities. Many whites may not have any idea about their family's genealogical history or even be aware of their surname's ethnic origin.

Furthermore, as communities become more racially diverse, the differences between different white ethnic groups become less noticeable or apparently important. If we imagine a community in which the only two groups are white Italians and whites of English descent, the differences between the Italians and the English will be salient, even if the two groups are only marginally different in terms of cultural and economic attributes. If the non-white population within that community were to substantially grow, particularly if these non-whites were substantially different from the native population in terms of cultural mores and political behavior, we could plausibly expect differences between white ethnic groups to appear increasingly irrelevant. As a result of non-white newcomers, all white ethnic groups may come to view themselves simply as white. Indeed, it has been argued that, as African Americans moved into many Northern cities in the aftermath of World War II, Italian Americans, Polish Americans, and Irish Americans merged into a single white entity in order to preserve their communities' racial integrity.[10]

For all of these reasons, it increasingly makes sense to view white Americans as a single group. Stanley Lieberson suggested "unhyphenated whites" actually represent a new ethnic group. He said this group, which represents an increasing share of the population, possesses the following characteristics:

> There is a recognition of being white, but lack of any clearcut identification with, and/or knowledge of, a specific European origin. Such people recognize that they are not the same as some of the existing ethnic groups in the country such as Greeks, Jews, Italians, Poles, Irish, etc. It is assumed at this point that the vast bulk of persons meeting these conditions are of older Northwestern European origins, but I also assume that there are some persons from newer European sources of immigration shifting into this group.[11]

There are a number of reasons to anticipate the growth of this group. As noted earlier, the mixing of various ethnicities is one powerful driver of this group's growth. The lack of new immigrants from Europe, who might otherwise have helped reinforce the ethnic ties of native-born Americans, is another potential explanation for this loss of genealogical memory and attachments to white Americans' ancestral homelands and cultural mores. It has been effectively argued that "European ethnicity is overshadowed by class and education and rarely proves the most salient factor in political decision-making."[12]

Robert Dahl noted in his important study of New Haven, Connecticut, in 1961 that, although there was clearly a great deal of voting along ethnic lines among whites in that city, "the strength of ethnic ties as a factor in local politics must surely recede."[13] Dahl formulated a three-stage model of ethnic assimilation. In the first stage, first-generation ethnics are at the bottom of the economic ladder and vote reliably as a bloc. In the second stage, later generations begin to make economic gains and many members of the ethnic group move into the middle class, which makes it more difficult to activate ethnic appeals. In the third stage, "large segments are assimilated into the middling and upper strata . . . [and] ethnic politics is often embarrassing or meaningless."[14] We can confidently say that large segments of all major white ethnic groups are represented in the nation's higher economic strata; thus we should expect that white ethnic voting has continued to diminish.

One explanation for this expected trend is that it was socially beneficial for white ethnics, especially those from more recent immigrant stock, to abandon their ethnic differences and embrace their identity as white Americans without an ethnic hyphen. That is, as the primary racial fault line in the United States became black versus white, white ethnics had an incentive to identify themselves exclusively as white Americans.

THE PERSISTENCE OF ETHNICITY IN WHITE POLITICS

The melting pot hypothesis, of course, never applied to African Americans, who have never been fully incorporated into American politics and culture; huge disparities between African Americans and whites have always been present in virtually all politically relevant variables. Political, economic, and cultural distinctions between Latinos and non-Hispanic whites also remain evident. One of the reasons the melting pot system presumably worked for whites was that the waves of European migration eventually ceased, making it more difficult for white ethnics to maintain strong ties to their ancestral culture. There is presently no indication that large-scale migration from Latin America and Asia into the United States is coming to an end, and some commentators have noted that this continuing influx raises questions about whether Latinos and Asians will assimilate into American culture at the same speed as European immigrants.[15]

A case can be made that the melting pot argument is overstated, even for white Americans. Even for whites, ethnicity may remain a more important influence on characteristics such as ideology and vote choice than scholars such as Lieberson have suggested. It is worth noting that models of cultural and political assimilation such as Dahl's have been successfully challenged in the decades since he wrote about voting patterns in New Haven.

Steven Martin Cohen challenged Dahl's hypothesis that upward economic mobility erodes ethnic cohesion, arguing for a cultural pluralist perspective that suggests ethnic ties will remain, even for the middle and upper middle social strata, and that we can expect ethnic homogeneity for as many as three or four generations.[16] His empirical analysis found little evidence that higher economic status leads to a weakened sense of ethnic identification, as measured by intermarriage and intraethnic friendship. However, he did find that higher education was associated with weaker ethnic ties.[17]

Gimpel and Cho found that, even in the 21st century, white ethnicity continues to play an important role in New England politics. While the explanatory power of white ethnic groups was not nearly as great as that for non-white groups (such as African Americans), the concentration of different white groups in different communities was associated with different political outcomes. Interestingly, they found that towns with high concentrations of Irish and Italian Americans were associated with higher rates of Republican voting.[18] This is notable because these white ethnic groups were once heavily Democratic. In this instance, it appears that ethnic groups politically realigned, but remained cohesive.

Mathew Frye Jacobson posited an intriguing argument for the survival of white ethnic identity in the United States. In his book *Roots Too*, Jacobson argued that a revival of interest in ethnicity among American whites following World War II was related to the civil rights movement.[19] Much of the narrative during this period was focused on the continuing effects of slavery on the African American community. This discussion provided contemporary whites an incentive to distance themselves from the slave-holding whites of the 18th and 19th centuries. That is, whites could skirt any personal sense of guilt for slavery by noting that their ancestors arrived after slavery had ended, and by further noting that their ancestors also suffered discrimination on their arrival—this point about the discrimination against white ethnic groups was subsequently used as an argument against Affirmative Action and other government programs designed to improve conditions for African Americans. By noting that their ancestors also experienced severe disadvantages, but nonetheless achieved substantial economic gains, they argued African Americans could accomplish the same thing without significant government assistance.

As a counter to the argument that the resurgence in interest in white ethnic identity is a sign that whites never truly merged in the melting pot, it has been suggested that this new interest was always superficial. As Richard Alba put it, "During the 1970s, ethnicity could be celebrated precisely because assimilation had proceeded far enough that ethnicity no longer seemed so threatening and divisive."[20] Whether the renewed interest in ethnicity was as superficial as Alba suggested is beyond the scope of this chapter, but we can consider whether or not there is still evidence for ethnic voting among whites.

DOES WHITE ETHNICITY STILL MATTER? EVIDENCE FROM THE GENERAL SOCIAL SURVEY

It is worth asking whether political differences between white ethnic groups remain and whether these differences have changed substantially in recent decades. Three questions the GSS has continuously asked relate to party identification, ideology, and ethnicity. Respondents are asked whether they

identify as a Republican, Democrat, or neither; the strength of their identification; and where they place themselves on the ideological spectrum
(a five-point scale from very liberal to very conservative).

GSS respondents are also asked, "From what country or part of the
world did your ancestors come?" Respondents have provided several dozen
different answers, but certain regions and countries are more common, as
reflected in the actual ethnicities of Americans. To reduce the number of
categories under consideration, and to increase the number of observations within each category, several nationalities were merged to conduct
the forthcoming analysis. England, Scotland, and Wales (hereafter ESW)
are now a single category. Austrians are included in the German category.
Respondents from any Scandinavian country, France, the Netherlands, and
Belgium are included in the "Other Northern Europe" category. All European countries east of the former "Iron Curtain," including Russia, are categorized as Eastern Europe. Southern Europeans include Italians, Spanish,[21]
and Portuguese Americans—though most people in this category identified
as Italian.[22] Those who did not provide an answer or simply described themselves as "Americans" were a separate category. Whites who provided any
other ethnicity beyond these categories were not examined separately.

These groups were then compared according to their ideologies and party
identifications. In the case of partisanship, Table 13.1 only includes those
who explicitly identified as Republicans or Democrats; those who identified as independents, but nonetheless admitted to leaning toward one party,
were treated as independents. Similarly, the strength of individual ideological inclination was not disaggregated. This analysis makes no distinction
between those who were very liberal and somewhat liberal, or very conservative and somewhat conservative.

Two points that immediately stand out are the substantial increase in the
percentage of whites who identified as Republicans in 2012 compared to 1976
and the even more dramatic decrease in the percentage of whites who identified as Democrats. Not all groups exhibited comparable change, however. It
is worth noting that the group that identified as Republican in the greatest
number in 1976—Americans of ESW descent—were still the most Republican
group in 2012. However, in terms of Republican identification they remained
virtually unchanged; only about 1 percent more of this group identified as
Republican in the latter year. All other white groups saw a greater increase
in their support for Republican candidates. Indeed, there is now virtually no
difference in support of Republicans between Americans of ESW heritage and
Americans who say their ancestors are from Germany or some other country
in Northern Europe. Americans from Ireland, Southern Europe, and Eastern
Europe remain less Republican, but the gap has substantially decreased.

We can take this as evidence that the process of assimilation for white
Americans from different European backgrounds has continued, and per-
haps all ethnic differences will fade away entirely as the century continues.
We should be careful not to infer too much from these descriptive statistics.

Table 3.1 White Political Attributes by Ethnicity

	1976				
	Observations	% Republican	% Democrat	% Conservative	% Liberal
All Whites	1,361	22.2	39.6	32.7	27.1
Southern Europe	108	13.9	39.8	25.5	35.9
Eastern Europe	117	9.4	53.0	36.6	26.8
Ireland	138	22.5	39.9	30.2	26.4
Germany	94	28.0	29.7	33.3	25.5
Other Northern Europe	94	22.3	37.2	31.9	30.8
England, Wales, & Scotland	232	35.8	32.8	40.0	21.3
"American" or Unknown Ethnicity	306	17.0	44.4	31.3	25.4

	2012				
	Observations	% Republican	% Democrat	% Conservative	% Liberal
All Whites	1,309	29.4	28.3	35.1	26.3
Southern Europe	106	21.7	30.2	27.4	29.3
Eastern Europe	78	21.8	30.8	33.3	23.1
Ireland	196	24.4	33.2	31.6	28.5
Germany	244	33.6	27.7	37.8	24.4
Other Northern Europe	78	35.9	26.9	46.2	28.2
England, Wales, & Scotland	197	36.6	28.4	43.3	27.3
"American" or Unknown Ethnicity	262	30.2	24.1	33.2	24.8

Independent "leaners" are treated as independents rather than partisans
Source: 1976 & 2012 General Social Survey

These differences in political attitudes may be driven by characteristics other than ethnicity per se. It is possible that, in the 1970s, white Americans of Southern or Eastern European ancestry were much more likely to be on the lower end of the economic spectrum or live in urban areas, and this accounts for their lower rates of Republican voting. Perhaps these economic and geographic differences have subsequently faded, and this is what accounts for the shrinking ethnicity gap among white voters. Once these other characteristics are accounted for, we may find that white ethnicity had already ceased to matter by 1976.

Two models (see Appendix 3.1) examined predictors of Republican identification and identifying as a conservative among whites. In addition to ethnic background, these models included many control variables such as income, marital status, age, religiosity, and education level. Conservatism was transformed into a dichotomous variable—those who identified as "somewhat conservative," "conservative," and "very conservative" were classified as 1; all other ideological responses were classified as 0. Republican identification was similarly coded as a dichotomous variable. Given the categorical nature of these variables, a logistic regression model examined the impact of ethnicity on white party identification and ideology in both 1976 and 2012.

Dichotomous variables for ethnicity were included in the model, with ESW respondents serving as the excluded base category. In all cases, if an ethnicity was statistically or substantively significant, we can say that, on average and controlling for all other variables, whites of that ethnicity were more or less likely to identify as conservative or Republican compared to ESW Americans—depending on the direction of the coefficient.

Again, coefficients are difficult to interpret in logistic regression models. A more useful measure is the odds ratio, which is what is reported in Appendix 3.1—as was the case in the logit model presented in Chapter 2. These models provide a number of interesting insights. The most important thing to note is that there were, and remain, important differences between white ethnic groups when it comes to party identification and ideology, and these differences remain even after controlling for a large number of individual characteristics.

When it comes to ideology, more ethnicities possessed statistically significant coefficients in 2012 than in 1976. In other words, after all other variables are taken into consideration, we do not see evidence that ethnicity ceased to matter in the latter election. The data from 2012 indicate that Irish Americans were only 0.64 times as likely to identify as conservative as the ESW; Americans descended from Southern Europeans were only 0.57 times as likely to identify as conservative; and those who identified as "American" or had an unknown ethnicity were only 0.60 times as likely. These coefficients were not dramatically different in 1976, but only the coefficient for Southern Europeans was statistically significant in 1976. As was the case in the models in the appendixes at the end of Chapter 2, we should be cautious when comparing coefficients in separate models—though in this case, because the sample size in both years was similar, it is less likely that different results were due to one year having a greater number of observations than another.

We also see that, in 2012, ESW Americans were no longer the white ethnic group most likely to identify as conservative after controlling for other characteristics. The coefficient for "Other Northern Europe" suggests that this group had a greater probability of being conservative than ESW Americans, after controlling for all other variables—though this coefficient did not achieve statistical significance, so we cannot say this with any confidence.

Turning to the models of party identification, we again see that ethnicity mattered in both 1976 and in 2012. But in all cases the coefficients were smaller in the latter election. That is, although most ethnicities were statistically discernible from the base category in both years, they were *less* different in 2012 than they were in 1976. We should not infer too much from this finding, as we cannot definitively say that these coefficients are statistically discernible from each other because they are in separate models. Nonetheless, it appears that ethnicity is less strongly predictive now than it was 30 years ago.

The lesson from these models is that white ethnicity still apparently matters when it comes to party identification and ideological inclination. Generally speaking, whites whose ancestors came to America in the more distant past (ESW, Germans, etc.) tend to be more ideologically conservative and Republican than whites whose ancestors arrived more recently (Southern and Eastern Europeans). These differences remain even when a host of additional individual-level variables are included in the models. That being said, it appears that the general trend toward assimilation is ongoing. All white groups have been converging toward the ESW in terms of party identification and ideology, though the ESW have remained largely unchanged in terms of both variables in the last several decades.

While these individual-level findings are interesting and suggest that European ethnicities continue to play a role in American politics, it is worth investigating whether these differences also appear in aggregate data. For this study, counties are a useful geographic unit to investigate. Unfortunately, the decennial census in 2010 was not as detailed as previous censuses and cannot be used to estimate the percentage of each ethnic group at the county level. However, the American Community Survey (ACS), which does gather this detailed information, is conducted annually. Although the ACS is less exhaustive in terms of the number of people it contacts, by aggregating the ACS results over a five-year period, it is possible to make reasonable estimates regarding the percentage of each ethnic group within a county.

Figure 3.1 shows the relationship between the percentage of a county that identified with particular European ethnicities and the county-level support for John McCain in the 2008 presidential election. The ethnic categories here are the same as those used for the individual-level data.[23] This relationship is once again plotted using LOWESS.

In most cases, there was not an obvious strong relationship between the size of certain European ethnicities and aggregate county vote choice. The one clear exception was for the size of the ESW population within a county. As the ESW population grew in size, so too did the support for McCain in 2008. This is congruent with what we saw when examining individual-level data.

This basic visual examination is inadequate for determining whether or not there is a meaningful relationship between white ethnicity and aggregate vote choice. It is important to remember that the percentage of an ethnicity within a county may be correlated with other characteristics more strongly

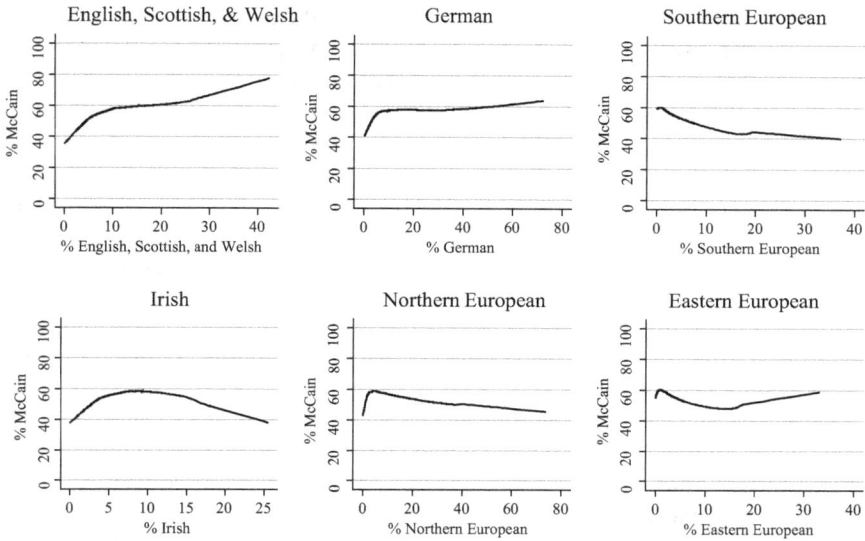

Figure 3.1   County Support for McCain by Percentage of European Ethnicities

related to vote choice. For example, some white ethnics may be more likely to live in urban areas, and urban voters are more likely to be Democratic. Similarly, some white ethnicities may be more likely to live in counties with a large African American or Latino population, and although those white ethnics are themselves likely to be Republican, the local non-white population drives down the aggregate support for McCain. For this reason, a regression model that controls for a myriad of other characteristics is necessary.

Creating and interpreting such a model provides its own challenges. A problem with using counties as the unit of analysis is the issue of spatial autocorrelation. To resolve this problem, the author created a spatial error model. See Appendix 3.2 for the full model and a discussion of this issue.

The spatial error model indicates that, even when controlling for many other variables, the size of different white ethnic groups within counties continued to exhibit statistical significance. Counties with larger ESW populations, German populations, and other Northern European populations gave more support, on average, to John McCain in 2008. The most substantively significant of these variables was the percent who identified as being of German descent. A 1 percent increase in the size of the German-identifying population was associated with a 0.23 percent increase in the county-level support for McCain. Those counties with larger Eastern European and Southern European populations gave less support to McCain. The effect was particularly strong for Southern Europeans. After controlling for all other variables, the size of the local Irish population did not have a statistically significant influence on the two-party vote.

While these variables achieve statistical significance, it is important to note that their substantive effect was dwarfed by the effect of the African American and Asian population. A 1 percent increase in the size of the African American population was associated, on average and controlling for all other variables, with a 0.64 percentage point decrease in support for McCain. A 1 percent increase in the Asian population was associated with a 0.94 percent decrease in support for McCain. It is interesting to note that the coefficient for Asian Americans was larger than the coefficient for African Americans—while both groups are predominantly Democratic in their voting behavior, a larger percentage of African Americans vote for Democratic presidential candidates compared to Asian Americans. This suggests that Asian Americans tend to be found in places where non-Asians also tend to be heavily Democratic.

Problems of ecological inference[24] make it difficult to confidently declare very much about the behavior of individuals based on aggregate data. However, the fact that the aggregate county data are largely congruent with the individual data from the GSS should assuage these concerns. The two examinations combined provide compelling evidence that ethnicity still plays a role in white voting patterns. White Americans who are descended from earlier European settlers (those from Britain or elsewhere in Northern Europe) today are somewhat more Republican than white Americans descended from more recent European immigrants (those from Eastern and Southern Europe).

Another caveat is in order. It is possible that the causal arrow is pointing in the wrong direction, at least for some people. That is, ethnicity may not be driving political attitudes. Instead, political attitudes may be influencing which part of a white American's ethnic background he or she chooses to identify with. It is important to remember that most white Americans have some choice when it comes to ethnic identity—an option not typically available to non-whites.[25] The GSS does not conduct a thorough genealogical analysis to prove that someone's true ethnic identity matches his or her stated ethnic identity. The ACS also takes respondents at their word when asking them to name their ancestry. Furthermore, the number of white Americans who can literally trace all of their ancestors to a single European country is small and getting smaller with each generation. Thus, many people who identify as Irish or Italian probably also have a few English or German ancestors somewhere in their family tree.

This is relevant because peoples' political attitudes may influence which part of their heritage they choose to emphasize. For example, a white American conservative, who wishes to stress her patriotic bona fides and familial identification with the country, may prefer to identify with her WASP ancestors who arrived decades or even centuries prior to the American Revolution. On the other hand, a strong progressive may not feel comfortable celebrating early American history and may not personally identify in any meaningful way with the earliest European immigrants; such a person may be more inclined to emphasize the part of his heritage that is least con-nected to the traditional WASP elite and perhaps identify as Polish, Irish, or some other ethnic group that experienced a substantial period as outsiders in America. In truth, the two people just described may be genealogically identical—both possessing a mix of different white ethnicities.

This is an interesting possibility that deserves greater study in the future. Unfortunately, testing this hypothesis is beyond the scope of this particular project. To this writer's knowledge, there are no recent survey data that verify the ethnic background of respondents and ask meaningful questions about politics. Without such data, it is not possible to definitively conclude whether or not politics drives ethnic identification, rather than the other way around.

REGIONAL CULTURES WITHIN THE UNITED STATES

The subject of regional culture and white voting patterns is, of course, intimately related to ethnicity and white voting, as different white ethnic groups tended to settle in particular regions of the country. The persistence of regional differences among whites in contemporary politics deserves fur-ther exploration. There is an extensive literature within political science, history, and sociology suggesting that there are different political cultures within the United States, and some have even argued that there are multiple distinct "nations" within the borders of the United States.

The most well-known and seemingly intractable regional political dis-tinction in the United States is between the South (usually defined as those states that joined the Confederacy during the 1860s, and sometimes as those states that immediately border these states) and the rest of the nation. The memory of the Civil War, Reconstruction, and the conflict over civil rights helped strengthen this crucial geographic fault line in American politics. While there are important differences between the Southern states and other states, to solely examine that particular geographic split would assume greater homogeneity outside the South than actually exists and disregard many of the important regional differences within the South itself.

This book does not make the argument that whites are the only group that exhibits political or cultural differences along regional or state lines—such an argument would be incorrect. However, whites are the primary focus of this book and for that reason will again be the only demographic category considered in this section. This section examines the degree to which whites vary along regional lines. It takes as its starting point a number of scholarly works that suggest that different areas within the United States exhibit dra-matic differences in political culture. Many of these works helpfully draw clear boundaries around each of these specified regions, which make it eas-ier to discern whether or not there really are coherent, and clearly different, patterns of political attitudes within them.

There are many reasons why voting patterns and political attitudes might vary by region even within the same racial and ethnic group. For example, geography might play a role in the types of economic activities that occur within a region, and people engaged in different industries may have different political preferences as a result. You will not find many farmers in Boston or software engineers in rural Oklahoma. One political party may be viewed as better for agriculture, and another may be viewed as better for high-tech industries, and people working in those separate fields may vote accordingly even if their average household incomes are similar. If their average household incomes are not similar, then economic disparities may explain their different voting patterns.

It has also been argued that differences in communities' built environments can shape political attitudes. Susan Bickford suggested gated communities tend to lead to more exclusionary attitudes, which leads to greater political conservatism. In contrast, crowded urban areas encourage people to hold more egalitarian and liberal political attitudes.[26] Thad Williamson argued that areas with younger housing stock and longer commuting times had, on average, more Republican voters.[27] This might explain why whites living in older American cities such as New York vote, on average, more heavily for Democrats than whites in newer American cities such as Phoenix.

The differing histories of various regions are a compelling explanation for persistent cultural and political differences. This argument suggests that many political and cultural patterns established decades or even centuries ago can persist to the present day, despite tremendous economic and demographic changes. That is, whether or not a region's first settlers came from Northern Ireland or southern England can tell us something about that region's contemporary political attributes, including the political attitudes of the people who live in these regions. This argument has been made by a number of prominent scholars in recent decades, though it is not without its critics.

This hypothesis builds on an argument made by Wilbur Zelinsky in *The Cultural Geography of the United States*.[28] Zelinsky made the case that the first settlers to a region will leave a lasting imprint, even if they are eventually displaced demographically. Zelinsky formulated the "doctrine of first effective settlement," which states that "variations in the cultures of the peoples that dominated the first settlement and the cultural traits developed by these people in the formative period" largely explain cultural differences in the present day.[29] This does not mean that a region's culture cannot change over time. However, it does suggest that the initial settlers to a region will have a greater long-term impact than those who follow.

Culture is a broad and perhaps nebulous term, but this section is predominantly interested in *political* culture. Political culture has been described as

> the set of attitudes, beliefs and sentiments which give order and meaning to a political process and which provide the underlying assumptions and rules that govern behavior in the political system. It encompasses

both the political ideals and operating norms of a polity. Political culture is thus the manifestation in aggregate form of the psychological and subjective dimensions of politics.[30]

Different political cultures have an impressive ability to survive in the United States because of the nation's federal nature. The U.S. Constitution clearly distinguishes between tasks that are the proper role of the national government and tasks that should be performed by the states and local governments. This has allowed different states to pursue divergent paths with comparatively little interference from the national government. The relative freedom enjoyed by different states and localities allows their different political cultures to inform their policies, and those policies to further entrench the established political culture. Perhaps if the United States had a more unitary form of government, these state and regional differences would be substantially smaller.

Among scholars who study variation in American political culture along regional lines, the work best known by political scientists was written by Daniel Elazar.[31] Elazar argued that there are three distinct political subcultures within the United States: individualistic, moralistic, and traditional. According to Elazar, the individualistic political culture tends to conceive of society as a marketplace. Government, to those living in such a culture, serves a utilitarian purpose. Intervention into private activity is kept to a minimum, and government exists to primarily ensure access to markets and to encourage productive economic activity.[32] The moralistic political culture is more inclined to view government as a crucial component of the effort to create a good society. It gives less weight to laissez-faire arguments about the proper limits of the state.[33] The traditionalistic political culture is also somewhat ambivalent about free markets and limited government, but it is less interested in advancing a conception of the common good than in maintaining the existing cultural order. It is a hierarchical society in which government serves to maintain the preexisting elite.[34]

Elazar argued that distant history plays an important role in contemporary political cultures. He claimed that understanding these differences requires an understanding of the "geology" of political culture.[35] The roots of political culture can often be traced back to the founding of the country or even to the Old World cultures from which the first settlers were derived. The moralistic political culture has roots in Puritanism and was most influential in New England. The individualist political culture was centered on the Mid-Atlantic states. Because this region has the longest history of ethnic and religious diversity, pluralism was a fact of life in this region of the country from the very beginning. The Southern states, with their plantation-based economy and rigidly hierarchical society, developed a traditionalistic political culture.

As groups that initially settled in one area began to move westward, such as the movement of Puritans out of New England into the Great Lakes region or the westward expansion of the Scots-Irish from Appalachia, they took their political cultures with them. Many states were destinations for migrants from states with differing political cultures, and these different political cultures mixed together.

It is important to note that a specific set of public policies do not flow inevitably from a particular political culture. This point is driven home by the case of New England. Since the first European settlers first arrived in New England, it has possessed a distinct political culture. However, it has also transitioned from being a society of devout Calvinist Puritans eager to build a "city on a hill" or even a Christian Sparta[36] to being one of the nation's most secular and progressive regions. Northern New England has now surpassed the Pacific Northwest as the least religious region of the country.[37] New England has nonetheless maintained its moralistic political culture—though the morals emphasized by people in the region have changed over time.

While Elazar's work had an important influence on political science, other prominent scholars from other disciplines have provided a similar view of American history and contemporary American political culture. *Albion's Seed* by David Hackett Fischer was one important work in this tradition. Fischer argued that the specific region of England from which an American region's first settlers derived tells us much about its history and its contemporary cultural characteristics. Fischer identified four major cultural groups who arrived in America from England or Scotland. The first group he examined was the Puritans. The Puritans were predominantly from East Anglia, and they moved to New England from 1629 to 1640. As noted earlier, this was predominantly a movement of devout Calvinists hoping to establish a Christian society in the New World.

The arrival of this group in America is a vital part of the nation's national myth. It was the Puritans who landed on Plymouth Rock and are often credited with celebrating the first Thanksgiving.[38] There were a number of reasons why the migration of Puritans to America was demographically interesting. Compared to other European settlers on the American continents, where single men were overrepresented by a substantial margin, Puritans were quite likely to move as family units, and there was not a substantial disparity between the sexes in terms of overall numbers.[39] This large number of women allowed New England to grow in population at an extraordinary rate. The Puritan settlers also tended to come from middle-class English families, rather than from the aristocratic class or from the bottom strata of society.[40]

It is still taught to American schoolchildren that the Puritans came to America in search of "religious liberty." There is some truth to this, but it must be emphasized that they were not seeking liberty in the contemporary sense. Individual liberty in terms of religious expression and lifestyle choices was not the primary concern of these settlers. Rather, when they spoke of liberty, they generally meant collective liberty. That is, they were concerned with New England's liberty to govern according to its own rules, not the liberty of each individual living in New England to live as he or she desired. Indeed, within the Puritan communities, the lives of individuals were subjected to a large number of legal restraints, congruent with the Puritan traditions. Religious and other dissenters were not welcome in New England and were often cast out in a brutal fashion.[41]

Fischer also described a Royalist elite that moved to Virginia from the south and west of England between 1642 and 1675. These settlers were fundamentally different from those who settled in New England.[42] The cultural mores of these colonists differed sharply from those in New England. For one, they did not share the same alienation from England expressed by many Puritans and were proud of their ancestral roots. Even after several generations had passed, Virginians continued to refer to England as the "mother country."[43] They were furthermore conservative in their religion in the sense that they remained loyal to the Church of England.

The culture of Virginia was less egalitarian than that of New England. This was the first region of the future United States to experience widespread racial slavery, as well as the extensive use of white indentured servants. The settlers in Virginia and the settlers in New England supported opposing sides during the English Civil War. The Puritans favored Cromwell, while the Virginians remained loyal to the king.

Like the Puritans of New England, these colonists also valued liberty, but their use of the term was different from both the contemporary meaning and how the term was understood by the Puritans. Indeed, to contemporary readers, the use of the term "liberty" by unrepentant slaveholders seems bizarre and hypocritical.[44] To the settlers of Virginia, however, liberty was conceived of as the power to rule, and it belonged to only a fraction of the population. In this hierarchical society, liberty was a privilege enjoyed by the highest ranking members of society, and their liberties were not to be encroached on by the state.[45]

A movement from Wales and the North Midlands of England to the Delaware Valley from 1675 to 1725 established a different culture in America, and probably the culture we would recognize as most congruent with contemporary American values. This region was initially settled by a large contingent of English Quakers. Thus, they were religiously distinct from both the Puritans of New England and the Anglicans of Virginia. This region was unique because of the remarkable degree to which it exhibited cultural pluralism and egalitarianism. The region quickly became a haven for a large number of non-British immigrants, notably Germans. This was a culture that rejected a formal hereditary social hierarchy.[46] A system of democratic politics, including political parties, also arrived in this region at an early date.[47] While Quakers ceased to be a majority in this region after a relatively short period, the culture of tolerance they established remained.

The settlers in the Delaware Valley also had their own conception of liberty, differing from the others, and perhaps most similar to our current understanding of the word. For the most part, Quakers genuinely believed in individual religious liberty. From an early date they also exhibited some of the greatest hostility to slavery. They also were jealous defenders of property rights and the right to trial by jury.[48]

The large movement of people from Northern Ireland and the English-Scottish border (a people generally referred to as the Scots-Irish) to the Appalachian backcountry took place from 1718 to 1775. Of the four groups Fischer examined, this was the poorest economically, both before departing Britain and after arriving in the New World. The region from which these settlers originated had for centuries been at the center of violent conflicts between English and Scottish rulers, and the region also suffered due to smaller battles between minor warlords. The incessant violence shaped the culture of this people. Family connections were exceptionally important to those in the Border region, and they had little trust in formal legal institutions.[49] These cultural patterns survived the unification of England and Scotland in 1707, and those who moved to America from this region carried these patterns with them.

From an early date, these Scots-Irish settlers were met with hostility from other American colonists. They were quickly encouraged to move west, far from the established coastal cities, and they settled in large numbers throughout the highlands of Appalachia and beyond. Being the vanguard of westward expansion, this group fought brutal wars with Native Americans from the late 17th century to the early 19th century. They maintained a strong clannish culture, as they had in Britain. In spite of their poverty, they were an exceptionally proud people and tended to practice a militant form of Presbyterianism or were Baptists.[50] Compared to other areas of what would later be known as the South, slavery was not as dominant of an institution in areas settled by this group—indeed, it was the region of Virginia dominated by the descendants of these settlers that split off during the Civil War to form the state of West Virginia.

The people of the backcountry were also concerned with the issue of liberty. This was the most radically libertarian of the four groups Fischer examined. They were seemingly skeptical of all ordering institutions. Patrick Henry, who famously declared, "Give me liberty or give me death!" was a product of this culture. This attitude did not imply that Americans in the backcountry were tolerant of individual dissent and the eschewing of cultural norms, but they were hostile to any outside attempts to restrain them.[51] The descendants of these settlers took longer to successfully assert themselves in national politics than other groups in the United States. It was not until the expansion of the franchise to virtually all white males and the ascendancy of Andrew Jackson that Americans in the backcountry became a powerful political force of their own.

James Webb, a former Democratic senator from Virginia, argued that the Scots-Irish had a greater impact on the development of American culture than is generally acknowledged. He noted that they have been overrepresented not only in the nation's military ranks but also among the most influential presidents:

> The fought the Indians and they fought the British, comprising 40 percent of the Revolutionary War army. They were the great pioneers—Daniel Boone, Lewis and Clark, and Davy Crockett among them—blazing the westward trails into Kentucky, Ohio, Tennessee and beyond, where other Scots-Irishmen like Kit Carson picked up the slack. They reshaped American politics, taking hegemony away from the aristocratic English-Americans and creating the populist movement. In this role they gave us at least a dozen presidents, beginning with the incomparable Andrew Jackson and including Chester Arthur, Ulysses S. Grant, Theodore Roosevelt (through his mother), Woodrow Wilson, Ronald Reagan (again through his mother), and, most recently, Bill Clinton. It is even said that the patrician George W. Bush has a Kentucky-born, Scots-Irish ancestor.[52]

These cultures and the regions they dominated generally correspond to the regions and political cultures identified by Elazar: The moralistic political culture dominates in areas initially settled by Puritans, the individualistic political culture corresponds to those regions settled by those from the Midland region, and the traditionalist culture corresponds to those regions settled by the aristocratic English royalists. Elazar did not apparently believe the Scots-Irish in the American backcountry had a particularly strong influence on later political cultures. According to his taxonomy, those regions dominated by the Scots-Irish in America exhibit a combination of the individualistic and the traditionalistic political cultures.

A more recent addition to this genre was *American Nations* by Colin Woodard. In this book, Woodard argued that there are 11 distinct "nations" within the continent of North America: Yankeedom, New Netherland, Tidewater, Deep South, First Nation, New France, Greater Appalachia, the Midlands, the Far West, the Left Coast, and El Norte. These nations, with one exception,[53] are geographically contiguous. All but one are at least partially contained within the United States.[54] As with Elazar and Fischer, Woodard argued that the characteristics of these separate nations are largely the result of the different cultural characteristics of the original settlers. Unlike Elazar, Woodard argued that these separate cultures do not correspond to state or even national boundaries; many states contain multiple nations within their borders.[55]

In many ways, Woodard's taxonomy mirrors that of Fischer, but he extended his analysis to the diaspora of American settlers out of their initial colonies and into the American West, noting the continuity of culture they carried into these new regions. Woodard argued that Yankeedom includes not just New England but also most of the region surrounding the Great Lakes, including all of Minnesota, Michigan, and Wisconsin. The Midlands is an unusually shaped "nation," extending from its original base in Pennsylvania and Delaware deep into the central Midwest, and then extending upward into parts of the Dakotas and south into parts of Kansas and Oklahoma. Greater Appalachia extends far west from its origins in the Appalachian backcountry into Missouri, Arkansas, Texas, and even eastern New Mexico. Only three of Woodard's nations have boundaries that have not substantially expanded since their original founding: Tidewater (in eastern Virginia, North Carolina, and Maryland), New Netherland (which still encompasses New York City and its surrounding counties), and New France (which includes those communities in Louisiana and Mississippi originally dominated by the French).

Woodard argued that some cultural patterns established by non-English settlers continued to have a lasting impact long after they were absorbed by either Britain or, later, the United States. He made the case that much of New York and New Jersey should be classified as "New Netherland" and that it remains culturally distinct from both "Yankeedom" and "The Midlands," which border the region. This was an area initially settled by the Dutch, and although Britain annexed this territory in 1674, the influence of the original settlers continued.[56]

The same is true of "New France," which was centered around Quebec in Canada, but also around New Orleans in the United States. Although Britain eventually conquered both elements of New France, and the formerly French regions of the Deep South have largely assimilated to Southern norms, Woodard argued that the region remains culturally distinct in a number of important ways.

El Norte was that region of the American Southwest first colonized by the Spanish. Although relatively few Europeans lived in the region prior to its annexation by the United States, Woodard argued that we continue to see old cultural patterns there. The large migration of Latin Americans to the region in recent decades, particularly Mexicans from northern Mexico, has only reinforced this cultural difference.

The Left Coast and the Far West were two of the relatively young nations Woodard identified. The Left Coast includes those counties on the Pacific Coast that are west of the Cascade Mountain range in the Pacific Northwest, extending downward into the coastal counties of northern and central California. The Far West encompasses those sparsely populated communities in the Mountain West—extending from those northwestern counties east of the Cascades all the way to the Dakotas in the east to northern Arizona and New Mexico in the south.

A critique of this kind of historical and cultural analysis from social scientists is that it contains arguments that are difficult to falsify. Elazar, Fischer, and Woodard relied heavily on the historical record of cultural attributes and migration patterns, as well as on a more qualitative examination of current trends, to build their arguments. Their respective studies provided relatively little in the way of quantitative analysis of contemporary data to demonstrate that these various regions continue to exhibit meaningful differences in terms of their political culture and other attributes.

While this is an important critique, there have been quantitative studies that largely confirm these arguments. Joel Lieske used a statistical methodology to measure American regional subcultures. He relied on principal component and cluster analysis to identify ten distinctive subcultures in the United States. These subcultures geographically correspond closely with the subcultures identified by Fischer and Elazar.[57] Lieske later created additional categories of political culture, in addition to those identified by Elazar. Lieske argued that these political cultures were moralistic, individualistic, pluralistic, bifurcated, and separatist.[58] The pluralistic category is generally culturally diverse. The bifurcated political culture is found in those areas settled by British migrants from the Border region and those areas that experienced extensive African slavery. The separatist category includes those areas largely dominated by Native Americans and Latinos who are protective of their native cultures and resistant to assimilation to Anglo-American political norms. Lieske categorized counties as belonging within a specific political culture, but states were often categorized as possessing a mix of different cultures.

Dante Chinni and James Gimpel also generated their own taxonomy of communities, using counties as the unit of analysis, in their book *Our Patchwork Nation*.[59] In this work, the authors used factor analysis to identify 12 community types in the United States that share important political, demographic, and cultural characteristics.[60] Like Woodard, this analysis paid little attention to state boundaries. Chinni and Gimpel's work is interesting and distinct from the others in that it did not assume, a priori, that different community types would be geographically contiguous. On the map of the different community types they generated, a "Boom Town" county may be right next to an "Evangelical Epicenter" county, which may border both an "Immigration Nation" county and a "Tractor Country" county. They further made the compelling argument that a county within a classification may have more in common with a county similarly classified hundreds of miles away than it has with a differently classified county right next door.

HOW MUCH DOES WHITE POLITICAL CULTURE VARY BY "NATION"?

This section examines white political behavior within the nation's various regions. It will specifically examine how whites differ in the categories specified by Woodard. It attempts to discern whether or not there really are differing political cultures within different geographic regions.

As noted previously, Woodard argued that the different American nations did not neatly fit within state boundaries. However, his suggested map of various nations did correspond to county lines. Thus, with few exceptions, each U.S. county can be placed within one of Woodard's specified nations.[61] Using survey data that include county codes for each respondent, it is possible to discern whether white Americans differ systematically according to their "nation."

Once again, the NAES data are useful for considering this issue. The NAES is not a perfectly representative sample, and thus these findings should not be used to infer the exact degree to which all whites in any particular "nation" support a political party or specific grouping of policies. Once again, party identification only includes those who explicitly identify with a particular political party and excludes those who initially described themselves as independents but admitted to leaning toward one party or the other. Table 3.2 shows how white political attitudes and party identifications vary according to region, using Woodard's geographic categories.[62] Conservatism is a five-point scale, ranging from "very liberal" to "very conservative." The favorability of the two presidential candidates in 2008 is ranked on a ten- point scale, with higher scores indicating higher levels of favorability.

The table also includes the percentage of white respondents in each "nation" who favored specific public policies, including both social and economic policies. It also shows the percentage of respondents with demographic characteristics known to shape political attitudes, such as religiosity—in this case, the percentage of respondents who attended a worship service once a week or more—and gun ownership.

From this analysis, we can discern whether there are substantial political and cultural differences among whites living in these separate nations, as categorized by Woodard. Answering whether or not whites in these different geographic categories are "polarized" is a somewhat tricky question, because there is not a clear-cut standard for this term. One thing we can say, however, is that the evidence for polarization differs according to the kind of question asked on the survey.

In the case of ideology, the case for geographic polarization is relatively weak. On the five-point ideology scale, the mean score in the most liberal region (the Left Coast) was 1.9. In the most conservative region (New France), the mean score for whites was 2.5. These scores do not indicate a gaping ideological chasm. However, we should keep in mind that the definition of an ideology is not fixed. A person living in Portland, Oregon, who feels she is conservative may be considered a liberal if she lived in rural Mississippi. Similarly, a white liberal in Alabama might be considered a strong conservative if she moved to San Francisco.

There were also relatively modest differences in terms of white attitudes toward the two competing presidential candidates in 2008. In no nation was there a uniform adoration or hostility toward either John McCain or Barack Obama. In terms of feelings toward McCain, the greatest difference was again between New France and the Left Coast. On the Left Coast, McCain's mean favorability was 5.1 and in New France it was 6.3. There

Table 3.2 Political Attitudes and Cultural Attributes in Woodard's *American Nations*

	Yankeedom	New Netherland	Tidewater	Greater Applachia	Deep South	New France	Midlands	Far West	Left Coast	El Norte
% Republican	25.1	27.8	32.5	34.3	40.3	40.9	32.3	37.5	25.9	40.3
% Democrat	32.4	33.4	28.1	30.4	24.3	29.4	32.0	24.6	41.2	27.3
Mean Conservatism	2.1	2.0	2.2	2.4	2.5	2.5	2.2	2.3	1.9	2.2
Mean Favorability of McCain	5.5	5.8	6.0	5.8	6.1	6.3	5.6	5.7	5.1	5.8
Mean Favorability of Obama	5.8	5.7	5.5	4.8	4.4	4.1	5.5	5.2	6.3	5.1
% Favor No Abortion Restrictions	35.2	44.2	36.8	22.0	25.3	16.3	28.7	32.6	51.0	38.6
% Favor Full Marriage Rights for Gays	36.0	40.2	31.2	19.8	21.9	22.2	27.5	28.9	45.6	31.7
% Favor a Fence on Mexican Border	56.5	62.8	58.9	64.7	66.4	65.0	62.5	60.5	49.5	62.3
% Believe Iraq War Was Worth It	30.4	29.7	38.5	43.0	48.1	58.7	34.5	42.3	25.7	40.3
% Favor Government Health Insurance	49.9	49.7	44.5	44.4	39.3	34.9	45.4	42.1	52.2	41.3
% Favor Free Trade Agreements	43.5	53.6	49.0	37.7	41.8	49.2	40.7	44.4	46.2	45.5
% Favor New Tax Cuts	34.1	38.5	31.3	38.2	38.4	45.7	36.4	33.2	25.8	34.1
% Own Gun	37.3	17.7	39.8	53.1	53.1	61.3	40.4	52.9	35.2	38.6
% Frequently Attend Religious Services	36.5	32.7	36.5	47.6	46.9	52.5	41.9	38.6	25.6	32.9
% Have Veteran as Member of Household	29.9	26.5	36.7	32.9	38.7	29.0	32.1	35.1	31.5	36.1

Sources: 2008 National Annenberg Election Survey and *American Nations* by Collin Woodard

was a slightly larger gap for the favorability rating of Obama, where his mean score was only 4.1 in New France but 6.3 in the Left Coast.

Party identification might be a better indication of polarization, as both parties are now relatively homogeneous nationwide in terms of their policy platforms—though again this should not be overstated, as the Republican Party of Tennessee is surely more consistently conservative than the Republican Party of Vermont. However, the two parties only have a single presidential candidate every four years, which forces a degree of ideological cohesiveness within them. There is furthermore a large degree of ideological cohesiveness within the two parties in Congress.[63]

We see that there are substantial differences between the most Democratic and the most Republican nations. Whereas more than 40 percent of white respondents in New France identified as Republican (again, excluding independents who leaned toward the GOP), only 25.9 percent of white respondents on the Left Coast did so. We should not infer that a region is monolithically Republican just because the white residents within that region score high on various measures of conservatism. We must remember that this analysis exclusively examines whites. Some of the areas where whites appear to be most conservative (the Deep South, New France, El Norte) are also regions where there is a larger than average non-white population that tends to support Democrats and prefer more liberal policies.

We see greater evidence of polarization when we turn to specific issues. Whereas more than 50 percent favor no restrictions on abortion in the Left Coast, and more than 44 percent similarly favor no limits in abortion in New Netherlands, fewer than 26 percent of respondents favored unlimited abortion access in Greater Appalachia, the Deep South, and New France. Almost 60 percent of white respondents in New France agreed that the Iraq War was "worth it" as of 2008, as did 48 percent of respondents in the Deep South. In contrast, only 25.7 percent of those in the Left Coast felt this way, and about 30 percent agreed with that statement in Yankeedom and New Netherland.

We also see significant cultural differences among white respondents living in these different regions. Religious observance is greatest in those regions that overlap with the South—New France, Greater Appalachia, and the Deep South. It was lower elsewhere, and considerably lower in the Left Coast, where only about one-quarter of white respondents reported attending a worship service once a week or more. Gun ownership also varies dramatically according to region. Whereas more than 50 percent of white respondents in the Far West, the Deep South, New France, and Greater Appalachia reported owning a gun, fewer than 20 percent of respondents owned a gun in New Netherland.

These results seem to indicate that there are important differences between whites living in the different regions identified by Woodard. There is considerably more variation among whites when categorized in this manner than when they are simply divided between Red States and Blue States. It also shows that the geographic divide among whites is more complicated than a simple South vs. non-South divide. Within the South, which includes most of Tidewater and Greater Appalachia and all of the Deep South and New France, there are meaningful differences between whites. By all measures, whites in the Tidewater region were less conservative than other whites in the South—this may help explain why Obama was able to win both Virginia and North Carolina in 2008. These states have experienced considerable immigration from Latin America in recent years, as well as an influx of white migrants from north of the Potomac. Both groups were considerably more Democratic than native-born white Southerners.[64]

CONCLUSION

This chapter considered whether white American voters remain divided along both ethnic and regional lines. Based on the analysis in the preceding pages, the answer can be answered unequivocally in the affirmative. Knowing the ethnic background of a white American conveys at least some information about which party that person identifies with and where that person will fall on the ideological spectrum. Knowing the region in which a white person lives can also tell us something about that person's party identification.

This finding should not be overstated. The trend since 1976 appears to have been toward further assimilation of white American ethnic groups, at least politically. The political differences between the average English American and the average Italian, Irish, and Polish American have continued to shrink. Furthermore, the ethnic origin of a white American's surname has less predictive power than other socioeconomic determinants of voting and ideology—characteristics such as marital status, education, and income. On the other hand, it is interesting that these ethnic distinctions continue to survive at all, given the great temporal distance between most white Americans and their European ancestors.

There are a number of useful ways the United States can be divided up and categorized geographically. Some of the most useful and interesting means to do so were developed by historians such as Fischer and Woodard, who argued that the earliest European settlers to a region had a lasting impact, even if they were eventually displaced demographically. We see this in the survival of the moralistic political culture in New England, despite the fact that this region later became a magnet for Irish, Italian, and other European immigrants who had few cultural similarities with the once-dominant Puritans. We further see it in the distinct political culture in those regions initially established by those borderland people from northern England, southern Scotland, and northern Ireland. The preceding analysis suggests that white Americans living in the different regions Woodard identified do have meaningful political differences from each other.

All of the preceding research indicates that we are not yet approaching the day when we can speak of a monolithic white political culture in the United States. Even in the face of major demographic changes sweeping the entire nation, whites remain divided by geography and history—though observers can disagree with each other on the importance of these distinctions and whether they will continue into the future. The next chapter examines a topic more familiar to political scientists: the relationship between class and politics.

NOTES

1. Samuel P. Huntington," The Hispanic Challenge," *Foreign Policy* 141(2004): 30.
2. Colin Woodard, *American Nations: A History of the Eleven Regional Cultures of North America* (New York: Viking Press, 2011).
3. Daniel J. Tichenor, *Dividing Lines: The Politics of Immigration Control in America* (Princeton, NJ: Princeton University Press, 2002), 49.
4. Raymond E. Wolfinger, "The Development and Persistence of Ethnic Voting," *American Political Science Review* 59(1965): 897.
5. Tichenor, *Dividing Lines*, 65.
6. Wolfinger, "The Development and Persistence of Ethnic Voting," 904.
7. This phenomenon may also explain the lag between the increasing number of Latinos in the United States and the degree to which Latino interests are served by government.
8. Pew Social and Demographic Trends, "Second Generation Americans," February 7, 2013, accessed December 10, 2013, www.pewsocialtrends.org/2013/02/07/second-generation-americans/.
9. Alexandra Chachkevitch, "Chicago's Irish Accent Fades a Bit: Ethnic Group Still Large, but Population Shrinks a Wee Bit as Immigration Slows, Some Move to Suburbs," *Chicago Tribune,* March 16, 2012, accessed November 7, 2013, http://articles.chicagotribune.com/2012-03-16/news/ct-talk-irish-chicago-20120316_1_irish-heritage-irish-americans-irish-ancestry.
10. Arnold R. Hirsch, *Making the Second Ghetto: Race and Housing in Chicago* (Chicago: University of Chicago Press, 1983), 81.
11. Stanley Lieberson, "Unhyphenated Whites in the United States," *Ethnic and Racial Studies* 8(1985): 159.
12. Louis DeSipio, *Counting on the Latino Vote: Latinos as a New Electorate* (Charlottesville, VA: University of Virginia Press), 4.
13. Robert A. Dahl, *Who Governs? Democracy and Power in an American City* (New Haven, CT: Yale University Press, 1961), 59.
14. Ibid, 35.
15. Huntington, "The Hispanic Challenge." 30–45.
16. Steven Martin Cohen, "Socioeconomic Determinants of Intraethnic Marriage and Friendship," *Social Forces* 55(1977): 999.
17. Ibid, 1008.
18. James G. Gimpel and Wendy K. Tam Cho, "The Persistence of White Ethnicity in New England Politics," *Political Geography* 23(2004): 1003.
19. Matthew Frye Jacobson, *Roots Too: White Ethnic Revival in Post-Civil Rights America* (Cambridge, MA: Harvard University Press, 2006).
20. Richard D. Alba, "The Twilight of Ethnicity Among American Catholics of European Ancestry," *Annals of the American Academy of Political and Social Science* 454(1981): 96.

21. A white American with ancestors predominantly from Spain is technically Hispanic and therefore should be excluded from the category of non-Hispanic white. This further underscores the difficulties associated with ascribing people to specific racial and ethnic categories. However, we might anticipate that Hispanic whites who came directly to the United States from Spain are, on average, more like white Americans politically than are Latinos who came from Latin America. Only a very small percentage of GSS respondents categorized themselves as racially white and said their ancestors predominantly came from Spain. The inclusion or exclusion of these respondents from the analysis did not change the substantive results.

22. It may be objected that these countries should not be lumped together in this manner, as we might anticipate important differences between Swedish Americans and French Americans, for example. However, the actual political differences within these groups were relatively small in all cases. Furthermore, to disaggregate any further would have reduced the number of respondents in each category to such a small number that they could not be used to draw meaningful inferences.

23. The one exception to this was the "American" category. A problem with this ethnicity is that it may not be exclusive to whites. African Americans, for example, may also indicate that their ancestors were American. Because this study exclusively examines white Americans, this ethnic classification was excluded from the aggregate analysis.

24. Ecological inference refers to the problems associated with inferring individual behavior from aggregate data. The problem was most famously explained in William Robinson's article, "Ecological Correlations and the Behavior of Individuals," *American Sociological Review* 15(1950): 351–357.

25. Mary C. Waters, *Ethnic Options: Choosing Identities in America* (Berkeley, CA: University of California Press, 1990), 10.

26. Susan Bickford, "Constructing Inequality: City Spaces and the Architecture of Citizenship," *Political Theory* 28(2000): 355–376.

27. Thad Williamson, "Sprawl, Spatial Location, and Politics: How Ideological Identification Tracks the Built Environment," *American Politics Research* 36(2008): 903–933.

28. Wilbur Zelinsky, *The Cultural Geography of the United States* (Englewood Cliffs, NJ: Prentice-Hall, 1973).

29. Raymond D. Gastil, *Cultural Regions of the United States* (Seattle: University of Washington Press, 1975), 26.

30. *International Encyclopedia of the Social Sciences* (New York: Macmillan, 1968, Vol. 12), 218.

31. Daniel J. Elazar, *Cities of the Prairie* (New York: Basic Books, 1970).

32. Daniel J. Elazar, *American Federalism: A View from the States,* 2nd Edition (New York: Thomas Y. Cromwell, 1972), 94.

33. Ibid, 97.

34. Ibid, 99.

35. Ibid, 103–104.

36. The fascination of many New Englanders with the Greek city-state of Sparta, and their hope that New England might emulate their devotion to an ideal—though in their case the ideal was a devout Christian society—is apparent in a number of documents from that period. One example worth noting was a letter written by the Boston patriot Samuel Adams: "But I fear I shall say too much. I love the People of Boston. I once thought, that the City would be the Christian Sparta. But Alas! Will men never be free! They will be free no longer than while they remain virtuous. Sidney tells us, there are times when People are not worth saving. Meaning, when they have lost their Virtue. I pray God, this may never be truly said of my beloved Town." Samuel Adams, "Samuel

Adams to John Scollay," *The Founder's Constitution, Volume 1, Chapter 18, Document 14*, accessed June 10, 2013, http://press-pubs.uchicago.edu/found ers/documents/v1ch18s14.html.

37. Boorstein, Michelle, "Number of U.S. Christians Declines, Survey Shows," *Seattle Times*, March 9, 2009, accessed October 15, 2013, http://seattletimes. com/html/living/2008829986_religion09.html.
38. Some states dispute the location of the first Thanksgiving. For example, there is some evidence indicating that the first Thanksgiving celebration in America actually occurred in Virginia. Charles E. Hatch, *The First Seventeen Years, Virginia, 1607–1624* (Charlottesville, VA, University of Virginia Press, 1957), 45.
39. David Hackett Fischer, *Albion's Seed* (New York: Oxford University Press), 25–26.
40. Ibid, 27–28.
41. Ibid, 199–205.
42. Ibid, 136.
43. Ibid, 253.
44. It seemed hypocritical to many observers at the time as well. Samuel Johnson famously asked, "How is it that we hear the loudest yelps for liberty among the drivers of negros?" Samuel Johnson, *Taxation No Tyranny: An Answer to the Resolutions and Address of the American Congress* (London, 1775).
45. Fischer, *Albion's Seed*, 410–418.
46. Ibid, 574.
47. Ibid, 591.
48. Ibid, 595–603.
49. Ibid, 628–629.
50. Ibid, 617.
51. Ibid, 777–782.
52. James Webb, *Born Fighting: How the Scots-Irish Shaped America* (New York: Broadway Books, 2004), 10.
53. "New France" includes French Canada as well as the region in Louisiana originally settled by the French.
54. The one exception is "First Nation," which is only in Canada and encompasses that region in which Native Americans remain comparatively dominant.
55. Indeed, Woodard seems to indicate that state boundaries played virtually no role in the geographic expansions of his separate nations. This view may be mistaken, especially when we consider the federal nature of the United States and the comparatively large amount of autonomy granted to states. We should not understate the degree to which state governments can encourage the development or maintenance of a political culture and force newcomers to assimilate to existing norms.
56. Woodard, *American Nations*, 66–72.
57. Joel Lieske, "Regional Subcultures Within the United States," *Journal of Politics* 55(1993), 910.
58. Joel Lieske, "The Changing Regional Subcultures of the American States and the Utility of a New Cultural Measure," *Political Research Quarterly* 63(2010): 533–534.
59. Dante Chinni and James Gimpel, *Our Patchwork Nation: The Surprising Truth About the "Real" America* (New York: Gotham Books, 2010).
60. These community types were named as follows: Boom Towns, Campus and Careers, Emptying Nests, Evangelical Epicenters, Immigration Nation, Industrial Metropolis, Military Bastions, Minority Central, Monied Burbs, Mormon Outposts, Service Worker Center, and Tractor Country.
61. Some counties do not fit neatly within Woodard's categories and are therefore excluded from this analysis. Woodard noted that Chicago does not fit within any single nation; thus Cook County, Illinois, is excluded. Woodard

also argued that Southern Florida should actually be considered part of the Spanish Caribbean—a nation he did not examine in any detail—and thus these counties are also excluded.

62. Some may object to the exclusion of independent leaners from this analysis, as people who fall in this category are often just as partisan as those who immediately identify with a party and in some cases are actually more partisan than those who only weakly identify with a party. To assuage this concern, I performed this same analysis including independents who lean toward a party. In all cases, the results were substantively identical.

63. McCarty, Poole, and Rosenthal, *Polarized America*, 23–32.

64. M. V. Hood, "What Made Carolina Blue? In-Migration and the 2008 North Carolina Presidential Vote," *American Politics Research* 38(2010): 266–302.

Appendix 3.1 Logit Models for Conservatism and Republican Identification

One important point to keep in mind when considering the effect of income in these models, particularly in the 1976 model, is that a large percentage of respondents do not have a reported income—in 1976, almost 45 percent of all respondents were not classified according to income. Rather than simply drop them from the analysis, they are categorized within the "income unknown" category.

Identify as Conservative	2012 Odds Ratio	Std. Err.	1976 Odds Ratio	Std. Err.
Germany	0.83	(0.17)	0.79	(0.16)
Other Northwest Europe	1.06	(0.30)	0.74	(0.20)
Southern Europe	0.52	(0.14)*	0.57	(0.15)*
Ireland	0.63	(0.14)*	0.64	(0.15)
Eastern Europe	0.68	(0.20)	0.91	(0.22)
"American" or Unknown	0.61	(0.12)*	0.73	(0.14)
Some Other Ethnic Group	0.59	(0.18)	0.63	(0.21)
Age	1.00	(0.00)	1.01	(0.00)*
Income Quartile 2	0.74	(0.19)	0.78	(0.18)
Income Quartile 3	1.32	(0.30)	1.21	(0.25)
Income Quartile 4	1.82	(0.46)*	1.42	(0.40)
Income Unknown	1.02	(0.21)	0.79	(0.15)
Maried	1.65	(0.21)*	1.24	(0.17)
Female	0.84	(0.11)	0.99	(0.14)
Frequently Attend Religious Services	2.68	(0.39)*	1.38	(0.18)*
BA	0.83	(0.12)	1.21	(0.21)
Constant	0.37	(0.11)*	0.26	(0.08)*
Observations	1250		1226	
Log Likelihood	−750.56		−752.19	

Identify as Republican	2012 Odds Ratio	Std. Err.	1976 Odds Ratio	Std. Err.
Germany	0.83	(0.17)	0.76	(0.16)
Other Northwest Europe	1.06	(0.30)	0.57	(0.17)
Southern Europe	0.52	(0.14)*	0.33	(0.10)*
Ireland	0.63	(0.14)*	0.52	(0.13)*
Eastern Europe	0.68	(0.20)*	0.19	(0.07)*
"American" or Unknown	0.61	(0.12)	0.42	(0.09)*
Some Other Ethnic Group	0.59	(0.18)*	0.34	(0.13)*
Age	1.00	(0.00)	1.02	(0.00)*
Income Quartile 2	0.74	(0.19)	0.64	(0.17)
Income Quartile 3	1.32	(0.30)*	0.90	(0.21)
Income Quartile 4	1.82	(0.46)*	0.83	(0.26)
Income Unknown	1.02	(0.21)	0.83	(0.17)
Maried	1.65	(0.21)*	0.99	(0.15)
Female	0.84	(0.11)	0.92	(0.14)
Frequently Attend Religious Services	2.68	(0.39)*	1.32	(0.19)
College Degree	0.83	(0.12)	1.56	(0.30)*
Constant	0.37	(0.11)*	0.23	(0.07)*
Observations	1250		1300	
Log Likelihood	−750.56		−642.56	

* $p < 0.05$
Conservatives include those who identify as "somewhat conservative," "conservative," and "very conservative" Republican excludes independent leaners
Source: 1976 & 2012 General Social Survey

Appendix 3.2 Spatial Error Model for Support for McCain

This model was created to consider whether or not differences in the percentage of various white ethnic groups within counties were associated with different support for the Republican presidential candidate in 2008. The size of the different ethnic groups was determined using the five-year estimates from the American Community Survey. As Figure 3.1 demonstrated, a simple visual examination of these data indicated that some ethnic groups were associated with higher levels of Republican voting at the aggregate level, a finding congruent with the individual-level data presented in Appendix 3.1.

To be more confident that any relationship between white ethnicity and aggregate vote choice was not spurious, a number of covariates were necessary. Most importantly, the size of the non-white population was critical. This model includes the percentage of the population that was black, Latino, and Asian. It includes a number of other covariates. For example, the degree to which a county is urban rather than rural was included, as rural voters are more likely to vote Republican, and some ethnic groups may be less likely to live in rural areas. This model controlled for this in two ways. The Office of Management and Budget defines what are called Core Based Statistical Areas (CBSAs), which are urban centers of at least 10,000 people and the surrounding areas that are tied to those urban centers. There are two subcategories of CBSAs: those with more than 10,000 people but less than 50,000 people (micropolitan areas) and those with more than 50,000 people (metropolitan areas). In this model, counties are classified as being metropolitan, micropolitan, or not containing a CBSA. Those counties not containing a CBSA were excluded as the base category. The other measure of this was simply the percentage of a county that was classified as rural—a variable that ranges from 0 percent to 100 percent. Some key economic indicators were also included, such as the county-level unemployment rate at the time of the 2008 election and the median household income.

Beyond including these covariates, it was equally important to control for the possibility of spatial autocorrelation. Using ordinary least squares (OLS) regression to examine these kinds of questions using geographic data is problematic because of the degree to which these variables tend to cluster together geographically—a county with a lot of Germans is likely surrounded by other counties with a lot of Germans, and a county that went heavily for McCain is likely surrounded by other counties that went heavily for McCain. As is the case with temporal autocorrelation (which requires the use of time-series models) the presence of spatial autocorrelation violates the OLS assumption of independence among the observations. This will tend to lead to an underestimation of the error term. A calculation of the Moran's I statistic confirmed that spatial autocorrelation was a serious problem.

Spatial error models are one of the primary means of correcting for spatial autocorrelation. In these models, the spatial dependence is found in the error term. Spatial error models can be written as follows:

$$y = \beta x + \varepsilon \text{ and } \varepsilon = \lambda We + u,$$

where λ is a coefficient for spatially correlated errors and W is a connectivity matrix. The connectivity matrix in this case was a queen weight matrix. That is, it defines a county's neighbors based on a shared border, rather than distance. This method requires that a county have a border with at least one other county in order to calculate a value. For this reason, this model was restricted to counties in the contiguous 48 states (that is, it excludes Hawaii and Alaska), and it excludes the small number of island counties that are not directly connected to another county.

To provide some indication of each variable's substantive significance, the size of the effect of a two-standard deviation change in each statistically significant continuous variable was also included.

	Coefficient	S.E.	2 Std. Dev. Δ
% English, Scottish, or Welsh	0.22	(0.04)*	2.19
% German	0.23	(0.03)*	5.70
% Other Northern Europe	0.15	(0.04)*	2.39
% Irish	0.00	(0.06)	
% Eastern European	−0.25	(0.07)*	−1.65
% Southern European	−0.50	(0.09)*	−3.22
% Hispanic	−0.12	(0.03)*	−3.07
% Black	−0.64	(0.02)*	−18.74
% Asian	−0.94	(0.11)*	−3.48
Median Household Income	0.00	(0.00)*	3.21
Unemployment Rate	−0.10	(0.06)	
% Rural	0.03	(0.01)*	1.97

(*Continued*)

	Coefficient	S.E.	2 Std. Dev. Δ
Metropolitan County	−0.62	(0.36)	
Micropolitan County	0.05	(0.31)	
Total County Population	0.00	(0.00)*	−0.69
Constant	53.89	(11.26)*	
λ	0.99	(0.01)*	
Observations	3103		
Lagrange Multiplier Test of λ	2568.08		

* p < 0.05

4 Class and the White Vote

INTRODUCTION

It is well established that race dwarfs class as a political cleavage in the United States.[1] That is, race is a considerably more powerful predictor of vote choice than class, however defined, and race remains a statistically and substantively significant predictor of vote choice even after economic characteristics are held constant. But this does not mean that there are not considerable class-based cleavages within each racial group. This chapter considers the degree to which whites remain divided by educational attainment, income, and union membership.

The opening chapter of this book suggested that whites can be classified as an understudied demographic group, at least when it comes to political behavior. This statement ceases to be true when we break down whites into smaller sub-categories. In particular, there has long been interest in the white working class. This chapter will build on that literature, considering how class divides white Americans politically, using a number of different definitions of class. This chapter will provide a survey of the existing literature on the white working class, as well as on whites higher up on the socioeconomic scale. It will also examine the degree to which class divides whites politically and whether these divisions have grown or receded in recent decades.

HOW TO DEFINE CLASS?

The study of social classes and the political behavior within different social classes has an extensive history dating back at least to Karl Marx. The Marxist model of class emphasized control over the means of production: Those who controlled the means of production were able to exploit those who did not. To Marx, this was the primary political cleavage of human history. However, as the United States transitioned to a largely post-industrial society, the traditional Marxist vision of economic divisions and their political consequences began to appear increasingly anachronistic. This is not to say that interest in class and voting waned. In their famous study of political cleavages in developed democracies, Lipset and Rokkan suggested that a great dividing line was between those who were owners (landowners and employers) and those who were not (tenants and workers). This cleavage ultimately took political shape, as parties formed around the interests of both groups.[2] The role of social class, however defined, in shaping political behavior has always been a key consideration of political science.

One problem with discussions of class and politics is that classes do not have universally agreed-on fixed definitions. The growth of the "service class" added a new level of complexity to questions about class and voting.[3] Richard Florida's "creative class"[4] potentially complicates our taxonomy of classes as well. Furthermore, while many public opinion surveys ask respondents to name the class to which they belong, Americans overwhelmingly describe themselves as middle class (whatever that actually means), even if their household income places them far above or below the national median.[5] Thus these self-categorizations are of relatively little value to social scientists. In their important book on working-class whites, Joel Rogers and Ruy Teixeira used the straightforward measure of college education as a proxy for class: Whites without a college degree were classified as working class or, to use their terminology, members of the "forgotten majority."[6] Rogers and Teixeira argued that college education was the "Great Divide" in American life[7] and thus is an appropriate, if crude, characteristic to measure whether an American should be classified as working class.

One may question whether or not this remains the most appropriate measure of class in American life. Some commentators recently suggested that college degrees are no longer as valuable as they once were. The costs of college have increased at a rate far greater than inflation, and the student loan debt that burdens many college-educated Americans has grown at an astonishing rate. This debt can have unfortunate consequences for individuals and may ultimately have disastrous consequences for the nation.[8] *Forbes* magazine recently reported on a poll indicating that only 16 percent of college seniors graduating in 2013 had jobs lined up prior to graduation.[9] Peter Theil, the co-founder of PayPal, has even argued that higher education, like real estate during most of the previous decade, is currently a "bubble" ready to burst, with tremendous negative ramifications.[10] Michael Barone, a conservative commentator and political analyst, has made a similar argument.[11] Many people disagree with this analysis, however.[12]

In spite of arguments suggesting college is no longer worth the expense, all reliable data demonstrate that those with a college education are less vulnerable to unemployment than those without a degree. They also earn considerably more money over the course of their lifetimes, on average.[13] However, determining a causal relationship between a college education and better economic outcomes may be more difficult than it first appears. It may be the case that those who earn degrees tend, on average, to have greater intelligence, better people skills, and a stronger work ethic than those who do not. These individuals would likely have done well economically even if they did not attend college. Examining this possibility is outside the scope of this project. For our purposes, all that matters is that a college education is a significant determinant of social standing, and this is unlikely to change in the foreseeable future.

Whether or not educational attainment alone is a valid measure of social class, the relationship between education and voting has long been studied by political scientists. Discerning the precise relationship between education and political attitudes and behavior presents a challenge, given that education is also associated with income. While there is evidence indicating that higher levels of education lead to a greater average preference for left-wing policies,[14] higher incomes are, on average, associated with greater levels of political conservatism, at least when it comes to economic issues.

While education is often a useful proxy, there are other valid measures of social class. For example, we could use income, but there are also problems with this measure. Low-income does not always mean lower class. Among the low-income you have retirees, students, and homemakers.[15] There is an additional problem resulting from the format in which most political surveys present income information. Rather than providing income data as a continuous variable (in which we know each respondent's exact annual household income), income in political surveys is often a categorical variable where respondents are asked to place themselves within a specific range of values. These categories often differ between surveys.[16] An additional problem is that on many surveys a large percentage of respondents decline to share their income—the reader likely noticed that in the regression models in the appendixes in Chapter Three, an independent variable for "income unknown" was included so that such respondents did not need to be dropped from the analysis. This tends to be less of a problem with education.

One might also consider the use of income percentiles (those in the bottom 25 percent in terms of household income, for example) to determine social class. This option has some attractive qualities, and the present author typically divides income into quartiles when examining individual-level data (and will do so later in this chapter). A problem with this option arises when examining time-series data, as the size of each quartile will always be fixed—there will always be 25 percent of the population in the bottom quartile, for example. This may mask changes in the conditions of the different quartiles—in one decade, life in the bottom 25 percent may be reasonably comfortable for many; in other eras, almost everyone in the bottom 25 percent may have to struggle a great deal. While the value of a college degree may have declined in recent years, it is a less fluid measure of class than income.

Occupation type is another variable that can serve as a meaningful measure of social class, and the present author's previous book demonstrated that occupation type can be a statistically and substantively significant predictor of political attributes.[17] That work built on scholarship by other scholars and journalists, including Ruy Teixeira and John Judis, whose book *The Emerging Democratic Majority* argued that successful professionals were a new important component of the Democratic coalition. This category of workers supports the party known for economic redistribution in spite of their relative affluence. The Democratic Party further benefits from the fact that this group is increasing as a percentage of the total electorate. These authors made the case that this growing support for the Democratic Party is not necessarily irrational on their part, given major changes in the U.S. economy:

> As long as professionals felt they had an opportunity to pursue excellence in their jobs, they identified with the successful entrepreneur and CEO. They saw themselves as case studies of how capitalism could reward quality. But as the numbers of professionals have grown within postindustrial capitalism, they have become subject to higher authority within the private and public sectors. And they don't like it. . . . As a result, they have increasingly made a distinction between their own priorities and those of business and the market. That has placed them much closer in outlook to the Democratic Party than to the unequivocally pro-market Republican Party.[18]

By professionals, Judis and Teixera were specifically referring to people with jobs such as "architects, engineers, scientists, computer analysts, lawyers, physicians, registered nurses, teachers, social workers, therapists, designers, interior decorators, graphic artists, and actors."[19] This work, along with others, indicated that to predict how a relatively affluent person will vote, it is helpful to know how that person made her money. However, once again it must be noted that not all political surveys include detailed information about occupation type.

Another problem with the use of occupation type when considering the issue of class in America is that the stereotypical view of the white working class now has relatively little basis in statistical reality. As Andrew Levison noted, when most people think about working-class whites, they generally imagine blue-collar industrial workers. Given the degree to which American manufacturing has declined, at least in terms of the number of people it employs, one might be forgiven for inferring that the white working class is disappearing. Levison argued that the working class is a much larger category than industrial workers, including occupations such as construction workers, mechanics, and truck drivers. Levison's examination of the Bureau of Labor Statistics' data indicated that almost half of the white male workforce remains employed in blue-collar occupations.[20]

Charles Murray, in his book *Coming Apart: The State of White America, 1960–2010*, generated a measure of class in America that incorporated both education and occupation type (though not income).[21] Murray examined two major classes in the United States, the upper class and the lower class, largely disregarding those who fell in between. This chapter will also examine the political trends of people within Murray's categories.

It is not controversial to state that Americans differ in their political behaviors and policy preferences according to social class—however defined. There is a long tradition of scholarship that makes this argument. In 1957, C. Wright Mills argued that ordinary Americans were powerless compared to the nation's military, corporate, and political elites, who had their own agenda and were able to see it implemented in spite of any popular disagreement.[22] However, in order for a wide preference gap to exist across classes, people in different classes need to have coherent and clearly defined preferences. As noted in Chapter 1, some political scientists have disputed whether most people have meaningful political opinions. Some scholars have questioned whether or not there really is an opinion gap across classes. Soroka and Wlezien[23] argued that the gap in public policy preferences is only present in certain issues. On most issues, differences between the preferences of higher and lower income Americans are relatively small. The only major exception they noted was welfare spending. Martin Gilens disagreed and presented evidence suggesting that the income gap in policy preferences is deep and extends to a large number of policies.[24]

THE POLITICS AND POLICY PREFERENCES OF THE WHITE WORKING CLASS: WHAT THE LITERATURE INDICATES

The white working class has been the subject of a great deal of study, and it causes a great deal of consternation for progressives who believe that the white working class consistently votes for Republicans at higher rates than their socioeconomic status suggests they "should." A classic of this genre was *What's the Matter With Kansas*, by the journalist Thomas Frank. Frank argued that the Republicans were able to build a dominant coalition consisting of business and blue-collar workers.[25] They did so largely by appealing to cultural wedge issues such as abortion and gun control. The success of this strategy suggests that the white working class is extraordinarily conservative on cultural issues, and their cultural conservatism drives their voting patterns, even if it means voting against their economic interests.

A look at the relationship between aggregate vote choice in presidential elections and income at the state level indicates that the poorest Americans are Republicans and the richest Americans are Democrats. In 2012, Mitt Romney won all of the ten poorest states in the nation. On the other hand, rich states such as Connecticut and New Hampshire voted for Obama by significant margins in both elections.

Frank's thesis received a great deal of criticism from political scientists. Larry Bartels, one of the most vocal critics of Frank's argument, argued that, however one wishes to define the white working class, Frank exaggerates this group's conservatism on social issues. Bartels also noted that the working class remains more aligned with Democrats than Republicans.[26] He demonstrated that, while cultural issues have become more important in recent decades, it is actually the higher class whites who have given these issues greater weight in recent years.

Andrew Gelman and his co-authors also challenged Frank's conclusions in their book *Red State, Blue State, Rich State, Poor State*. They found that, across the nation, the poor remain quite supportive of the Democratic Party. The real geographic political split is among the rich. In rich states, rich voters are considerably more Democratic than the rich in poorer states. They argued that this is the case because rich voters in wealthier states tended to be more liberal on social issues, and they were thus willing to vote against their presumed economic interests by voting for the party that is in favor of redistribution but also in favor of liberal social policies. The wealthy in poorer states tended to be conservative on both social and economic issues; thus the Republican Party was their natural home.[27]

Regardless of whether or not the Republican leanings of the white working class have been overstated, it is undeniable that this demographic group is *far* more Republican than working-class members of other races. Many scholars and pundits have speculated on why this is the case.

An argument one frequently hears is that many whites abandoned the Democratic Party for racist reasons. That is, as the Democratic Party embraced its role as the party of civil rights, poor whites with anti-black sentiments abandoned the party because of this issue, even if their personal economic circumstances make them more prone to prefer redistributionist policies. This argument should not be cavalierly dismissed. The political realignment of Southern whites in the 1960s and 1970s was definitely related to the civil rights movement. That being said, this argument is somewhat problematic. If racism is the only explanation for this phenomenon, then why has this trend continued despite the fact that all indicators suggest whites are, on average, less racist now than ever before?

Stanley Greenberg, a Democratic pollster and strategist, has long studied the white working class, the group once known as "Reagan Democrats." These are poorer whites who, although they may have identified with the Democratic Party, nonetheless voted for Ronald Reagan in the 1980s and have subsequently voted for other Republicans in presidential elections. In a report published prior to the 2008 presidential election, Greenberg and his co-authors argued that Obama also had a problem with these voters. Many of these members of the white working class were suspicious of Obama on issues of national security. There was also a racial element to their lower levels of support for Obama; many believed that Obama only cared about minority interests.[28]

Another argument is that working-class whites are turned off by the perception of Democrats as the party of upper class elitists with contempt and hostility for working-class whites. Stereotypical images of Democrats as latte-sipping, overeducated urbanites incapable of physical labor, and

Republicans as hard-working, domestic-beer-drinking country boys may have little basis in statistical reality, but they may be sufficiently entrenched in the culture to affect political attitudes among the white working class. Progressive author Joe Bageant, author of *Deer Hunting With Jesus*, argued that liberals largely have themselves to blame for the exodus of working-class whites out of the progressive coalition:

> The political left once supported these workers, stood on the lines taking its beatings at the plant gates alongside them. Now, comfortably ensconced in the middle class, the American left sees the same working whites as warmongering bigots, happy pawns of the empire. That is writing working folks off too cheaply, and it begs the question of how they came to be that way—if they truly are.
>
> . . . From where we stand, knee-deep in doctor bills and hoping the local Styrofoam peanut factory doesn't cut the second shift, you ARE elite. Educated middle class liberals (and education is the main distinction between my marginal white people and, say, you) do not visit our kind of neighborhoods, even in their own towns. They drink at nicer bars, go to nicer churches and for the most part, live, as we said earlier, clustered in separate areas of the nation, mainly urban. Consequently, liberals are much more familiar with the social causes of immigrants, or even the plight of Tibet, than the bumper crop of homegrown native working folks who make up towns like Winchester. Liberal America loves the Dalai Lama but is revolted by life here in the land of the pot gut and the plumber's butt.[29]

This argument suggests that many working-class whites are opposed to the Democratic Party because the Democratic Party is hostile to them or because they perceive the Democratic Party as being hostile to them. Even if it is true that working-class whites are generally anti-Democrat, accurately discerning the reasons for this is beyond the scope of this chapter. What we can consider in the pages ahead, however, is the degree to which white voters really are divided by class.

WHITE POLITICAL ATTITUDES ACROSS THE "GREAT DIVIDE"

This section considers the degree to which whites are politically divided along class lines, using college education as a proxy for class. This was the "great divide," according to Teixeira and Rogers. It relies on the most recent ANES study (2012) to discern major political differences between whites at different levels of education. About one-third of non-Hispanic whites have college degrees, and this is reflected in the ANES data. Because this analysis relies on educational attainment as a proxy for class, respondents under the age of 25 were removed. This is because people of that age are less likely to have earned a college degree, but they may currently be enrolled and may earn a degree within a few years. See Appendix 4.1 for the complete table of values for both class groups.

Party identification is a good place to begin considering this issue. Among the college educated, about 36 percent of respondents identified as Republican and 28 percent identified as Democrats. Among those without a college degree, about 34 percent identified as Republican and 27 percent identified as Democrats. In other words, there was very little difference among whites with college degrees and those without college degrees when it comes to party identification—both whites with a college degree and those without were more Republican than Democratic, and there was not much of a gap between the two groups.

The preceding numbers excluded independent leaners; that is, those who initially identified as independents, but when pushed they admitted to leaning more strongly toward one party than the other. What happens when leaners are combined into the partisan categories? The results are largely the same. Among whites without a college degree in 2012, about 48 percent were Republican or leaned toward the Republican Party, and 37 percent were Democrats or leaned toward the Democratic Party. Among whites with a college degree, 51 percent were Republican or leaned toward the Republican Party, and 39 percent were Democrats or independents who leaned toward the Democrats. In other words, once again we see relatively small differences, but again, the college educated identified as Republicans in slightly greater numbers. Perhaps treating college education as a dichotomous variable is too crude a measure, however. It may be useful to disaggregate those who have some college but have not graduated from those who have, at most, a high school diploma. When this categorization is used, we see virtually no change.

This rudimentary analysis indicates that, at least when it comes to party identification, the notion that white Democrats are predominantly overeducated members of the upper class and white Republicans are dominated by the white working class is mistaken. This finding is congruent with Bartel's argument against Frank's thesis.

There is more to politics than party identification, however. Perhaps if we consider characteristics such as ideological disposition and policy preferences we will find a greater class divide. Turning to ideology, we can again use a seven-point scale (0–6), in which higher values are associated with greater conservatism. Among less educated whites, the mean conservatism score was about 3.5—or slightly more conservative than liberal. Among whites with higher levels of education, the mean conservatism score was about 3.3. In this case, we see that lower levels of education were associated with higher levels of conservatism, but the difference was not dramatic.

Identifying as a conservative does not necessarily imply strong support for all conservative policies, however. Perhaps an examination of different policy preferences will reveal a greater educational divide. The ANES asked respondents whether they favored, opposed, or neither favored nor opposed reducing the federal budget deficit by raising corporate taxes. Here we see virtually no difference according to education. About 57 percent of whites favored this policy, and this was the case for both those with a college diploma and those without. The ANES asked respondents whether they favored a higher tax rate on those who make one million dollars a year or more. Once again, strong majorities of both educational categories agreed with this policy (78 percent of those without a college degree and 76 percent of those with a college degree).

We see that there is also not much of a class division when it comes to taxes. What about spending? Respondents were asked whether they believed federal spending on Social Security should be increased, decreased, or kept about the same. Here some important differences begin to emerge. Whereas 53 percent of whites without a college degree favored increased spending on Social Security, only about 30 percent of whites with a college degree agreed. Those without a college degree were more likely to favor increased spending to fight crime (54 percent) compared to those with a degree (35 percent), perhaps because poorer, less educated whites are more likely to live in neighborhoods in which crime is a serious problem. Those without a college degree were also more likely to favor additional spending on the poor (33 percent compared to 20 percent). On the other hand, those with a college degree were much more likely to favor increased federal spending on science and technology (55 percent) than those without (42 percent).

There was virtually no difference of opinion when it comes to increasing federal spending within schools—both groups agreed by large margins that spending should be increased. There was also widespread agreement among both groups that federal spending on welfare should not be increased— only 11 percent of those without a college degree wanted welfare spending increased, and 8 percent of those with a college degree wanted it increased. Nor did either group wish, on average, for increases in federal spending on childcare—though those without a college degree were slightly more favorable to this policy (28 percent rather than 26 percent). Only minorities of both groups favored more spending on the environment (38 percent of those with a degree and 34 percent of those without).

All of these data indicate that there is not a gaping class/education gap among whites when it comes to taxation and spending policies. What about social policies? Is there evidence for the stereotype that poor, uneducated whites are Bible-thumping fundamentalists and the upper class is entirely made up of post-modern secular liberals? This can also be considered using the 2012 ANES.

On the issue of abortion, we do see evidence of an education-based gap. The 2012 ANES asked respondents which of the following statements they agree with: "By law, abortion should never be permitted"; "The law should permit abortion only in case of rape, incest, or when the woman's life is in danger"; "The law should permit abortion for reasons other than rape, incest, or danger to the woman"; "By law, a woman should always be able to obtain an abortion as a matter of personal choice." It is interesting to note that, of the 2012 ANES respondents, there were far more white pro-choice purists than pro-life purists. Only about 12 percent of whites believed abortion should be completely prohibited, but approximately 44 percent said they favored no restrictions at all on abortion. We see further divisions among whites when we break them up according to educational attainment. Among whites with a college degree or more, a slim majority of whites favored no restrictions on abortion (51.3 percent), whereas only 41 percent of whites with no college degree favored this policy. Of those with a college degree, about 9 percent favored a complete prohibition on abortion, whereas 12 percent of those without a degree favored prohibition.

We see a similar gap when it comes to gun control. Respondents were asked if they thought it should be easier to obtain a gun, more difficult to obtain a gun, or whether the policy should remain the same. Approximately 47 percent of whites over 25 with a college degree felt that it should be more difficult to obtain a gun, but only 39 percent of those without a college diploma agreed.

Large majorities of whites from all classes favored federal laws to protect homosexuals from discrimination, but this support was especially strong among those whites with a college degree. Eighty-two percent of whites with a college degree or more favored laws protecting gays and lesbians from job discrimination, compared to 72 percent of those without a degree. There was almost no class difference among whites when it comes to Affirmative Action: Both groups were overwhelmingly opposed to Affirmative Action for African Americans in hiring.

To summarize, educational attainment appears to be a relatively poor predictor of white social policy preferences. If a majority of whites on the higher end of the educational scale approve of a policy, it is a good bet that a majority of whites at the lower end of the scale approve of that policy as well. Abortion was the lone exception, where a slim majority of those with a college degree favored no restrictions on abortion access, but only 41 percent of whites with a high school diploma or less favored this policy. Although the gaps on social policy issues were not typically large, we do see some differences, and in all cases working-class whites were more conservative than whites with higher levels of education.

On the other hand, on most issues related to taxing and spending, whites with higher levels of education tended to be more conservative. This is not a novel or surprising finding, as groups with lower levels of education are surely more likely to benefit from redistributive policies.

The use of education as a measure of class indicates that there is not a dramatic class-based gap among whites, at least in terms of party identification, ideological self-placement, and policy preferences. Perhaps this is because we are considering an inappropriate measure of class. The next section examines how whites differ in terms of income.

It is interesting to note that, although college education does not appear to be an especially powerful predictor of white political attitudes at the individual level, it does appear quite powerful at the aggregate level. That is, there is a rather strong positive correlation between the percent of whites with a college degree in a state and the percent of whites who voted for Barack Obama in 2008.[30]

THE INCOME GAP IN WHITE POLITICS

The previous section considered the possible political gap between whites with at least a college degree and whites with no more than a high school diploma. There are sound reasons for using education as a proxy for class, but this does not preclude the possibility that income actually conveys more meaningful information than education. By restricting the analysis to the 2012 ANES, it is possible to get around problems associated with looking at income and vote choice across multiple surveys and multiple years. The easiest place to look for major differences would be between those at the bottom of the economic scale and those at the top—that is, those in the lowest quartile and those in the highest quartile. Once again, see Appendix 4.1.

When we rely on income rather than education, we see a more significant gap between the wealthiest and the poorest whites when it comes to party identification. About 36 percent of whites with the highest incomes identified as Republican, compared to 28 percent of those with the lowest incomes—though there was virtually no difference between the two groups when it comes to Democratic self-identification. When we include leaners, we see an equally impressive gap. A majority of white respondents (51 percent) in this highest income category identified as Republican, compared to 39 percent of those in the lowest category. In terms of Democratic identification when leaners were included, the difference was again modest (38 percent for the wealthiest and 40 percent for the least wealthy).

The ideology gap is similar when income rather than education is used to demarcate the different classes. What is especially interesting to note, however, is that in this case the wealthiest whites were not the most likely to identify as conservative. The most ideologically conservative (in terms of self-placement) were those whites in the middle two income quartiles. In other words, there is not a linear relationship between wealth and conservatism, on average.

We also see slightly greater differences when it comes to government spending. Once again, one of the greatest differences was on government spending on Social Security. Fifty-three percent of those in the lowest income group favored more Social Security spending, compared to 30 percent of those in the highest income category. There was also a nearly 30 percentage point gap in terms of preferences for spending on the poor—approximately

48 percent of those in the lowest income category favored increased spending on the poor versus 18 percent among the richest.

We see that income is a relatively strong predictor of political attitudes among whites, and we see more variation according to income than we see according to education. This suggests that, while college education may represent a "great divide" when it comes to a large number of individual economic attributes, it is not a particularly strong divide on most political attributes compared to income.

ARE WHITE AMERICANS *COMING APART* POLITICALLY?

Charles Murray's recent book *Coming Apart* examined major trends among white Americans, making the case that whites are becoming increasingly divided along class lines. Murray focused on whites exclusively in order to demonstrate that the changes he was documenting were not strictly a function of demographic change nationwide. Murray argued that in many ways lower class whites are increasingly exhibiting dysfunctional behaviors—fewer intact families, lower levels of workforce participation, greater crime rates, etc. This, according to Murray, is a relatively new phenomenon. Murray made the case that, although there have always been major economic disparities among whites, they once shared a common culture. Now, according to Murray, the upper class and the lower class largely occupy completely different social worlds and rarely interact:

> I do not argue that America was ever a classless society. From the beginning, rich and poor have usually lived in different parts of town, gone to different churches, and had somewhat different manners and mores. It is not the existence of classes that is new, but the emergence of classes that diverge on core behaviors and values—classes that barely recognize their underlying American kinship.[31]

Interestingly, although the push for counter-cultural values largely originated from upper class whites, the upper class has changed relatively little in terms of how it actually lives. According to Murray, when it comes to characteristics such as marriage and family formation, the white upper class is today very similar to how it was in the 1960s. It is only in the bottom rung of society that we see these tremendous changes.

In *Coming Apart*, Murray offered a novel new classification of social classes. He described the members of the new white lower class as residents of "Fishtown"—named after a neighborhood in Philadelphia that has long been dominated by the white working class. He described upper class whites as residents of "Belmont"—named after a wealthy suburb near Boston. As noted previously, Murray categorized individuals using both their income and their occupation. White Americans were classified as residents of Fishtown if they had no more than a high school diploma (and, if they were married, if their spouse also had no more than a college education) and if they worked in a blue-collar profession. Whites were classified as residents of Belmont if they had a college degree (or their spouse had a college degree) and they worked in a high-status profession.[32]

While Murray relied on a large number of data sources to show how these two categories have diverged since the 1960s, most of his examination of public opinion within these two categories relied on the GSS, which has asked similar questions since 1972. It is interesting that Murray focused relatively little on the political characteristics of these two categories.[33] This section considers whether the trends Murray identified extend to politics— that is, if the political characteristics of Belmont and Fishtown have increasingly diverged.[34]

Party identification is one useful place to begin to consider this issue. Have the party affiliations of whites in these two classes increasingly diverged since 1972 (the first year of the GSS)? Figure 4.1 shows the trend in party identification for both residents of Fishtown and Belmont since 1972, using LOWESS—the same technique frequently used by Murray throughout his book. The category of party identifiers once again excludes independent leaners, though when these figures were generated with leaners included, the substantive results did not change.

Murray argued that white Americans are coming apart along class lines across a wide spectrum of sociological attributes. Party identification, however, is not one of those characteristics. Indeed, the trend in the last 40 years

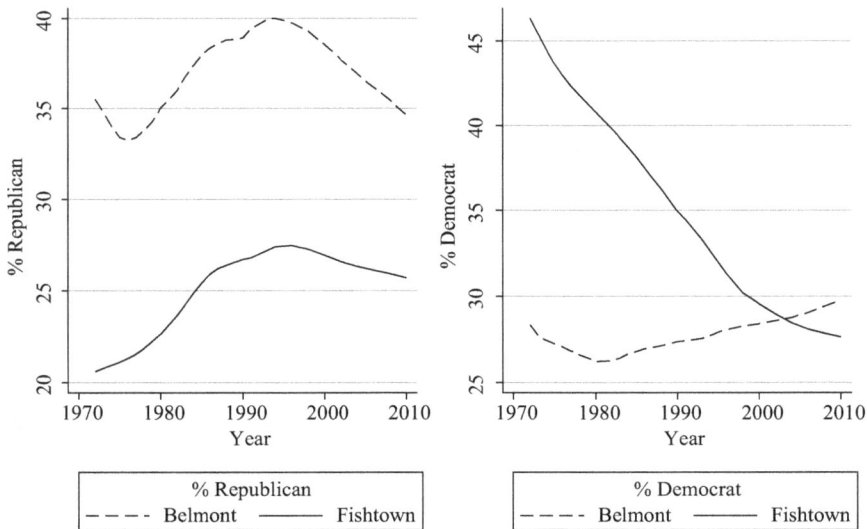

Figure 4.1 Trends in Party Identification in Belmont and Fishtown

has been toward fewer differences between the upper class and the lower class in terms of party identification. While the class gap in Republican identification has shrunk modestly in recent decades, the gap between the two groups in Democratic identification has all but disappeared. This is largely because Democratic identification in Fishtown has plummeted since the 1970s, and Democratic identification in Belmont has been inching upward. As of 2010, a greater percentage of Belmont than Fishtown residents aligned with the Democratic Party.

This is a curious finding. According to Murray's analysis, the white Americans who fit within the Fishtown category have been increasingly exhibiting demographic characteristics associated with higher levels of Democratic voting (being unmarried or infrequently attending religious services, for example), and their weakening economic standing (as demonstrated by their shrinking workforce participation) should encourage them to support the party of economic redistribution. This is not what we see. The people of Fishtown may have been, on average, more culturally conservative in how they actually lived their lives in the early 1970s than they are now, but they were considerably more liberal in their voting patterns.

We see similar findings when we consider the trend in ideology. Using the five-point ideology scale (0–4) ranging from "extremely liberal" to "extremely conservative" we can examine the trends in both Belmont and Fishtown. These trends can be found in Figure 4.2. We see that there has been less movement over time in terms of ideology than party identification. Throughout the entire period under consideration, both groups were more conservative than liberal.

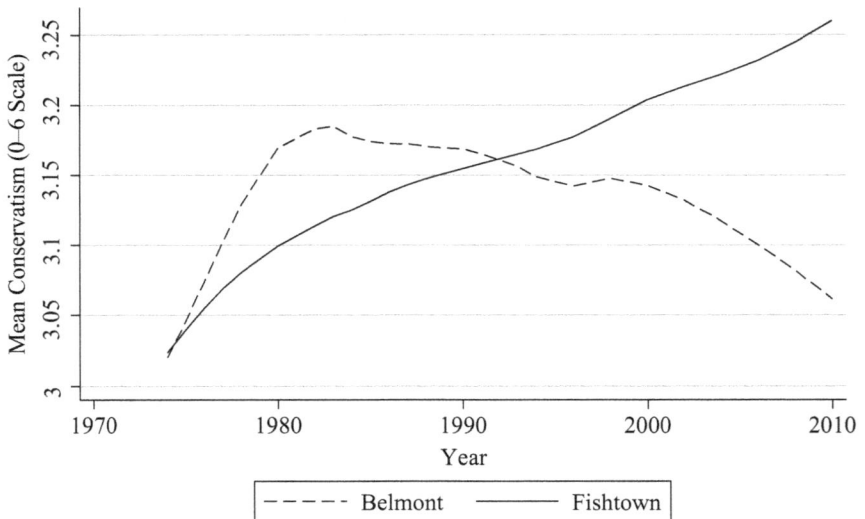

Figure 4.2   Mean Conservatism in Belmont and Fishtown

Here we could with some justification say that white Americans are "coming apart," but the trend has not been uniform. Whereas the two groups were nearly identical in terms of their mean ideological self-identification in the early 1970s, Belmont whites became meaningfully more conservative, peaking in the early 1980s, and then became consistently less conservative as time went on. On the other hand, the consistent trend in conservatism among Fishtown whites has been upward—these whites have only grown more conservative since the 1970s and on average are now more conservative than whites in Belmont.

The main thing to note about these two figures is that, if one believes Murray's class distinctions are valid, white Americans are clearly not dividing along class lines politically. To the extent that they are diverging, they are doing so because the poorest and least educated whites are abandoning the Democratic Party and identifying as more conservative at a greater rate than the wealthiest and most educated whites.

UNIONS AND THE WHITE VOTE

It is relatively infrequent that state-level political disputes make national headlines and continue to hold national interest for months at a time. However, during the early months of 2011, all eyes were on Wisconsin and the struggle between Republican Governor Scott Walker and public employee unions in that state. In the face of major budget shortfalls, Wisconsin Republicans backed a bill to deny public sector unions the ability to collectively bargain over pensions and health care. The bill also limited pay raises and denied public sector unions the ability to automatically collect dues from public sector employees.

This legislation set off a firestorm of controversy, leading to massive protests and counter-protests. Tens of thousands of protesters assembled in Madison on multiple occasions.[35] After a contentious political battle, Governor Walker was ultimately successful, but the drama continued when the governor was forced to stand for a recall election. Walker narrowly won his recall election—though interestingly he increased his share of the vote compared to his previous gubernatorial campaign.

Stories like this seem somewhat anachronistic in contemporary America. The days of great struggles between unions and employers now seem a distant memory. Union membership in the United States has declined dramatically since the 1950s: As of 2012, only 11.8 percent of American workers belonged to a union.[36] The ability of unions to effectively organize has been further weakened by the proliferation of right-to-work legislation at the state level. While different states have passed different legislation, generally speaking, right-to-work laws forbid compulsory union membership as a basis of employment. Although these laws are usually defended using the language of individual freedom, rather than with the use of anti-union rhetoric, anyone familiar with the collective action problem understands why "closed shops" can be essential to union success.[37] According to the National Right to Work Legal Defense Foundation, 24 states now have some form of right-to-work legislation.[38] Tope and Jacobs argued that there are other political explanations for the decline of unions. They made the case that conservative appointees to key regulatory agencies such as the National Labor Relations Board have hindered union efforts since the 1980s.[39]

There are also non-political economic explanations for the decline in union membership in the United States. Farber and Western argued that much of this decline can be explained by the different growth rates between union and non-union employment.[40] The deindustrialization of the United States and other economically developed nations led to a decline in those industries in which workers have traditionally been represented by strong unions.

The decline in union membership obviously has economic consequences, but it also has political consequences. Unions have always been strong proponents of redistributive policies, as well as policies that protect workers from abuse from employers. As a result, they have always been a vital component of the Democratic Party's electoral coalition. A decline in union membership is therefore problematic for Democrats and represents a potential windfall for Republicans.

Given the substantial decline in union membership and in the degree to which white voters do not exhibit strong class-based divisions in terms of ideology and party identification, one might infer that unions now play a relatively small role in American politics, at least at the national level. One

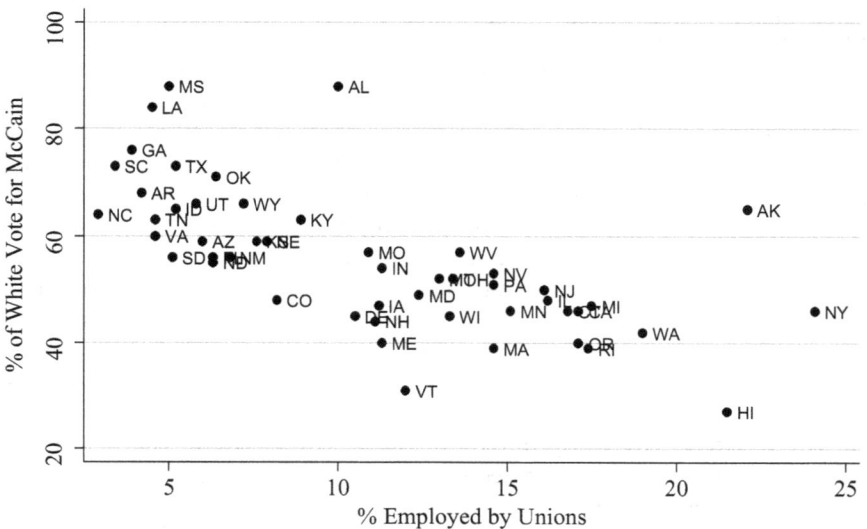

Figure 4.3   Percentage of State Employed by Unions and McCain Share of White Vote

way we can consider this issue is by examining the relationship between the percent of the population employed by a union at the state level, and the state-level support for John McCain among white voters in 2008, as measured by exit polls.[41]

In Figure 4.3, we see a clear linear relationship between the percentage of a state employed by unions and the percent of whites in the state who supported John McCain in the 2008 presidential election. While unions may be experiencing a long-term decline, they clearly remain important to electoral politics. We should be careful before immediately inferring a strong causal relationship between union membership rates and aggregate vote choice. It could be that states with large numbers of Republicans also tend to be states that implement anti-union legislation that discourage union formation and membership.

While the aggregate-level data indicate that union membership is a strong predictor of vote choice, it is worth returning to individual-level data to see if this is the case, and whether or not the relationship between union membership and voting among whites has grown stronger or weaker in recent decades. These differences for all political characteristics in 2012 can be found in Appendix 4.1. Once again these results were based on the 2012 ANES. About 17 percent of whites in the ANES, after applying the appropriate weights, were members of a union. This analysis does not make any distinction between public-sector and private-sector union membership.

When we compare the union-membership gap in politics and the other potential class gaps, we see that there is a far greater gap in terms of party identification between union members and non-union members than between the highly educated and less educated, or between the wealthiest and the poorest. There is also a comparatively large gap in ideology.

Even more interesting, however, is that when it comes to actual policy preferences, the gap between whites in union households and whites not in union households is negligible. Across all policy questions, the mean difference between union and non-union whites in percentages supporting particular policies was 2.7 percent. In contrast, the mean percentage difference between those with college degrees and those without was an impressive 7.8 percent, and the mean difference between those in the highest income group and the lowest was 11.1 percent. This indicates that unions play an important role in white party identification, but do not seem to have a strong influence on policy preferences.

Figure 4.4 shows how the union-membership gap among whites has changed since the 1970s. The figure was generated using the GSS cumulative file, and it shows the trend in Republican identification among both whites with a union member in their household and whites without a union member in their household. The figure shows that, while whites in unions and whites not in unions have both become much more likely to identify as Republicans since the 1970s (though that number has slightly declined in recent years for both groups), the gap between whites with a union member in their household and whites without remains substantial.

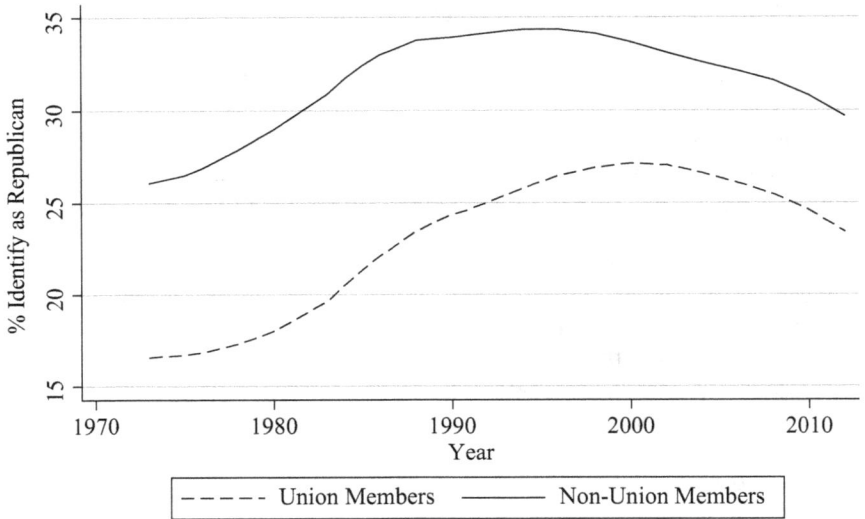

Figure 4.4   Trends in Republican Identification for Union and Non-Union Members

WHAT ACTUALLY INFLUENCES PARTY IDENTIFICATION AND IDEOLOGY?

The preceding descriptive statistics indicate that whites are divided along traditional economic lines, defined by educational attainment, income, and union membership. We see that in some cases these gaps are relatively small—such as the party identification gap in education. In other cases, they are quite significant—such as the party identification gap in union membership. Drawing meaningful inferences from these findings is difficult given the degree to which these characteristics are correlated (there is a particularly strong correlation between educational attainment and income). For this reason a regression analysis is necessary in order to determine which economic traits strongly influence white political attitudes and party affiliations.

Appendix 4.2 provides a logistic regression model in which vote choice was the dependent variable. It provides two models, one that only includes economic and educational traits and a second model that includes additional demographic variables that may be correlated with economic traits. Both models suggest that income is a substantively and statistically significant predictor of vote choice—higher incomes were associated with a greater probability of voting for Romney. However, the effect of income is considerably weakened when other demographic attributes were included, and its effect on vote choice does not appear to be linear. Union membership appears particularly important: A white voter in a union household was only about 0.64 times as likely to vote for Mitt Romney compared to a white voter not in a union household. This was true even after controlling for various other economic and demographic attributes.

Education appears to matter very little when it comes to vote choice. Compared to whites without a high school diploma, whites with a high school diploma, whites with some college, and whites with a college degree were no more or less likely to support Romney. However, there was a substantial difference between whites without a high school diploma and whites with an advanced degree (such as an M.A. or doctoral degree). Interestingly, whites with the highest level of education were 0.56 times as likely to support Romney compared to whites with less than a high school education. This was only true in the model that did not control for other individual attributes, however. Once age, gender, and marital status were included, no education variables remained significant.

It is worth noting that most of the non-economic and non-educational variables contributed little to the model. There was no strong evidence for a gender gap after controlling for other attributes. However, there was an age gap, and older respondents were more likely to vote for Romney than the youngest respondents. There was also a large and statistically significant marriage gap—married voters were much more likely to support Romney. This gap in the white vote will be considered in greater detail in the next chapter.

Just as economic attributes contribute to white vote choice, they may also contribute to ideology. The models in Appendix 4.3 use the same independent variables, but the dependent variable was ideology (measured on a seven-point scale from "extremely liberal" to "extremely conservative"). In the model excluding other demographic variables, the measures of income and union membership proved statistically significant, and in the expected direction—higher incomes were associated with greater conservatism, and union membership was associated with lower levels of conservatism. Education again appeared to have little influence, though whites with an advanced degree were more liberal than whites without a high school diploma. After additional demographic variables were included in the model, income played no substantive role in ideology—in the full model, union membership and possession of an advanced degree were the only economic variables that predicted ideology among whites.

CONCLUSION

The findings in this chapter indicate that, as of 2012, the class gap among whites when it comes to political behavior—however one chooses to define class—was relatively small for many political attributes. For example, there is not a substantive education gap in terms of party identification, ideology, or vote choice. On the other hand, when it comes to actual policy preferences, there were substantial differences according to educational attainment.

Although Charles Murray may be correct that across a wide range of sociological characteristics white Americans are "coming apart" along class lines, this is decidedly not the case politically. If anything, upper and lower class whites are coming together, and the two classes Murray identified have never been closer to each other politically.

The relationship between union membership and politics has held relatively steady and continues to be a powerful predictor of white vote choice. No matter how many additional control variables were included, belonging to a household with a union member dramatically decreased the probability that a white person voted for Romney. We see similarly strong results when we examine the relationship between union membership and white vote choice at the aggregate level. This suggests that, if the Republican Party really is waging a "war on unions,"[42] it has compelling political reasons to do so. Unions remain a definite boon to the Democratic Party. One might object that this has the causal arrow backward. That is, perhaps Republicans are not battling labor unions because their members are so Democratic; instead, perhaps union members became Democrats because of recent Republican hostility to unions. A problem with this alternative hypothesis is that the union gap in party identification has changed relatively little since the 1970s.

While not the main focus of this chapter, the reader may be interested in the findings in Appendix 4.2 that indicate that several non-economic demographic characteristics predicted white vote choice. For example, even after controlling for other variables, there was a statistically and substantively significant difference between whites under 30 and whites over 65 when it comes to vote choice. The next chapter considers the scope of the political generation gap among contemporary whites.

NOTES

1. For a thorough discussion of this topic, see Robert Huckfeldt and Carol Weitzel Kohfeld, *Race and the Decline of Class in American Politics* (Urbana: University of Illinois Press, 1989), 16.
2. It is worth noting that Lipset and Rokkan considered other major cleavages, such as the cleavage between church and state, between the nation's center and periphery, and between land and industry. Seymour Martin Lipset and Stein Rokkan, "Cleavage Structure, Party Systems, and Voter Alignments: An Introduction," In *Party Systems and Voter Alignments*, eds. Seymour Martin Lipset and Stein Rokkan (New York: Free Press, 1967), 1–64.
3. The idea of a service class, which is an intermediate class between the lower and upper classes, was first introduced by John Goldthorpe. The conditions of this class are generally much better than that of the traditional proletariat, and its members typically possess greater levels of specialized knowledge. John Goldthorpe, "On the Service Class, Its Formation and Future," in *Social Class and the Division of Labour*, eds. Anthony Giddens and Gavin Mackenzie (Cambridge: Cambridge University Press, 1982), 162–185.

4. Florida defines the "Creative Class" as follows: "I define the core of the Creative Class to include people in science and engineering, architecture and design, education, arts, music, and entertainment whose economic function is to create new ideas, new technology, and/or creative content. Around the core, the Creative Class also includes a broader group of *creative professionals* in business and finance, law, health, and related fields." Richard Florida, *The Rise of the Creative Class: And How It's Transforming Work, Leisure, Community, and Everyday Life* (New York: Basic Books, 2002), 8.
5. Benjamin Sosnaud, David Brady, and Steven Frenk, "Class in Name Only: Class Identity, Objective Class Position, and Vote Choice in American Presidential Elections," *Social Problems* 60(2013): 81–99.
6. Ruy Teixeira and Joel Rogers, *America's Forgotten Majority: Why the White Working Class Still Matters* (New York: Basic Books, 2000), 15.
7. Ibid, 12–14.
8. Some of these individual consequences include delayed family formation and homeownership, and weaker prospects for retirement security. Consumer Financial Protection Bureau, *Student Loan Affordability: Analysis of Public Input on Impact and Solutions,* May 8, 2013, accessed June 13, 2013, http://files.consumerfinance.gov/f/201305_cfpb_rfi-report_student-loans.pdf.
9. Susan Adams, "College Graduates' Expectations Are out Of Line with Reality, Says Study," *Forbes,* May 2, 2013, accessed June 13, 2013, www.forbes.com/sites/susanadams/2013/05/02/college-graduates-expectations-are-out-of-line-with-reality-says-study/.
10. Sarah Lacy, "Peter Thiel: We're in a Bubble, and It's Not the Internet. It's Higher Education," *TechCrunch,* April 10, 2011, accessed June 13, 2013, http://techcrunch.com/2011/04/10/peter-thiel-were-in-a-bubble-and-its-not-the-internet-its-higher-education/.
11. Michael Barone, "College Bubble Bursts After Years of Extravagance," *Washington Examiner,* May 7, 2013, accessed July 30, 2013, http://washingtonexaminer.com/michael-barone-college-bubble-bursts-after-decades-of-extravagance/article/2529082.
12. For one counter argument to the suggestion that higher education is a "bubble," see Jeffrey Dorfman, "There's No College Education 'Bubble': College Education Is Underpriced," *Forbes,* September 12, 2013, accessed October 15, 2013, www.forbes.com/sites/jeffreydorfman/2013/09/12/theres-no-college-tuition-bubble-college-education-is-underpriced/.
13. Catherine Rampbell, "Once Again: Is College Worth It?" *New York Times,* May 20, 2011, accessed June 13, 2013, http://economix.blogs.nytimes.com/2011/05/20/once-again-is-college-worth-it/.
14. There are a number of studies that verify this. For an older work in this genre, see Fred M. Kaiser and Robert Lilly, "Political Attitudes Among Students: A Small College Experience," *Adolescence* 10(1975), 287–295. For a more recent study confirming the relationship between education and liberalism on social issues, see Alan S. Gerber, Gregory A. Huber, David Doherty, Coner M. Dowling, and Shang. E. Ha, "Personality and Political Attitudes: Relationships Across Issue Divides and Political Contexts," *American Political Science Review* 104(2010), 111–133.
15. Though in the case of homemakers, it is possible to work around the fact they personally have low incomes by relying on overall household income when classifying individuals according to class.
16. Ruy Teixeira and Alan I. Abramowitz, "The Decline of the White Working Class and the Rise of a Mass Upper-Middle Class," *Political Science Quarterly* 124(2009): 193–194.
17. George Hawley, *Voting and Migration Patterns in the U.S.* (New York, Routledge, 2013), 120–124.

18. John B. Judis and Ruy Teixeira, *The Emerging Democratic Majority* (New York: Lisa Drew/Scribner, 2002), 43–44.
19. Ibid, 29.
20. Andrew Levison, *The White Working Class Today: Who They Are, How They Think, and How Progressives Can Regain Their Support* (Lexington, KY: Democratic Strategist Press, 2013), 22–23.
21. Charles Murray, *Coming Apart: The State of White America, 1960–2010* (New York, Crown Forum, 2012), 144–146.
22. C. Wright Mills, *The Power Elite* (New York, Oxford University Press, 1956).
23. Stuart N. Soroka and Christopher Wlezien, "On the Limits to Inequality in Representation," *PS: Political Science and Politics* 41(2008): 319–327.
24. Martin Gilens, "Preference Gaps and Inequality in Representation," *PS: Political Science and Politics* 42(2009): 335–341.
25. Thomas Frank, *What's the Matter With Kansas: How Conservatives Won the Heart of America* (New York: Metropolitan Books, 2004), 8.
26. Larry Bartels, "What's the Matter With *What's the Matter With Kansas,*" *Quarterly Journal of Political Science* 1(2006): 205–219.
27. Andrew Gelman, David Park, Boris Shor, Joseph Bafumi, and Jeronimo Cortina, *Red State, Blue State, Rich State, Poor State: Why Americans Vote the Way They Do* (Princeton, NJ: Princeton University Press, 2008), 167.
28. Stanley B. Greenberg, James Carville, Andrew Baumann, Karl Agne, and Jesse Contario, "Back to Macomb: Reagan Democrats and Barack Obama," *Democracy Corps*, August 25, 2008, accessed October 15, 2013, www.demo cracycorps.com/Archive/back-to-macomb/.
29. Joe Bageant, "Poor, White, and Pissed: A Guide to the White Trash Planet for Urban Liberals" *JoeBageant.com*, February 18, 2005, accessed June 14, 2013, www.joebageant.com/joe/2005/02/poor_white_and_.html.
30. Scott Keyes, "Obama Swept States with most Educated Workforces and Highest Paid Teachers," *Think Progress*, November 9, 2012, accessed August 7, 2013, http://thinkprogress.org/education/2012/11/09/1170241/obama-educa tion-2012/.
31. Murray, *Coming Apart*, 11–12.
32. Ibid, 321–325.
33. The lengthiest discussion in *Coming Apart* on politics was in the section on "SuperZips"—those zip codes where wealthy, highly educated Americans have increasingly clustered. The most important thing Murray notes was that the SuperZips are not politically homogeneous. While there are some SuperZips in which the Democratic Party is dominant (such as the SuperZips around San Francisco and Silicon Valley), this is not the case in SuperZips elsewhere, such as those in and around Los Angeles and New York City. See pages 94–97.
34. I am grateful to Charles Murray and his assistant Caroline Kitchen for sharing their coding for each GSS respondent with me. This not only saved me a great deal of time but also ensured that my findings are not the result of a coding error.
35. It was estimated that at least 25,000 people assembled to protest this legislation on February 16, 2011. Lila Shapiro, "Wisconsin Protests: State Police Pursue Democratic Lawmakers Boycotting Vote," *The Huffington Post*, February 17, 2011, accessed June 18, 2013, www.huffingtonpost.com/2011/02/17/wiscon sin-protests-scott-walker-police_n_824697.html.
36. Alana Semuels, "Union Membership in U.S. Continues Its Long Decline," *Los Angeles Times*, January 23, 2013, accessed November 7, 2013, http://articles. latimes.com/2013/jan/23/business/la-fi-mo-union-membership-20130123.
37. One of the primary stumbling blocks to any form of collective action is the problem of free-riding. That is, when a good is non-excludable, it is rational for an individual to choose not to exert any effort toward seeing that good's

creation. For that reason, some collective goods, such as better working conditions from an employer, can only be effectively lobbied for if every potential beneficiary is forced to contribute to the effort. Labor unions represent one of the classic examples of the free-rider problem. Even if a worker supports a union's goals, individual union members have little incentive to pay union dues. Since unions cannot restrict benefits exclusively to union members, the best choice option for individual workers is not to join the union, but nonetheless enjoy the benefits of the union's efforts. A compelling argument can be made that unions are completely ineffectual in the absence of mandatory membership. Mancur Olson wrote the most famous work explaining this issue. Mancur Olson, *The Logic of Collective Action: Public Goods and the Theory of Groups* (Cambridge, MA: Harvard University Press, 1965).

38. To see a list of states with some form of right-to-work law on the books, visit the following website: www.nrtw.org/rtws.htm (accessed June 18, 2013).
39. Daniel Tope and David Jacobs, "The Politics of Union Decline: The Contingent Determinants of Union Recognition Elections and Victories," *American Sociological Review* 74(2009): 858.
40. Henry S. Farber and Bruce Western, "Accounting for the Decline of Unions in the Public Sector: 1973–1998," *Journal of Labor Research* 22(2001): 459.
41. The 2008 election was the election used in this case rather than 2012 because exit polls were not conducted in many states in 2012.
42. The claim that the GOP is fighting a war on unions is frequently made by political commentators. For one example, see Harold Myerson, "The GOP's War on Labor Unions," *Washington Post*, December 1, 2012, accessed June 20, 2013, http://articles.washingtonpost.com/2011–12–01/opinions/35285194_1_machinists-union-nlrb-chairman-mark-pearce-national-labor-relations-board.

Appendix 4.1 The College Degree Gap, Income Gap, and Union Membership Gap in Party Identification, Ideology, and Policy Preferences

This appendix provides a table demonstrating the political differences between whites who have a college degree and those who do not. Those who have a degree include those with just a four-year college degree, as well as those with an advanced degree such as an M.A. or Ph.D. Those without a college degree include those with less than a high school diploma, those with just a high school diploma, and those with some college (including an associates degree) but no four-year college degree. These results for the portion of the table focused on education exclude respondents under the age of 25, as a large percentage of the population in this cohort may still be in the process of getting a degree; this also may be the case for those in older age cohorts, but the majority of college undergraduates are under the age of 25. The income categories are based on annual household income and are as follows: Income category 1: under $5,000–$19,999; 2: $20,000–$49,999; 3: $50,000–$99,999; 4: $100,000 or above. The union membership portion of the table makes no distinction between types of union—those in public- and private-sector unions are in the same category.

	Degree Gap			Income Gap					Union Gap		
	No College Degree	College Degree	Difference	Income Group 1	Income Group 2	Income Group 3	Income Group 4	Difference between Group 1 & Group 4	Non-Union Household	Union Household	Difference
% Republican	34.2	36.0	1.8	27.7	34.4	36.8	36.4	8.7	35.7	28.1	7.6
% Democrat	26.6	27.7	1.1	28.7	26.3	27.0	27.3	1.4	25.2	35.8	10.6
% Republican with Leaners	47.8	51.7	3.9	38.4	47.6	52.8	50.6	12.3	50.1	41.4	8.7
% Democrat with Leaners	37.1	38.7	1.6	40.4	37.8	37.1	38.3	2.1	36.4	44.7	8.3
Conservatism Scale (0–4)	3.5	3.3	0.2	3.2	3.5	3.4	3.3	0.1	3.4	3.1	0.3
% Favor Greater Corporate Taxes	56.8	56.6	0.1	59.4	60.6	54.5	54.1	5.4	56.5	59.3	2.7
% Favor Greater Tax on Millionaires	78.0	76.0	2.0	78.8	79.9	74.9	73.2	5.6	75.7	80.6	4.9
% Favor Increased Spending in Social Security	53.0	30.4	22.6	54.3	50.6	46.4	28.2	26.1	45.0	44.8	0.1
% Favor Increased Spending on Public Schools	57.3	56.8	0.5	60.2	57.6	61.1	54.8	5.4	58.1	60.6	2.5
% Favor Increased Spending on Science and Technology	42.0	55.2	13.2	41.5	42.2	47.3	52.6	11.1	45.9	49.2	3.4

(Continued)

	Degree Gap			Income Gap					Union Gap		
	No College Degree	College Degree	Difference	Income Group 1	Income Group 2	Income Group 3	Income Group 4	Difference between Group 1 & Group 4	Non-Union Household	Union Household	Difference
% Favor Increased Spending on Crime	54.5	35.2	19.3	50.1	52.9	48.3	35.9	14.1	48.2	47.4	0.8
% Favor Increased Spending on Welfare	10.7	7.8	2.9	18.8	10.9	6.8	5.5	13.3	10.0	8.9	1.1
% Favor Increased Spending on Childcare	28.4	26.4	2.1	36.5	27.0	27.8	23.8	12.7	28.1	32.0	4.0
% Favor Increased Spending on the Poor	33.1	20.2	12.9	47.7	32.4	24.7	18.4	29.3	29.2	31.9	2.7
%Favor Increased Spending on the Environment	34.3	37.8	3.5	43.0	36.7	30.3	37.6	5.4	35.6	41.1	5.5
% Favor No Restrictions on Abortion	41.1	51.3	10.2	41.0	35.9	44.9	56.9	15.9	43.5	47.6	4.2
% Favor Complete Abortion Prohibition	12.1	8.9	3.2	16.5	11.1	12.1	6.6	9.9	12.0	9.0	3.0
% Favor Making it More Difficult to Purchase a Gun	39.4	46.6	7.3	43.3	39.2	40.8	46.4	3.1	41.3	44.6	3.2
% Favor the Death Penalty	83.2	70.0	13.2	75.7	79.5	79.5	74.5	1.2	77.8	78.0	0.3
% Favor Civil Right Protections for Gays	71.8	81.7	9.9	67.6	71.9	78.8	77.6	10.1	74.4	78.3	3.9
% Favor Affirmative Action	10.5	12.3	1.8	18.2	10.6	10.7	9.1	9.1	11.3	11.9	0.6

2012 ANES

Appendix 4.2 Logit Model for Voting for Romney in 2012—Economic Characteristics

In models in previous chapters, respondents with an unknown income were included in the analysis, but coded as "income unknown." In the models in Tables 4.2 and 4.3, respondents who did not provide their income were excluded from the analysis.

	Odds Ratio	Std. Err.	Odds Ratio	Std. Err.
Union Household	0.64	(0.09)*	0.64	(0.09)*
Income Quartile 2	1.77	(0.29)*	1.53	(0.25)*
Income Quartile 3	2.49	(0.39)*	1.97	(0.32)*
Income Quartile 4	2.28	(0.38)*	1.62	(0.29)*
High School Diploma	1.11	(0.27)	1.13	(0.29)
Some College	0.91	(0.22)	1.05	(0.26)
College Graduate	0.91	(0.22)	1.10	(0.28)
Advanced Degree	0.56	(0.15)*	0.63	(0.17)
Female			0.90	(0.09)
Married			1.74	(0.19)*
Age 30–44			1.40	(0.29)
Age 45–64			1.68	(0.32)*
Age 65 Plus			2.00	(0.41)*
Constant	1.00	(0.26)*	0.28	(0.09)*
Observations	2658		2649	
Log Likelihood	−2028.0778		−1975.1837	

* $p < 0.05$
Source: 2012 ANES

Appendix 4.3 OLS Regression Model for Ideology

	Coeff.	Std. Err.	Coeff.	Std. Err.
Union Household	−0.33	(0.09)*	−0.32	(0.09)*
Income Quartile 2	0.30	(0.11)*	0.15	(0.10)
Income Quartile 3	0.38	(0.10)*	0.15	(0.11)
Income Quartile 4	0.39	(0.11)*	0.10	(0.12)
High School Diploma	0.05	(0.15)	0.05	(0.15)
Some College	−0.06	(0.15)	0.01	(0.15)
College Graduate	−0.07	(0.16)	0.01	(0.16)
Advanced Degree	−0.55	(0.17)*	−0.52	(0.17)*
Female			−0.19	(0.07)*
Married			0.51	(0.07)*
Age 30–44			−0.05	(0.12)
Age 45–64			0.05	(0.10)
Age 65 Plus			0.30	(0.11)*
Constant	3.21	(0.15)*	3.08	(0.17)*
Observations	2935		2935	
R-Squared	0.03		0.07	

* $p < 0.05$
Source: 2012 ANES
The Ideology variable is based on a seven-point scale, with higher values associated with greater conservatism.

5 The White Generation Gap, Gender Gap, and Marriage Gap

INTRODUCTION

This chapter will consider other possible "gaps" in the white vote: the gap between young and old, between men and women, and between the married and unmarried. All three have attracted significant attention in recent years, though some of these gaps are more substantive than others and their size has changed over time.

The political "generation gap" has long interested political scientists and other political observers, and this interest has only grown in recent years. This renewed interest is largely thanks to Barack Obama's overwhelming victories among young voters, especially in 2008. According to LexisNexis Academic, the words "Obama," "generation gap," and "election" have appeared together in 592 news stories, including 192 newspaper articles. Journalists have given a great deal of attention to the political views of the generation known as the "Millennials."[1] *Time* magazine declared 2008 the "year of the youth vote."[2] This chapter will examine the degree to which whites exhibit a political generation gap, drawing on the extensive literature on the subject. It will examine what the most recent data tell us about the political behavior of whites of different ages. It will also look at changes over the last several decades.

The gender gap has similarly attracted great attention recently. In 2012 multiple commentators claimed the Republican Party had declared a "war on women." Those making this argument pointed to the Republican opposition to abortion.[3] There was also justification for this attention on gender and voting, as there was a gender gap in vote choice in 2012. According to exit polls, 52 percent of men voted for Romney, but only 44 percent of women did so. The gender gap remains when we consider whites alone, but the gap is smaller, and a majority of both white men and white women voted for Romney—62 percent of white men versus 56 percent of white women. This chapter will also examine the political gender gap among whites and attempt to discern what explains these political differences.

The marriage gap is a subject the present author has explored on multiple occasions.[4] Marital status is one of the more useful predictors of vote choice and other political attributes—married Americans are much more likely to vote Republican. Although this subject has received less attention from political scientists, the forthcoming analysis will demonstrate that it is a powerful determinant of party identification among whites.

These issues are important. Discerning the degree to which political gaps are widening or closing among whites in different demographic categories can help us further ascertain whether whites are beginning to coalesce into a single major voting bloc or whether they will remain highly divided for the foreseeable future. This is additionally important because, if these gaps are persistent and show no signs of closing, we can examine demographic trends to consider whether whites will, in the aggregate, become more Republican or Democratic as the century progresses. For example, if marriage remains a powerful predictor of Republican voting among whites, and marriage is on a long-term decline, then we can anticipate further troubles for the Republican Party in the decades ahead.

THE MILLENNIALS AND POLITICS: THE CONTEMPORARY DISCUSSION

Much has been written about the political attributes of the Millennial Generation by both scholars and journalists. This subject deserves serious attention, as this generation will become increasingly politically powerful as it matures. In most of these articles, the comparatively progressive attitudes and behaviors of this group are emphasized. On many issues, particularly social issues such as gay marriage, the youngest generation of voters is, on average, more liberal than any generation that preceded it.[5] They voted overwhelmingly for Barack Obama in 2008—66 percent for Obama versus 32 percent for McCain according to some estimates.[6] A majority of voters under 30 voted for Obama again in 2012—though Obama's victory in this demographic category was more modest in the latter election. A 2009 study conducted by the Center for American Progress (a liberal think tank) found that, ideologically, young Americans were much more liberal than older Americans and they tended to prefer progressive public policies.[7]

On the other hand, recent survey data indicate that Millennials are becoming less trusting of all government institutions other than the military. They were also increasingly skeptical of Wall Street and the media. A May 2013 poll conducted by the Harvard University Institute of Politics indicated that only 22 percent of Millennials trusted the federal government to do the right thing all or most of the time. Only 18 percent indicated trust in Congress.[8] For this reason, it is not surprising that libertarians are also optimistic that the rising generation will be more interested in their message of limited government. The Ron Paul movement, for example, was demographically remarkable because of the great deal of enthusiasm Congressman Paul was able to generate among many young voters and activists. While Paul always performed poorly among primary Republican voters overall, his showing among the youngest cohort of Republicans was consistently high.[9]

When discussing the generation gap in American politics, it is crucial to emphasize that much of this gap is actually a racial and ethnic gap. That is, among older Americans, non-Hispanic whites are still a huge majority. The youngest generation of voters, however, is much more racially diverse, and this shows in their aggregate voting patterns. This is not to say that young whites are as conservative, on average, as their parents, but the current political and cultural generation gap is qualitatively different from previous generation gaps—the Baby Boomer generation may have been politically and cultural distinct from the World War II generation, but both generations were overwhelmingly white. This is not the case today. It is possible that, among white Americans today, the generation gap is actually rather small when it comes to politics, but the overall gap is large because of the large number of non-whites under the age of 30 and the comparably few non-whites in the oldest age cohorts.

THE GENERATION GAP: WHAT THE LITERATURE SUGGESTS

The political generation gap has long been studied by political scientists, and different explanations for this phenomenon continue to compete with each other. To some extent, a gaping generation gap should not be expected given what we know about the origins of party identification. It is well established that peoples' political views are largely shaped by their parents. This was one of the key findings of the earliest work by scholars of political behavior: "It is apparent . . . that an orientation towards politics begins before an individual attains voting age and that this orientation strongly reflects his immediate social milieu, in particular his family."[10]

Early scholars of political behavior established that party identification tends to be quite stable for most people throughout their adult lives.[11] This finding has been consistently verified since the 1960s.[12] As a result, we might not expect to see much of a generation gap emerge unless there was a dramatic difference in birthrates between members of different political parties or people with different ideological inclinations. That being said, age is often a meaningful predictor of political attitudes and party identification, and some explanation must be provided for this phenomenon.

Interest in the political generation gap is not new. It was particularly salient during the 1960s, when the nation was rocked by a series of protests on a number of major issues such as civil rights and the Vietnam War. Young Americans were overrepresented in all of these major protest movements. This led to some speculation that young people were rebelling against their parents' generation. On its face this is a plausible argument. However, a study of student activists in the late 1960s indicated that there was actually a great deal of generational continuity when it came to political activism:

Conservative activists tended to be the children of conservatives, and liberal activists were the children of liberals.[13]

We should also not overstate the degree to which party identification is inherited from parents. Green and colleagues examined the relationship between individual party identification and parental party identification. They found a relationship, but it was not dramatic—it was certainly too weak to explain all of party identification. This relationship also appears to dissipate over time. Those authors examined a panel study that provided the party identification of respondents' parents as of 1965, as well as the party identification of their children at different points of their lives (in 1973, 1982, and 1997). By 1997, there was still a relationship between individual party identification and the party identifications of their parents in the 1960s, but this relationship was not strong. By 1997, a respondent with Republican parents was 1.6 times as likely to be a Republican compared to a respondent without Republican parents.[14]

Life-cycle effects are one common explanation for differing political attitudes across the generations. This theory holds that as individuals become older, their circumstances change, and their political views change accordingly. Usually their incomes increase, they become more likely to own property, and they have a higher tax burden. This should make people less likely to support redistributive economic policies and become generally more conservative.

However, there is little evidence that people actually become more conservative as they grow older. As Donald Kinder put it, "Do individuals grow more conservative as they age? No. Aging is generally unaccompanied by movement to the right (or the left)—not on matters of economics or foreign policy and not on partisanship either."[15] People do tend to become more strongly attached to their parties as they age. People in their twenties may switch back and forth between parties. People in their fifties are less likely to do so.

Age gaps can open up because of specific policy issues that affect different age cohorts differently. These gaps are not necessarily ideological. Different age groups can be mobilized to engage in action to advance their specific interests—the young can be mobilized to oppose the draft, and the old can be mobilized to support Medicare, for example.[16]

The political science literature is in widespread agreement that there is not a clear linear relationship between a person's age and that person's political conservatism. This does not preclude, however, the possibility of a political generation gap.

IS THERE A WHITE GENERATION GAP?

It is worth considering whether or not an age gap among whites with regard to party identification is immediately apparent, as well as whether or not that gap has been consistent over time. To begin to answer this question, we can again turn to the GSS. Figure 5.1 shows the percentage of whites of different age cohorts who have identified with the two major parties since the early 1970s. Once again only respondents who immediately identified with a party were counted as partisans. True independents and independent leaners were not classified as belonging to a party.

Figure 5.1 shows that there is a generation gap among whites, and this has been the case since the 1970s. This gap has never been particularly large—especially if we compare it to racial and ethnic gaps. However, the differences between white age cohorts have changed over time. Since the 1970s, the generation gap in Democratic identification has held relatively steady, though the percentage of whites who identify with the Democratic Party has decreased substantially among all age cohorts. There has been an uptick in Democratic identification among whites under 30 recently, but it nonetheless remains far below the levels seen in the 1970s.

The changes in identification with the Republican Party have been more dramatic. In the mid-1970s, there was a massive gap between the oldest white Americans and the youngest white Americans when it came to identification with the Republican Party. Compared to the percentage of whites under 30 who identified as Republican, the percentage of Republicans among whites over 65 was almost twice as large. This rapidly changed. Republican identification among whites under 30 exploded in the subsequent decade, and by the mid-1980s, a greater percentage of whites in this age category were Republican than in any other group other than the oldest

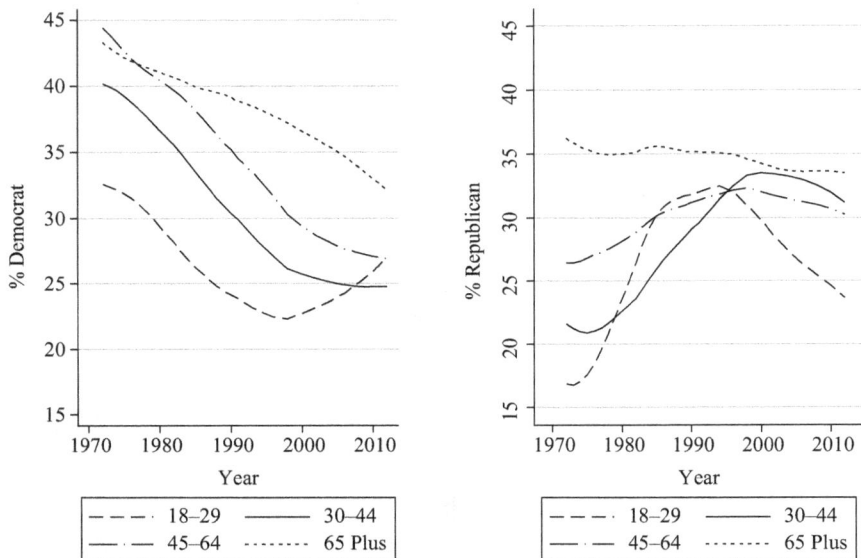

Figure 5.1 Trends in Party Identification by Age

cohort. Throughout much of the 1990s, there was almost no age gap among whites when it came to Republican identification. Since 2000, however, the age gap in Republican identification has begun to open up again, due largely to a recent drop in Republican identification among young whites. This gap nonetheless is still smaller than it was in the 1970s.

What about ideology? Are older whites substantially more conservative than younger whites? If so, has this always been the case? We can again turn to the GSS to consider this question and again use a seven-point ideology scale to consider changes over time. Those in older cohorts have been, on average, more conservative than those in younger cohorts. However, again, these differences have been rather modest. For all cohorts in all years, the mean conservatism score was closer to the moderate position than the "extremely conservative" score (equal to six) or "extremely liberal" score (equal to zero): Most cohorts in most years averaged between "moderate" and "slightly conservative." The ideological age gap has shrunk since the 1970s, largely because the youngest Americans have become more likely to identify as moderate or conservative and less likely to identify as liberal.

What we can say from this is that there is evidence of an ideological gap between young and old whites, but it is not gaping nor is it growing. The next question worth investigating is whether or not this contemporary gap has origins in issue preferences. To consider this question the 2012 ANES is a useful source. Appendix 5.1 shows how whites with different demographic attributes differ on party identification, ideology, and policy preferences.

Based on what we see in the 2012 ANES, it is apparent that there are few interesting or substantive gaps between whites of different ages. The difference in party identification between the youngest and the oldest whites was particularly insubstantial. At all age levels, about 35 percent of all whites identified as Republican.[17] The difference among age groups for Democratic identification was slightly greater, but in all age cohorts the percent identifying as Democratic was between 25 and 30 percent. There were similarly only minor differences in terms of ideology. The oldest cohort was slightly more conservative than the youngest cohort, but they both were quite moderate, on average.

For most policy issues, the differences were rather small. When differences do appear, it is not the case that older whites are always more conservative. A greater percentage of the oldest whites, for example, favored higher taxes on millionaires than whites in other age cohorts. The same is true for government spending on science and technology. We see the greatest opinion gaps when we look at spending issues that specifically benefit young people: Young whites were *far* more likely to favor additional spending on education and also more likely to favor additional spending on childcare.

While we might expect to see the greatest differences when it comes to social issues, this is apparently not the case. In fact, a greater percentage of whites under 30 favored the complete prohibition of abortion than any other age cohort—though this was still a small minority. Compared to the oldest cohort, they were less likely to say it should be more difficult to purchase a gun. While young whites were slightly more likely than older whites to favor gay rights, overwhelming majorities of all age cohorts were in agreement on this issue.

Based on the 2012 ANES, it appears we can answer the question of whether there is a substantial political generation gap among whites: There is not. In terms of party identification, ideology, and public policy preferences, whites do not differ a great deal, on average, according to age. When they do differ, it is not the case that young whites are always more liberal than older whites.

This analysis indicates that the striking degree to which Millennials are politically distinct is due to that generation's demographic features: It is less white, and the non-white elements are less Republican and less conservative. Among whites, the recent trend has not been toward high levels of generational polarization.

THE GENDER GAP IN POLITICS: THE CONTEMPORARY DISCUSSION

As noted in the introduction to this chapter, there was much discussion of a "Republican war on women" in the run-up to the 2012 presidential election. A number of minor scandals in that year caused a great deal of media attention to focus on gender issues. Much of the narrative of that year indicated that there was substantial gender polarization in the electorate.

In February 2012, Sandra Fluke first began to make headlines. Fluke was at the time a law student at Georgetown University and was invited by Democrats to speak to the House Oversight and Government Reform Committee about contraception. The Republican committee chairman denied Fluke the opportunity to speak, but she did eventually give a speech to the House Democratic Steering and Policy Committee. Fluke's primary argument was that religious organizations, such as Georgetown University, should be forced to offer health insurance that covered contraceptive drugs, despite their religious objections.[18]

Responding to Fluke's commentary, conservative talk radio show host Rush Limbaugh made comments suggesting Fluke behaved like a prostitute or slut.[19] These comments only expanded the controversy and proved to be a gift to the Democratic Party and feminist organizations in terms of fundraising in an election year. Other Republicans made rhetorical gaffes that year. When attempting to explain his stance on abortion, Missouri Republican Todd Akin, a candidate for the U.S. Senate, suggested that abortion in the case of rape is rare because women's bodies block unwanted pregnancies in cases of "legitimate rape."[20]

Beyond rhetorical differences between parties, it has been argued that certain policies promoted by many Republicans undermine women's rights.

For example, in 2011 and 2012 some states passed legislation requiring women who wish to undergo abortion to first receive an ultrasound—with the expectation that this would discourage abortion.[21] In 2011, House Republicans passed legislation designed to cut federal funding to Planned Parenthood.[22]

Democratic candidates and feminist organizations pounced on these comments made by Republican candidates and the conservative media, as well as the policies pushed by many Republican legislators. They furthermore helped boost a media narrative of gender polarization in American politics. These stories do not prove definitively that there is an enormous gender gap in American politics, though it is interesting to note that, according to one estimate, more than 60 percent of Obama campaign volunteers were women.[23]

Unlike the generation gap, in the case of the gender gap we cannot say that any aggregate findings are really the result of racial or ethnic differences. Men and women each make up approximately 50 percent of the population for all racial and ethnic groups in the electorate. Interestingly, the voting gap between white men and white women in the 2012 presidential election was slightly smaller than the voting gap between men and women overall. In other words, whites were less politically polarized by gender than other races and ethnicities in that election.[24]

THE GENDER GAP: WHAT THE LITERATURE SUGGESTS

As noted earlier, much of the recent discussion of the political gender gap has been attributed to Republican policies that are characterized by some as anti-woman, whereas the Democratic Party is more favorable toward women and their interests. Such discussions usually focus on policy issues such as abortion and other issues related to reproductive rights. A problem with this analysis is that it assumes a significant gap between men and women when it comes to important women's issues, but some research indicates that this is not the case.[25] Men are not uniformly reactionary when it comes to women's issues such as abortion, and women are not all progressive. At the time of this writing, a recent poll showed that a greater percentage of women than men support a complete ban on abortions after 20 weeks of pregnancy.[26]

Previous scholarship indicates that men and women do differ, on average, on a number of policy preferences and in their vote choice.[27] Women are both more likely to vote according to their view of the national economy and to be more pessimistic about the national economy, making them more prone to vote against incumbents.[28] There tends to be a gap on questions dealing with violence (war, the death penalty, police brutality, etc.) in which women are less inclined to support violent policies.[29] There is also research indicating that women are less favorable toward economic conservatism.[30]

One scholar suggested that the enfranchisement of women is largely responsible for the creation of welfare states in developed countries.[31]

Pratto and Stallworth argued that these political differences were ultimately the result of differing average social-psychological orientations between men and women. Specifically, they postulated that men possessed a greater Social Dominance Orientation, which influenced how they viewed policies relating to intergroup relations.[32] Margaret Trevor argued that the political gender gap has roots in different socialization patterns for men and women.[33] Hatemi, Medland, and Eaves presented evidence suggesting that some of the political differences between men and women can be explained by genetic differences between men and women.[34] If men and women differ according to hormonal or neurochemical pathways, and if these different pathways are associated with different political attitudes, then to a certain extent the political gender gap may be due to hard-wired differences between men and women.

Much of the discussion of the gender gap seems to begin with the assumption that the Republican Party has become increasingly unattractive to women. An equally plausible explanation for a gender gap is that the Democratic Party has become unattractive to men. This was suggested by Daniel Wirls in 1986, who noted, "[W]hile both men and women have been defecting from the Democratic Party and moving away from liberal values, rates of defection among men have been greater than rates among women. Hence the gender gap."[35] In his book, *The Neglected Voter*, David Paul Kuhn argued that Democratic hostility toward males, particularly white males, drove them from the Democratic Party:

> These [white] men were no longer "forgotten," as Franklin D. Roosevelt put it. That implies that Democrats accidentally left these men behind. In 1968, liberals began to purposely disregard white men, and they paid for it. They reaped the whirlwind of their illiberal intolerance in presidential election losses. But then they thought that these losses were simply the byproduct of fighting the good fight. Because, to be sure, the fight for black and female equality was fought and won by Democrats, and it was the greatest of fights.[36]

An examination of trends in party identification over time can indicate whether Republicans have been losing white women, Democrats have been losing white men, or both.

IS THERE A WHITE GENDER GAP?

As was the case with the preceding analysis, the GSS is a useful starting point if we wish to know if the gender gap among whites has grown in recent decades. Figure 5.2 shows how party identification has changed for

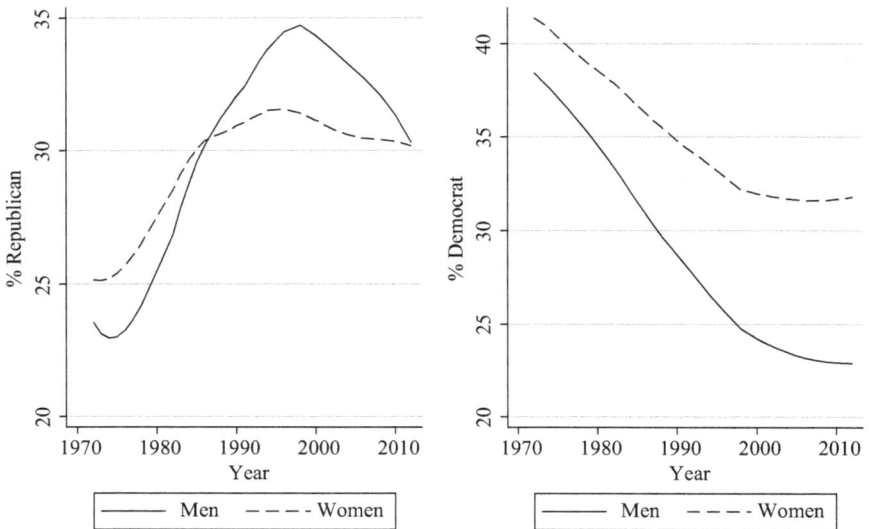

Figure 5.2   Trends in Party Identification by Gender

both men and women since the early 1970s. It demonstrates that, in most periods, there has been a gender gap in party identification among whites, but it has not been consistent over time.

We see that men have shown a greater variability in terms of their affiliation with the Republican Party. According to the GSS, in the early 1970s, fewer men than women identified as Republicans. Because of the growth in Republican identification among white men in the 1980s and 1990s, a significant gap between men and women developed. However, during the Bush years and beyond, Republican identification among white men fell at a faster rate among white men than it did among white women. As of 2012, there was virtually no gender gap when it came to Republican identification.

We see a different trend when we look at Democratic identification among whites of both sexes. Figure 5.2 also shows that Democratic identification declined for both white men and women since the 1970s, but it fell much faster for men. This provides further evidence that the gender gap, at least when it comes to whites, is more the result of men rejecting the Democratic Party than of women rejecting the Republican Party.

Figure 5.3 shows the trend for both sexes in mean ideology. As with the examinations of other groups in terms of ideology, the differences between men and women have long been rather modest, and the means for both have always been somewhere between "moderate" and "slightly conservative." It is worth noting that, in the 1970s, there was virtually no ideological difference between white men and women (at least if we are considering the mean value for both groups). Both groups became more conservative during

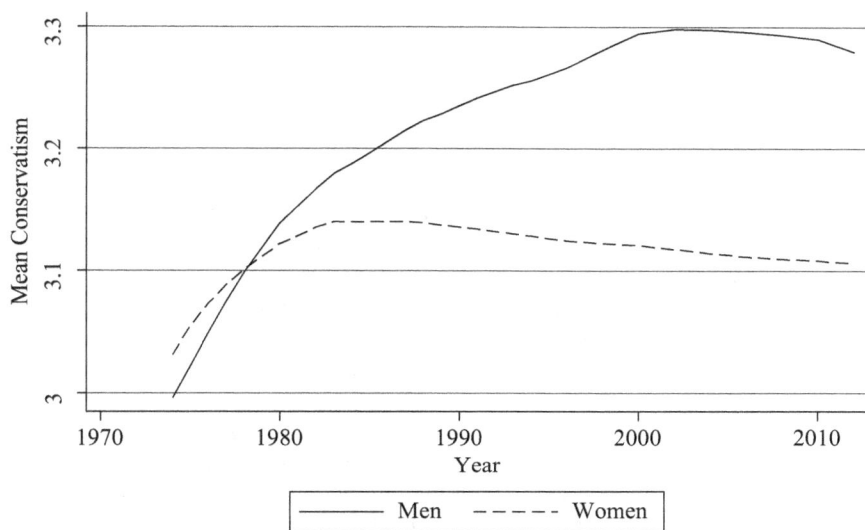

Figure 5.3   Trends in Ideology by Gender

this period, but the increase in conservatism for white women ceased in the 1980s. White men, on the other hand, continued to become, on average, more conservative throughout the 1990s, and this increase has only recently begun to level off.

Once again, all of this suggests that, to the extent that a gender gap exists among whites, it appears to be largely driven by the fact that white men have become more conservative and Republican, rather than because white women have become more liberal and Democratic. Since the 1970s, whites of both genders have become more conservative and less likely to identify as a Democrat on average, but the change was more dramatic for white men.

Although these results indicate that there is not a dramatic gender gap when it comes to party identification and ideology, and the regression models in the previous chapter indicate that gender was not a statistically significant determinant of vote choice in 2012, this does not mean that white men and women do not differ when it comes to support for specific public policies. Appendix 5.1 shows where both genders stood on important public policy issues in 2012, according to the ANES.

Congruent with the findings from the GSS, there is not presently a large gap between men and women when it comes to Republican identification. However, when we include independent leaners in the Republican category, the gap increases somewhat—51.6 percent of white men identified as Republican compared to 45.9 percent of white women. We see different effects when we include independent leaners who lean toward Democrats in the Democratic category. When we do this, the gap between men and women shrinks slightly—though in both cases the gap is around 5 percent. Men were also slightly more conservative in their ideological leanings, but as usual the mean for both groups was between "moderate" and "slightly conservative."

Given these modest differences in party identification and ideology, it is somewhat surprising that there are substantial gender gaps among whites on a number of important policies. For virtually all questions, a greater number of white women than white men preferred the more liberal position. The difference was especially remarkable on gun control (50 percent of white women favored greater restrictions on gun ownership compared to 33 percent of white men). For all questions regarding spending, with a single exception, a greater percentage of women than men preferred higher spending levels. The one exception to this was with regard to spending on science and technology—42.5 percent of white women wanted more spending on this, compared to 50.3 percent of white men.

The results for the abortion question are interesting because a greater percentage of white women than white men favored both placing no restrictions on abortion and the complete abolition of abortion—though the difference was only 1 percent for the latter question and within the margin of error. In contrast, a greater percentage of white men preferred one of the more moderate stances on abortion—again the difference was modest. In other words, it appears white women are slightly more polarized on this perennial culture war issue than white men.

THE MARRIAGE GAP IN AMERICAN POLITICS

While the gender gap and generation gap have generated a tremendous amount of interest from journalists, the marriage gap has received comparatively less attention. This is interesting because it is arguably far more substantive, particularly among whites. While it is true that Romney performed poorly overall among women—capturing only 46 percent of the female vote—he was crushed among single women: Only about 31 percent of single women voted for Romney according to the Reuters/Ipsos exit poll. On the other hand, Romney actually won among married women, capturing about 55 percent of the married female vote.[37]

The marriage gap in politics is partially a function of the marriage gap in terms of race and ethnicity. Whites have a much higher rate of marriage than African Americans and Latinos and also vote Republican in much greater numbers. This substantial marriage gap between whites and blacks was not always present. Indeed, within living memory the marriage rate among African Americans was actually higher than the marriage rate for non-Hispanic whites; however, as of 2010, 20 percent of black women over

44 had never been married, compared to 7 percent of white women.[38] The journalist Kay Hymowitz recently made this point:

> Analysts offer a number of theories about the marriage gap: married women are more financially stable and therefore less reliant on government assistance; they care less about reproductive issues than about their pocketbooks and security; when they marry, they adopt their husbands' political preferences. But the obvious reason for the marriage gap is that for several decades now, married women have become likelier to be white, educated, affluent, and older—demographic groups that leaned Republican in this election. Romney lost the black, Hispanic, and Asian vote, while he won the college-educated vote (though not post-grads), the votes of those making over $50,000 a year, and the votes of older Generation X-ers, Baby Boomers, and voters over 65. In other words, married women voted less as part of a sisterhood than as part of a cohort of white people holding college diplomas, earning more than $50,000 a year, and wearing reading glasses.[39]

While Hymowitz raises an important point, it is not true that marriage ceases to matter after we control for other variables—as we saw in the regression models in Appendix 4.3. Indeed, even if we restrict ourselves to whites alone, the marriage gap is enormous. According to exit polls, Romney lost among unmarried white women (gaining only about 44 percent of this group's votes), but won big among married white women (about 62 percent). Romney won among both married and unmarried white men, but he won by a larger margin among married white men—65 percent compared to 51 percent.

There was a greater than usual interest in the marriage gap in the 2012 presidential election. This was partly due to research conducted by the Quinnipiac University Polling Institute, which provided polling data indicating that there was going to be a massive marriage gap in 2012. While that poll was not able to provide a definitive answer as to why the marriage gap exists, Peter A. Brown, assistant director of the Quinnipiac University Polling Institute, said, "Married voters are more likely to focus on the economy and health care, while single voters are more focused on issues such as gay rights and reproductive issues."[40]

Steve Sailer is one of the few journalists who began writing extensively on the marriage gap long before the 2012 presidential election. Sailer argued that one of the key differences between Red States and Blue States was the relative affordability of family formation—in places where it is relatively inexpensive to form a family, people do so and ultimately end up voting for Republican candidates. While some costs of family formation are relatively fixed across the nation, one important element of starting a family, for many people, is home ownership. Thus, according to Sailer, areas where housing is relatively inexpensive tend to also have higher rates of marriage and higher rates of Republican voting.[41]

THE MARRIAGE GAP: WHAT THE LITERATURE SUGGESTS

There is a reason why the marriage gap has received less attention than other gaps: The marriage gap is actually a relatively recent phenomenon. In 1987, Herbert Weisberg conducted a study showing that, while there was a marriage gap, it disappeared after controlling for other variables.[42] In a different 1987 study, Kingston and Finkel could find only modest evidence that marriage per se influenced political attitudes and behavior after controlling for other characteristics.[43] Plutzer and McBurnett similarly found little evidence for a strong marriage gap in most presidential elections in a 1991 study; they furthermore were unable to discern a causal mechanism for the marriage gap when it appeared.[44]

From these humble beginnings, the marriage gap in American politics grew consistently, and by the early 2000s, marriage rates were one of the most powerful predictors of state-level vote choice in presidential elections.[45] The substantive significance of this variable may have reached a historical high in 2012. It is not immediately obvious why we see a marriage gap in politics, and there are a number of plausible explanations for the strong correlation—at both the individual and the aggregate level—between marriage and vote choice. Edlund and Pande made an economic argument: Because men, on average, have higher incomes than women, marriage tends to represent a redistribution of wealth from men to women. Thus marriage increases the economic standing of women and decreases the degree to which they favor redistributive policies. Because marriage has declined, women are, again on average, experiencing lower levels of economic security and thus are more inclined to support progressive economic policies.[46] However, the economic gap between men and women has also shrunk dramatically in recent decades, which makes such an argument potentially problematic.

There are also non-economic explanations for the marriage gap among women. It has been argued that marriage re-orders individual preferences when it comes to public policies. That is, single women are more concerned with issues such as access to contraception and gender equity, but married women are less concerned with these kinds of issues.[47]

On the other hand, it is important not to discount the possibility that the causal arrow points in the opposite direction. That is, perhaps marriage does not cause people to become more conservative and more likely to vote Republican. Instead, conservatives may be more likely to get married. If a marriage gap has grown, it may be that more progressive Americans are simply eschewing marriage as an institution. There is some evidence for this. Those who are more religious are more likely to get married at a young age[48] and are more likely to vote Republican. Marriage is also increasingly correlated with higher socioeconomic status.[49]

Disentangling the precise causal mechanism of the marriage gap is beyond the scope of this chapter.[50] What we can determine, however, is the scope of the marriage gap among whites, how long it has been an important force in American politics, and whether or not married and unmarried whites differ substantially on important policy issues.

IS THERE A WHITE MARRIAGE GAP?

The trend in party identification among men and women, married and unmarried, can be found in Figure 5.4. According to the GSS, the marriage gap in party identification, while present since at least the 1970s among whites, has grown in the last two decades. This helps explain why scholars in the 1980s found little evidence for a marriage gap once other variables were included in the model. Among whites, we see that every group became considerably less likely to identify as Democratic since the 1970s with one exception: unmarried women. In the early 1970s, a smaller percentage of unmarried women identified with the Democratic Party than was the case for married women and married men. Throughout that decade, unmarried women were similar to other groups in that their Democratic identification rate continued to decline. However, in the 1980s, unmarried white women began to return to the Democratic Party, whereas other groups continued to abandon the party—including married women.

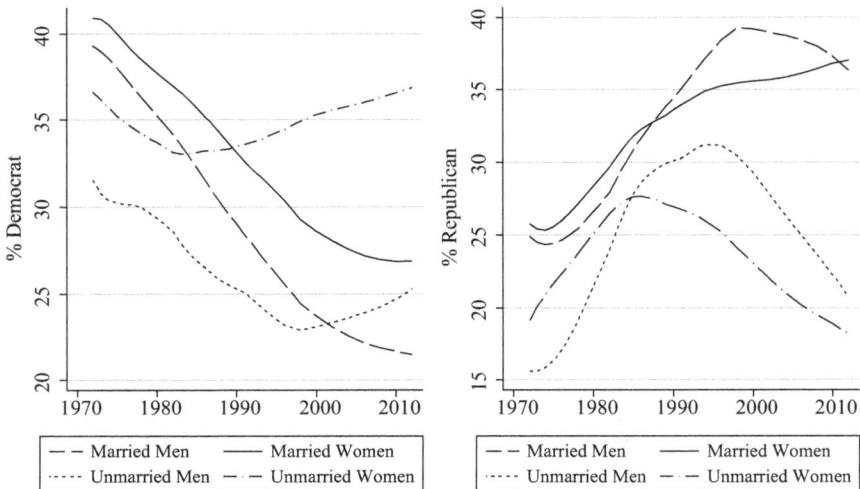

Figure 5.4 Trends in Party Identification by Marital Status

We see other interesting results when we consider the trend in Republican identification. Here we see that all groups experienced substantial growth in Republican identification throughout the 1970s, but the trend reversed for unmarried women in the 1980s and for unmarried men in the 1990s. By 2012, white married men were more like white married women (and white unmarried men were more like white unmarried women) when it came to Republican identification—and the difference was enormous.

Turning to the trend in ideology, we see similar findings. The trend in ideology can be seen in Figure 5.5. Unlike the preceding figure, this figure shows that the marriage gap has always been substantial—though as usual the mean for all groups was close to the moderate position. At the start of the 1970s, the mean ideological placement for unmarried white men and women was between "slightly liberal" and "moderate." The mean ideological placement for married white men and women was between "moderate" and "slightly conservative." Whereas the mean score for all groups is more conservative now than it was in the 1970s, men of both categories increased their conservatism more than women in either category. However, once again we see that, on average, married white men and women have more in common ideologically with each other than with unmarried members of their own gender.

All these data indicate a strong and steadily growing partisan and ideological marriage gap among whites in the United States. A gap in party identification does not necessarily imply a strong difference in term of public policy preference, however. In the case of union membership in the previous chapter, we saw that having a union member in his or her household made

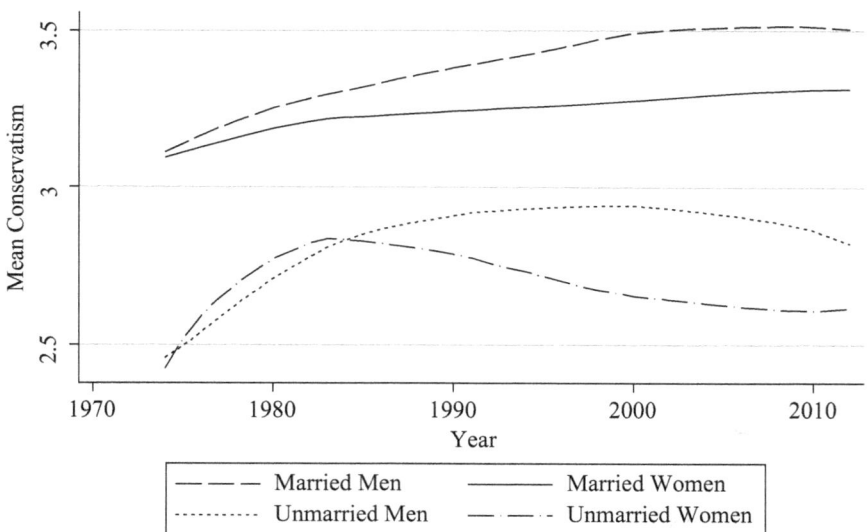

Figure 5.5   Trends in Ideology by Marital Status

a white person much more likely to support the Democratic Party, but it did not seem to have much of an influence on actual policy preferences. Perhaps the same is true of marriage.

A complete list of how married and unmarried whites differed on major policy questions can be found in Appendix 5.1. This closer examination of the policy preferences of married and unmarried whites indicates that the marriage gap extends far beyond party identification and applies to all kinds of public policy preferences. Indeed, the average difference between the percentage of married and unmarried whites who favored a particular policy was greater than the average difference between white men and women and equal to the average difference between whites under 30 and whites over 65.

On all policy questions, a greater percentage of unmarried whites preferred the more liberal position compared to married whites. Unmarried whites were more likely to prefer greater government spending on the poor (a difference of 13.1 percentage points), greater spending on the environment (6.8 percentage point difference), and higher taxes on corporations (5.7 percentage point difference). On social issues, the unmarried were considerably more likely to favor greater civil rights protections for homosexuals—though in both cases support for this policy was greater than 70 percent—and more likely to favor unrestricted access to abortion. Whereas 39.08 percent of married white American believed it should be more difficult to obtain a gun, 45.54 percent of unmarried whites believed this.

All of these findings indicate that the marriage gap is significant among white Americans, and today it is as least as important as the gender gap and the age gap. Of course, disentangling all of this is somewhat problematic, given that age and marriage are correlated—older Americans are also more likely to be married than younger Americans. For this reason, a regression model controlling for all of these different characteristics is necessary in order to discern which variable actually influences white Americans' political attributes.

To some extent, we have already seen the answer to this question in Appendix 4.2, which also included age, marital status, and sex in the regression model of presidential vote choice. However, there are a few additional individual characteristics worth considering. For example, marriage also tends to be associated with another major life event: home ownership. It may be that owning a home is associated with greater conservatism, and this partially explains the correlation between marriage and Republican voting. Finally, we might anticipate that born again Christians are both more likely to get married at a relatively young age and vote Republican. For these reasons, a new logit model of vote choice including these additional covariates can be found in Appendix 5.2.

This new model confirms what we already saw in previous models and also provides some new insights. Once again, gender was not a statistically discernible predictor of vote choice in 2012—although the direction of the coefficient suggested women were slightly less likely to vote

Republican. Marriage was once again highly significant—both substantively and statistically—as were home ownership and identifying as a born again Christian. All of these variables were positively and strongly associated with Republican voting. Identifying as a born again Christian was a particularly powerful predictor of vote choice on average: Controlling for all other variables, identifying as born again was associated with being 2.46 times as likely to vote for Romney. The relationship between religion and white political characteristics will be explored in greater detail in the next chapter. Although there is an age gap in that those older than 65 were more likely to vote Republican than those under 30, the difference was not dramatic. Finally, it is worth noting that after controlling for this additional religious variable and home ownership, no education variable proved statistically significant.

CONCLUSION

This chapter considered the degree to which whites were split politically on a number of key demographic attributes: age, sex, and marital status. The preceding findings reveal that, although the gender gap has received a great deal of attention, gender is not a statistically significant predictor of white vote choice once other characteristics are held constant. While white men and women differ politically, on average, there is not a political "battle of the sexes" among whites. We also see that there is not a tremendous generation gap among white Americans when it comes to politics. While older white Americans are more likely to vote Republican than younger white Americans, the differences are too small to reasonably describe white Americans as polarized by age. Marriage is a powerful predictor of vote choice, ideology, and policy preferences among whites. This has not always been the case, and it is not immediately apparent why this gap has developed. One plausible explanation is that, as the Republican Party worked to establish itself as the party of "family values," its message was much more compelling to married rather than unmarried Americans. Similarly, as the Democratic Party established itself as the political home for America's counter-cultural movements, it may have turned off married Americans but became more attractive to the unmarried, on average. On the other hand, it could be entirely an issue of self-selection: People with attributes correlated with Republican voting (religiosity, belief in more traditional gender roles) are now more likely to get married than people with other attributes. This may be especially true today now that the social stigma associated with cohabitation as an alternative to marriage has largely been removed. However, we should note that the inclusion of the religiosity variable had very little impact on the size and significance of the coefficient for marriage. That is, marriage continued to matter even after we control for whether a respondent identified as a born again Christian.

Regardless of the marriage gap's cause, it is an important phenomenon in American politics, and it underscores an additional demographic dilemma for the Republican Party. While marriage is strongly associated with Republican voting, marriage is on the decline. This is true for whites and non-whites. In 1960, 72 percent of all adults over the age of 18 were married. In 2010, this was true of only 51 percent of American adults.[51] This decline has been accelerating in recent years. This development should be a major concern for the GOP, as it shows yet another way in which the party is fighting an uphill battle demographically—the groups that are most likely to vote Republican (the white, the highly religious, and the married) are all shrinking as a percentage of the overall population.

From this, we see little evidence indicating that one party enjoys a massive advantage over another among whites of any particular age group or gender. In the last several decades, Republican identification has grown among both men and women and the young and old, though Republican gains have slowed and even reversed for some groups in recent years.

The growing Democratic identification among unmarried whites, particularly unmarried white women, is one of the most important political developments uncovered in these data. This finding represents the greatest challenge to the hypothesis that whites, as a group, are going to become even more Republican in the years ahead. The problem this trend represents for the Republican Party is compounded by the fact that marriage is declining for all racial groups in America, including whites. According to the National Marriage Project, marriage rates among whites, particularly whites with lower levels of education, have plunged since the 1970s.[52] If this trend continues, and unmarried whites remain generally supportive of the Democratic Party, a major increase in the Republican share of the white vote is unlikely in the near future.

NOTES

1. There is no consistent definition for the Millennial Generation, a term used interchangeably with "Generation Y." Speaking generally, this is the generation born between the early 1980s and the early 2000s.
2. David Von Drehle, "The Year of the Youth Vote," *Time*, January 31, 2008, accessed June 21, 2013, www.time.com/time/magazine/article/0,9171,1708 836,00.html.
3. *U.S. News & World Report* actually sponsored a debate on the question of whether Republicans were engaged in a war on women. "Is There a Republican War on Women?" *U.S. News & World Report*, April 10, 2012, accessed June 24, 2013, www.usnews.com/debate-club/is-there-a-republican-war-on-women.
4. See Hawley, *Voting and Migration Patterns in the U.S.*, and "Home Affordability, Female Marriage Rates, and Vote Choice in the 2000 Presidential Election: Evidence from U.S. Counties," *Party Politics* 18(2012), 771–789.
5. Peter Leyden, Ruy Teixeira, and Eric Greenberg. "The Progressive Politics of the Millennial Generation," *New Politics Institute*, June 21, 2007, accessed

June 20, 2013, http://ndn-newpol.civicactions.net/sites/ndn-newpol.civicac
tions.net/files/NPI-Millennials-Final.pdf.

6. Patrick Fisher, "The Age Gap in the 2008 Presidential Election," *Society* 47(2008): 295–300.
7. Halpin, John, and Karl Agne, *The Political Ideology of the Millennial Generation* (Washington, DC: Center for American Progress, 2009), 3–5,
8. "Survey of Young Americans' Attitudes Toward Politics and Public Service: 23rd Edition," Institute of Politics, Harvard University, April 30, 2013, accessed June 20, 2013, www.iop.harvard.edu/sites/default/files_new/spring_ poll_13_Exec_Summary.pdf.
9. Alexis Levinson, "Why is Ron Paul So Appealing to Younger Voters?" *The Daily Caller*, November 19, 2011, accessed June 21, 2013, http://dailycaller. com/2011/12/19/why-is-ron-paul-so-appealing-to-younger-voters/.
10. Angus Campbell, Philip E. Converse, Warren E. Miller, and Donald E. Stokes, *The American Voter* (New York: Wiley and Sons, 1960), 146–147.
11. Ibid, 148–149.
12. See Charles H. Franklin and John E. Jackson, "The Dynamics of Party Identification," *American Political Science Review*, 77(1983): 957–973, for a model of party identification that predicts high levels of stability. For a more recent discussion on this topic, see Benjamin Highton and Cindy Kam, "The Long-Term Dynamics of Partisanship and Issue Orientations," *Journal of Politics* 73(2011): 202–215.
13. L. Eugene Thomas, "Political Generation Gap: A Study of Liberal and Conservative Activist and Non-Activist Students and their Parents," *Journal of Social Psychology* 84(1971): 313–314.
14. Donald Green, Bradley Palmquist, and Eric Schickler, *Partisan Hearts and Minds: Political Parties and the Social Identities of Voters* (New Haven, CT: Yale University Press, 2002), 80.
15. Donald R. Kinder, "Politics and the Life Cycle," *Science* 312(2006), 1906.
16. Angus Campbell, "Politics Through the Life Cycle," *The Gerontologist* 11(1971): 112–117.
17. On this point, the ANES and the GSS data were not consistent. In the GSS, the percentage of young whites who identified as Republicans was considerably smaller (about 22 percent), though the percentage identifying as Democrats was similar in both surveys. However, the number of observations in the GSS was also considerably smaller (there were fewer than 200 white respondents in this age category in 2012 in the GSS, compared to more than 400 in the 2012 ANES); for this reason the author considers the ANES to be a more reliable measure, though the GSS is still useful for looking at trends across multiple years.
18. Meghan McCarthy, "How Contraception Became a Train Wreck for Republicans," *National Journal*, March 4, 2012, accessed June 24, 2013, www. nationaljournal.com/healthcare/how-contraception-became-a-train-wreck-for-republicans-20120304.
19. Jack Mirkinson, "Rush Limbaugh: Sandra Fluke, Woman Denied Right to Speak at Contraception Hearing, a 'Slut,'" *The Huffington Post*, February 29, 2012, accessed June 24, 2013, www.huffingtonpost.com/2012/02/29/rush-limbaugh-sandra-fluke-slut_n_1311640.html.
20. John Eligon and Michael Schwirtz, "Senate Candidate Provokes Ire with 'Legitimate Rape' Comment," *New York Times*, August 19, 2012, accessed June 24, 2013, www.nytimes.com/2012/08/20/us/politics/todd-akin-provokes-ire-with-legitimate-rape-comment.html?_r=0.

21. Lucy Madison, "Virginia Gov. Bob McConnell Signs Virginia Ultrasound Bill," *CBS News*, March 7, 2012, accessed June 24, 2013, www.cbsnews.com/8301–503544_162–57392796–503544/virginia-gov-bob-mcdonnell-signs-virginia-ultrasound-bill/.
22. David Nather and Kate Nocera, "House Votes to Defund Planned Parenthood," *Politico*, February 18, 2011, accessed June 24, 2013, www.politico.com/news/stories/0211/49830.html.
23. Liz Halloran, "2012 Gender Gap Could Be Historic, but Maybe Not for the Reason You'd Think," *NPR*, September 27, 2012, accessed July 10, 2013, www.npr.org/blogs/itsallpolitics/2012/09/27/161818462/2012-gender-gap-could-be-historic-but-not-necessarily-why-you-think.
24. The notion that the gender gap differs among racial and ethnic groups is not a novel finding. For a useful introduction to this topic, see Pei-Te Lien, "Does the Gender Gap in Political Attitudes and Behavior Vary Across Racial Groups?" *Political Research Quarterly* 51(1998): 869–894.
25. Jane Mansbridge, "Myth and Reality: The ERA and the Gender Gap in the 1980 Election," *Public Opinion Quarterly* 49(1985): 164–178.
26. Jennifer Rubin, "Abortion Polling," *Washington Post*, July 25, 2013, accessed July 30, 2013, www.washingtonpost.com/blogs/right-turn/wp/2013/07/25/abortion-polling/.
27. R. Michael Alvarez, Carole Chaney, and Jonathan Nagler, "Explaining the Gender Gap in U.S. Presidential Elections, 1980–1992," *Political Research Quarterly* 51(1998): 311–339.
28. Ibid.
29. Tom Smith, "The Polls: Gender and Attitudes Towards Violence," *Public Opinion Quarterly* 48(1984), 384–396.
30. Jim Sidanius and Bo Ekehammer, "Sex-Related Differences in Socio-Political Ideology," *Scandinavian Journal of Psychology* 21(1980): 17–26.
31. Graziella Bertocchi, "The Enfranchisement of Women and the Welfare State," *European Economic Review* 55 (2011): 535–553.
32. Felicia Pratto and Lisa M. Stallworth, "The Gender Gap: Differences in Political Attitudes and Social Dominance Orientation," *British Journal of Social Psychology* 36(1997): 49–68.
33. Margaret C. Trevor, "Political Socialization, Party Identification, and the Gender Gap," *Public Opinion Quarterly* 63(1999): 62–89.
34. Peter K. Hatemi, Sarah E. Medland, and Lindon J. Eaves, "Do Genes Contribute to the 'Gender Gap'?" *Journal of Politics* 71(2009): 262–276.
35. Daniel Wirls, "Reinterpreting the Gender Gap," *Public Opinion Quarterly* 50(1986): 317.
36. David Paul Kuhn, *The Neglected Voter: White Men and the Democratic Dilemma* (New York: Palgrave MacMillan, 2007), 227.
37. The Reuters/Ipsos poll is an excellent resource for anyone examining the 2012 presidential election, as it provides a user-friendly means to generate crosstabs for various demographic and geographic groups in the electorate. It can be accessed at: http://elections.reuters.com/ (accessed July 10, 2013).
38. Diana B. Elliott, Diana B., Kristy Krivickas, Matthew W. Brault, and Rose M. Kreider, "Historical Marriage Trends from 1890–2010: A Focus on Race Differences." In SEHSD Working Paper Number 2012–12, p. 14.
39. Kay S. Hymowitz, "The Misunderstood Gender Gap," *City Journal*, November 16, 2012, accessed July 10, 2013, www.city-journal.org/2012/eon1116kh.html.
40. Quinnipiac University Polling Institute, "Big Marriage Gap Keeps Obama Ahead by a Nose, Quinnipiac University National Poll Finds; American Voters

Give Supreme Court Best Scores in DC," media release, July 11, 2012, accessed July 10, 2013, www.quinnipiac.edu/institutes-and-centers/polling-institute/national/release-detail?ReleaseID=1770.

41. Steve Sailer, "Value Voters," *The American Conservative*, February 11, 2008, accessed October 22, 2013, www.theamericanconservative.com/articles/value-voters/.

42. Herbert F. Weisberg, "The Demographics of a New Voting Gap: Marital Differences in American Voting," *Public Opinion Quarterly* 51(1987): 342.

43. Paul William Kingston and Stephen E. Finkel, "Is There a Marriage Gap in Politics?" *Journal of Marriage and the Family* 49(1987): 60–62.

44. Eric Plutzer and Michael McBurnett, "Family Life and American Politics: The 'Marriage Gap' Reconsidered," *Public Opinion Quarterly* 55(1991), 126.

45. Hawley, "Home Affordability," 771–789.

46. Lena Edlund and Rohini Pande, "Why Have Women Become Left Wing?" *Quarterly Journal of Economics* 117(2002): 917–961.

47. Kathleen Gerson, "Emerging Social Divisions Among Women: Implications for Welfare State Politics," *Politics and Society* 15(1987): 213–221.

48. Arland Thornton, William G. Axinn, and Daniel H. Hill, "Reciprocal Effects of Religiosity, Cohabitation, and Marriage," *American Journal of Sociology* 98(1992): 628–651; Evelyn L. Lehrer, "Religion as a Determinant of Economic and Demographic Behavior in the United States," *Population and Development Review* 30(2004): 707–726.

49. Murray, *Coming Apart*, 149–167.

50. Indeed, determining the cause of the marriage gap is actually a much greater challenge than it first appears. To this writer's knowledge, the only way to do this with any precision would require a longitudinal study that demonstrated that peoples' political beliefs actually changed after getting married or by finding an instrumental variable to conduct a two-stage least squares regression. While the latter method is not particularly difficult statistically, the present author has not yet been able to think of a variable that is meaningfully correlated with marriage but is in no way correlated with politics.

51. D'Vera Cohn, Jeffrey Passel, Wendy Wang and Gretchen Livingston, *Barely Half of U.S. Adults Are Married—A Record Low* (Washington, DC: Pew Research Center, 2011), accessed July 14, 2013, www.pewsocialtrends.org/2011/12/14/barely-half-of-u-s-adults-are-married-a-record-low/?src=prc-headline.

52. W. Bradford Wilcox, Paul Taylor, and Chuck Donovan, *When Marriage Disappears: The Retreat from Marriage in Middle America* (Charlottesville, VA: The National Marriage Project, 2010), 55.

Appendix 5.1 The Generation Gap, Gender Gap, and Marriage Gap in Party Identification, Ideology, and Policy Preferences

	18–29	30–44	45–64	65 Plus	Difference between Youngest & Oldest	Men	Women	Difference	Unmarried	Married	Difference
% Republican	34.9	34.3	34.4	34.6	0.2	35.1	34.0	1.2	26.91	40.38	13.47
% Democrat	25.7	25.5	27.4	29.3	3.6	24.4	29.4	5.0	32.28	22.83	9.45
% Republican with Leaners	48.7	48.5	47.8	50.1	1.4	51.6	45.9	5.7	39.62	55.61	15.99
% Democrat with Leaners	35.1	37.3	38.5	39.2	4.1	35.3	40.0	4.7	45.48	31.81	13.67
Conservatism Scale (0–6)	3.2	3.3	3.4	3.6	0.4	3.5	3.3	0.2	3.09	3.58	0.49
% Favor Greater Corporate Taxes	58.6	57.6	58.6	52.3	6.3	54.9	58.9	4.0	60.11	54.46	5.65
% Favor Greater Tax on Millionaires	70.1	75.9	79.6	77.0	6.9	72.7	80.3	7.6	80.33	73.72	6.61
% Favor Increased Spending in Social Security	40.7	42.7	51.0	40.3	0.4	40.3	49.4	9.2	61.18	56.76	4.42
% Favor Increased Spending on Public Schools	72.1	67.2	54.1	46.3	25.9	54.9	62.3	7.5	61.18	56.76	4.42
% Favor Increased Spending on Science and Technology	42.7	44.6	46.8	49.8	7.1	50.3	42.5	7.9	47.28	45.54	1.74
% Favor Increased Spending on Crime	41.7	45.9	51.0	49.9	8.2	45.5	50.5	5.0	49.40	47.03	2.37
% Favor Increased Spending on Welfare	9.3	11.2	11.1	6.5	2.8	9.3	10.2	0.8	12.39	7.72	4.67
% Favor Increased Spending on Childcare	33.5	32.8	27.1	21.7	11.8	27.2	30.2	3.0	32.61	25.81	6.80
% Favor Increased Spending on the Poor	31.1	30.7	30.4	25.2	6.0	27.1	32.0	4.9	37.02	24.01	13.01

% Favor Increased Spending on the Environment	44.0	39.3	34.2	31.2	12.8	35.9	37.4	1.6	42.16	32.46	9.70
% Favor No Restrictions on Abortion	39.5	49.0	47.6	37.5	2.0	43.1	45.1	2.0	48.52	40.76	7.76
% Favor Complete Abortion Prohibition	16.3	11.8	9.9	10.0	6.3	11.1	12.1	1.0	10.04	12.78	2.74
% Favor Making it More Difficult to Purchase a Gun	40.0	40.6	40.9	46.1	6.2	33.0	50.3	17.3	45.54	39.08	6.46
% Favor the Death Penalty	74.4	79.4	79.3	75.8	1.4	78.5	77.2	1.4	75.65	79.50	3.85
% Favor Civil Right Protections for Gays	75.7	81.1	72.6	71.9	3.8	71.8	78.2	6.4	79.17	71.95	7.22
% Favor Affirmative Action	13.5	12.3	11.8	8.4	5.1	11.4	11.3	0.1	14.43	9.04	5.39

Source: 2012 ANES

Appendix 5.2 Logit Model for Voting for Romney in 2012—Family Characteristics

The model below is identical to that in Appendix 4.2 with three exceptions. First, unlike the model in the former appendix, this model does not exclude those respondents with an unknown income—this inclusion led to no substantive change. Because it is associated with marriage and family formation, the author included a variable indicating home ownership. The author also included a variable indicating whether the white respondent identified as a born again Christian for the same reason.

	Odds Ratio	Std. Err.
Union	0.64	(0.09)*
Income Quartile 2	1.50	(0.26)*
Income Quartile 3	1.99	(0.34)*
Income Quarile 4	1.76	(0.33)*
Income Unknown	1.60	(0.43)
High School Diploma	1.05	(0.26)
Some College	0.98	(0.24)
College Graduate	1.04	(0.26)
Advanced Degree	0.63	(0.17)
Female	0.86	(0.09)
Married	1.56	(0.17)*
Home Owner	1.48	(0.20)*
Born Again	2.46	(0.27)*
Age 30–44	1.24	(0.25)
Age 45–64	1.38	(0.26)
Age 65 Plus	1.74	(0.35)*
Constant	0.20	(0.06)*
Observations	2779	
Log Likelihood	−2025.82	

* $p < 0.05$
Source: 2012 ANES

6   Religion and the White Vote

INTRODUCTION

Religion has always been a fault line in American politics. Throughout the colonial period, different regions of the United States were dominated by different religious groups, and in many ways these religious differences explain why the various regions of the United States developed unique political cultures. As was noted in Chapter 3, over the course of the 19th century, new immigrants changed the religious landscape of America—thanks to widespread immigration from Catholic countries, the nation ceased to be overwhelmingly Protestant. The Catholic-Protestant divide played a major role in partisan politics in the United States until the latter years of the 20th century. The crucial religious divide in America is no longer between Catholics and Protestants, but between the religiously committed and the secular and the nominally religious. Americans exhibiting high levels of religious commitment tend to vote for the Republican Party, whereas those with no religious affiliation are more likely to support the Democratic Party.[1]

As is the case throughout the developed world, the United States has experienced a serious decline in religiosity in recent decades—though this trend is less pronounced in the United States than in Western Europe. This is true of white Americans as well as other demographic groups in the United States. This trend presents a problem for the Republican Party. If the trend toward secularization continues, the portion of the electorate attracted to the party associated with traditional Christian values will shrink.

That being said, although white Americans have become less religious in recent years, white America has not, in the aggregate, become more Democratic. This is a curious finding. One possible explanation for this is that, although secular whites have always been predominantly Democratic, whites who take their religion seriously are now much more likely to identify as Republicans and there are now few strongly religious white Democrats. If this political-religious sorting process is now complete, then the Republican Party may have reached a ceiling in its support from white voters. If white Americans become progressively more secular as this century continues, then the Republican base of support will continue to erode.

However, it may also be the case that whites are not as divided along religious lines as many commentators imply. In other words, non- or weakly religious whites may not be as overwhelmingly Democratic as much contemporary commentary implies. If this is the case, then the trend toward secularization among whites does not necessarily represent a major problem for the GOP. If religion is no longer a key determinant of white party identification and political behavior, then trends in religion will not be a useful predictor of trends in party politics. This chapter will consider this issue, looking at the current relationship between religion and politics among white voters, as well as how this relationship has evolved in recent decades.

RELIGION AS A DIVIDING LINE IN AMERICAN POLITICS

The political-religious divide in the United States seemed to reach new heights in the 2004 presidential election. Policy questions strongly related to religious concerns, such as the issue of gay marriage, were particularly salient in that year; in 11 states, anti-gay marriage initiatives were on the ballot, and these initiatives easily passed in all cases. The incumbent president, George W. Bush, was an outspoken Christian who publicly discussed his religious convictions with greater frequency than other recent presidents. Both devoted Christian conservatives and secular liberals made the case that religion was a critical issue in American politics. The so-called God Gap was a leading story in the national media.

Prominent Evangelical Christians were eager to take credit for Bush's victory and emphasized their own importance as they urged the president and Republicans in Congress to implement their agenda. Dr. James Dobson was one particularly aggressive player in American politics during this period. According to Michael Crowley, writing in *Slate* just days after the 2004 election:

> [Dobson is] already leveraging his new power. When a thank-you call came from the White House, Dobson issued the staffer a blunt warning that Bush "needs to be more aggressive" about pressing the religious right's pro-life, anti-gay rights agenda, or it would "pay a price in four years." And when the pro-choice Pennsylvania Sen. Arlen Specter made conciliatory noises about appointing moderates to the Supreme Court, Dobson launched a fevered campaign to prevent him from assuming the chairmanship of the Senate Judiciary Committee, which until then he had been expected to inherit. Dobson is now a Republican kingmaker.[2]

Shortly thereafter, Dobson issued a warning to Democratic senators who threatened to block Bush's judicial nominees, suggesting that they would be in his "bulls eye" the next time they stood for election.[3] Many progressives in the United States were concerned that the tremendous political power of

Evangelical Christians represented a threat to the divide between church and state. Kevin Philips wrote a best seller titled *American Theocracy*, in which he argued that radical Christianity was playing a dangerous role in American politics.[4]

During this period, some commentators who were not writing about politics per se noted that religious devotion seemed to be experiencing an upswing. Rich Karlgaard suggested in 2004 that America was experiencing a new "Great Awakening."[5] Given the degree to which devout Christians were vocal about both their theology and their politics, such sentiments were understandable.

However, the fact that conservative Christians were both vocal and an important part of the Republican coalition was not itself proof that religion was on the rise in the United States. The reality is that religious observance has been declining since at least the 1990s. According to Robert Putnam and David Campbell in their book *American Grace*, 17 percent of Americans identified with no religion as of 2006. More Americans identified with no religion than with a mainline Protestant denomination—though they were still outnumbered by Evangelical Protestants (about 30 percent of the population) and Catholics (about 25 percent of the population).[6] While it is true that Evangelical Christians have not been declining in absolute numbers, their share of the total U.S. population has not been increasing. The real explosive growth in religious affiliation has been among those who identify with no religion, and this growth really took off in the last two decades.[7] During the 1990s alone, the percentage of Americans who identified with no particular religion more than doubled.[8]

There are different theories that seek to explain the decline in religious observance among Americans and those in other developed countries. It may be the case that modernization necessarily leads to a shift away from traditional values, including religious values. Such arguments were particularly prevalent in the 19th century, as thinkers like Marx and Nietzsche predicted the demise of religion. The persistence of religion as a force in the world to the present day demonstrates that these predictions were premature, if not mistaken entirely. That being said, the fact that religion has declined in post-industrial societies indicates that the arguments for a positive relationship between modernization and secularization were not completely off base.[9]

Hout and Fischer argued that the rapid decline of religious affiliation in the United States during the 1990s was directly related to politics. This was a period in which organizations affiliated with the Religious Right, such as the Christian Coalition, increasingly flexed their political muscles. As a result, many liberal or moderate Americans who were only weakly attached to their religion responded to the politicization of Christianity by renouncing organized religion. Further bolstering their case was the fact that there has actually been little change in stated religious *beliefs*, even among those who do not identify with a religion. There was not a corresponding decline in belief in God or the afterlife among Americans during this period, and atheists remained a minority even among those unaffiliated with a particular religion.[10]

In the years after the 2004 election, commentary on religion and politics began to catch up with the demographic facts on the ground. Evangelical Christians did not have the electoral clout to control American politics, nor was there much threat of a looming theocracy. In 2006, Jacob Weisberg wrote:

> Bush has indeed allied himself with his party's evangelical wing. But while Karl Rove's pander-to-the base strategy got Bush narrowly re-elected, the entente hasn't truly served Bush or the religious right. The appearance of extremism on issues of church-state separation and stem-cell research has helped dig a deep hole for the president and his party, alienating secular and libertarian Republicans uncomfortable with the revival-tent atmosphere. And evangelical power appears to have peaked. Since the Terri Schiavo debacle, the religious right has mainly embarrassed itself by battling evolutionary theory.[11]

Other commentators have remarked on the recent decline of the Evangelical Christians as political powerbrokers. In *The New Republic*, Michael Kazin declared the "end of the religious right."[12] Paul Waldman made a similar declaration in *The American Prospect*.[13] Further weakening the clout of Evangelical Christians is the fact that they may no longer be as uniformly Republican as was once the case. There is evidence that Obama made important inroads with this demographic group in 2008.[14] The Religious Right also appears to have declined in the years following the 2004 election due to the loss of key figures in that movement—Jerry Falwell and D. James Kennedy passed away prior to the 2008 presidential election, and Pat Robertson, while still living, is now in his 80s. There is not presently a new group of leaders in the Religious Right with a comparable level of political influence, leaving a leadership vacuum in the movement.[15]

None of this is to say that religion no longer plays a role in American politics—it clearly does. However, how much it matters or how it will continue to influence politics in the years ahead remains to be seen. Before considering how the relationship between religion and politics will continue to develop in the future, it is worth briefly examining the historical relationship between religion and politics in the United States.

While religion received much attention in 2004, this was obviously not the first year in which religion played a prominent role in American politics. Religion and politics were closely intertwined during the colonial period, and religion played a major role in the American Revolution.[16] While the British colonies in North America were all overwhelmingly Protestant, different Protestant denominations dominated different regions, and in many ways these religious differences informed their politics—the comparative tolerance exhibited by early settlers to the Delaware Valley, for example, cannot be understood without knowledge of the Quaker religion that dominated the region. The development of the moralistic political culture in New England was clearly a direct result of the Puritan culture of the original settlers.

Religion became a salient feature of American politics very early on and has been an important predictor of voting behavior since the early 1800s. However, it is worth questioning whether an apparent religious divide might actually be the result of a racial or ethnic divide. Throughout the 19th century there were major tensions in New England between Irish Catholic immigrants and Protestants descended from earlier migrations. The Protestants tended to support the Whig Party, whereas the Irish Catholics supported the Democrats. This does not necessarily indicate that there was anything in Catholic doctrine that led these newcomers to support the Democratic Party's policy platform. The correlation between religion and vote choice may be more about ethnoreligious social identification than theology.[17] Even if the religious divide was actually the result of some other dividing line in American politics, however, the correlation was nonetheless real and played an important role in party politics.

Furthermore, religious disagreements directly influenced American politics. Protestant leaders in the 19th century and later were concerned about the growing number of Catholics in the country due to immigration from Ireland and Germany, and later from Southern and Eastern Europe. The hierarchical nature of the Catholic religion and Catholic loyalty to the Pope caused many to doubt their attachment to republican values. There was also a stark religious divide when it came to the Temperance Movement and Prohibition. Evangelical Protestants, on average, tended to favor alcohol restrictions, whereas Catholics were more opposed to this policy.[18]

Different Christian denominations continued to exhibit strikingly different voting patterns well into the 20th century. Catholics remained loyal Democrats through the 1930s and 1940s. The gap between different denominations subsequently shrunk, however. The once-substantial Catholic-Protestant divide has grown smaller; the real political divide today is what Laura Olson and John Green called "the worship-attendance gap."[19] Today, the more important question is not whether one identifies primarily as a Catholic a Protestant or a Jew, but whether or not one regularly attends religious services. This gap is relatively new and did not become a major element of American politics until 1992.[20] Republicans now tend to perform well with committed Evangelicals and committed Catholics (those who attend religious services once a week or more), whereas the Democrats do well among those who never or infrequently attend religious services, even if they identify with a particular religion. Those who attend religious services with some frequency (a few times a month) are about evenly split in their politics.[21]

Examining the contemporary political-religious divide, Putnam and Campbell also argued that this gap is due to different policy preferences of the highly religious and the secular. Specifically, questions about abortion and same-sex marriage strongly divide the religious from the less religious, and these policy preferences help explain their political affiliations.[22] Putnam and Campbell also demonstrated an impressively large "grace gap." A majority of Americans who say a prayer before meals on a daily basis identify as Republican, and an overwhelming majority of Americans who never "say grace" identify as Democrats.[23]

Scholars have attempted to ascertain the precise role that religion played in recent elections. Guth et al. examined a number of variables in order to determine exactly how religion influenced the outcome of the 2004 presidential election. They argued that religious affiliation and the degree to which voters were religious traditionalists were powerful predictors of vote choice.[24] Lewis and de Bernardo noted some of the difficulties of properly classifying Christians as Evangelical or non-Evangelical: Do you make this determination according to their actual religious denominations or based on whether they identify themselves as Evangelicals? The question is not as straightforward as it may seem. Some people belong to denominations that are not generally categorized as Evangelical—such as Methodists—but many people within that religious tradition may actually classify themselves as Evangelical. Lewis and de Bernardo found that people who technically belong to mainline Protestant churches, but self-identify as Evangelical Christians, behave more like Christians within an Evangelical denomination than Christians within other mainline denominations when it comes to politics.[25]

When considering the relationship between religion and voting, the degree to which different religious groups should be disaggregated may not be entirely clear. The most simplistic measure would be to compare the religiously devoted to the secular or marginally religious. Such a measure, however, may inappropriately lump together different religious groups that exhibit dramatically different voting patterns—as mentioned before, Catholics have traditionally been politically distinct from Protestants. Thus, Catholics and Protestants should be examined separately.

This approach may mask some further heterogeneity among Protestants, however. So-called mainline Protestants (which include the Evangelical Lutheran Church of America, the Episcopalian Church, the United Church of Christ, and several others) tend to be both theologically and politically less conservative than Evangelical Protestants (which include denominations like the Southern Baptists and the Missouri Synod Lutherans). A problem with relying on more detailed breakdowns of Christian groups is that many political surveys do not ask respondents their specific denominational affiliation. However, it is common for surveys to ask Christians whether they consider themselves "born again," which can be a useful tool for disaggregating mainline Protestants from Evangelical Protestants.

A new development in American Christianity must also be considered. In recent decades there has been a serious growth in "mega churches"—religious establishments that have more than 2,000 members; while many of these churches are expressly Evangelical Protestant, a majority of them are explicitly non-denominational or "unspecified Christian."[26] The growth in the number of non-Catholic Christians who do not necessarily call themselves Protestants may present an additional difficulty when attempting to categorize Americans according to their religion.

To be clear, this chapter is not arguing that all religious Americans, even all white religious Americans, are Christians. Jews have lived in America since the colonial period, for example. However, in terms of aggregate numbers, non-Christian religious minorities have always been a relatively small percentage of the religious population in the United States, and this is especially true of white Americans. In surveys with a small sample size, it is often not possible to estimate the political preferences of these religious minorities with any accuracy—though it is well established that a majority of Jewish Americans tend to vote for Democratic presidential candidates.[27]

Looking at the entire electorate to discern the size and significance of the religious-political gap poses some challenges. The effect of religion on vote choice seems to vary according to racial and ethnic groups. One racial group that overwhelmingly supports the Democratic Party (African Americans) is also the most religious racial group in the electorate; another racial group that overwhelming votes for Democrats (Asian Americans) is by far the least religiously observant racial group in America.[28] This is not to say that religion does not influence the political behavior of racial and ethnic minorities. It does. Republicans tend to perform better with Latinos who identify with Evangelical Christianity than with Latinos who identify with the Catholic Church, for example.[29] The effect of religion on party identification and vote choice seems to vary by racial group. For this reason, a study of religion focused on whites alone can provide greater clarity.

THE PARTY IDENTIFICATION PATTERNS OF DIFFERENT RELIGIOUS GROUPS

The 2008 National Annenberg Election Study was one survey with an exceptionally high number of respondents, which allows for a more detailed look at smaller religious categories among white Americans. Figure 6.1 shows the percentages of different religious groups that identified with the Republican Party in that year. It demonstrates the degree to which religion is a strong predictor of party identification among whites.

Rather than use denominational affiliation to disaggregate Evangelical from non-Evangelical Protestants, Figure 6.1 was based on respondent self-categorization: Protestants who described themselves as Evangelicals were so classified regardless of their actual denominational affiliation. The figure also disaggregated those non-Catholic Christians who do not identify with any particular denomination from those who explicitly affiliate with a

Protestant church. The figure also shows the Republican identification rates of Mormons.

In Figure 6.1, we see that Mormons who attended religious services on a weekly basis were *overwhelmingly Republican.* The fact that more than two-thirds of these Mormons identified as Republican is even more remarkable when we remember that this percentage does not include those independents who leaned toward the Republican Party. When we count independent leaners in the Republican category, we see that 85 percent of Mormons who attend services on a weekly basis were Republicans. No other religious category was so heavily Republican.

Three other religious categories were majority Republican even when independent leaners were excluded: Evangelical Protestants who attended services on a weekly basis, non-denominational Evangelical Christians who attended services weekly, and non-denominational non-Evangelical Christians who attended services weekly (the last category are likely members of the growing non-denominational "mega churches" mentioned earlier). There were two Christian groups that were less than majority Republican, even when restricted to those who attended services every week—Catholics and non-Evangelical Protestants.

For all religious groups, those who attended services every week were more Republican than those who did not. It is worth noting that secular white Americans were not the least Republican category according to this survey. These data indicate that Jewish Americans who do not attend religious services once a week or more were the least Republican category—fewer than 12 percent of less observant Jews identified as Republican. Jewish Americans who did attend services weekly were scarcely more Republican—fewer than 19 percent of whites in this category identified as Republican.

The data demonstrate that there is a both a denomination gap and an attendance gap among whites. Mormons, Evangelical Protestants, and non-denominational Protestants are more Republican than Catholics, Jews, and

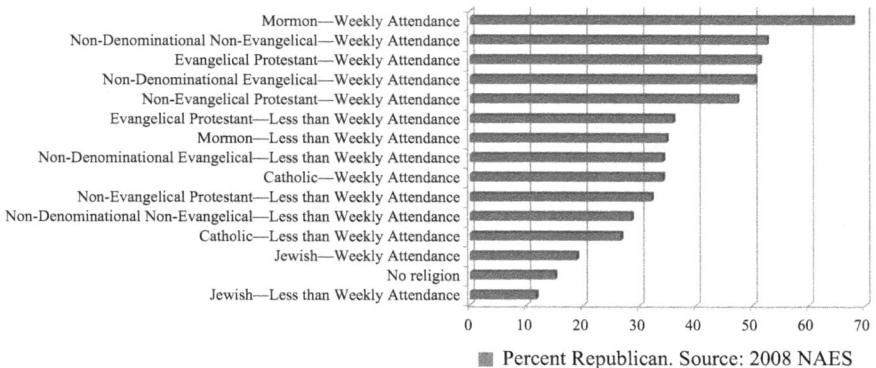

Figure 6.1   Republican Affiliation by Religious Denomination and Service Attendance

the secular, and in every case attending services with greater regularity is associated with higher Republican identification. While examining these data at a single point in time is useful, it is important to examine the long-term trends in religion and party identification.

THE SHRINKING DENOMINATION GAP AMONG WHITES

As was mentioned earlier, denominational differences were once the salient political-religious divide in American politics. Current social science research indicates that the primary political-religious schism today is between those who are highly involved in their religion and those who only nominally affiliate with a religion or have no religion at all. But, this does not necessarily mean that the gap between white Catholics and Protestants has disappeared.

Figure 6.2 was generated using the GSS cumulative file. It shows trends in party identification among white Protestants and Catholics. It would have been ideal to disaggregate Protestants further—showing the trend for both mainline and Evangelical Protestants—but the small sample size of each annual GSS makes this problematic. For this reason all Protestants are combined together. This figure also does not disaggregate those who regularly attend worship services from those who do not—that is, it includes both the devout and those who only weakly identify with their particular Christian denomination. From this figure we see that both groups have exhibited similar trends: Both are much more likely to identify as Republicans and less likely to identify as Democrats. We also see that the gap is smaller now than was once the case. In the early 1970s, a majority of white Catholics identified as Democrats and fewer than 20 percent identified as Republican until the early 1980s. This advantage is even more remarkable when we again note that this figure does not include independent "leaners" within the partisan categories. If we include independents who leaned toward the Democrats in the Democratic category, then the Democratic advantage among this religious group was even more dramatic; in 1972, 64.27 percent of all white Catholics either identified as Democrats or leaned toward the Democratic Party.

Since that time, Democratic affiliation among white Catholics has plummeted. Since the late 1990s, the percentage of Democratic affiliation among white Catholics has been in the mid-30s or below—dropping as low as 28 percent in 2006. Throughout the 1970s, 1980s, and 1990s, Republican identification among white Catholics also increased dramatically. Since the late 1990s, Republican identification has changed little for Catholics.

Although the gap between white Catholics and white Protestants has shrunk, it has not disappeared. This gap is still present because we see a similar trend among Protestants. This group also became more Republican and less Democratic during these years, but they started at a different baseline.

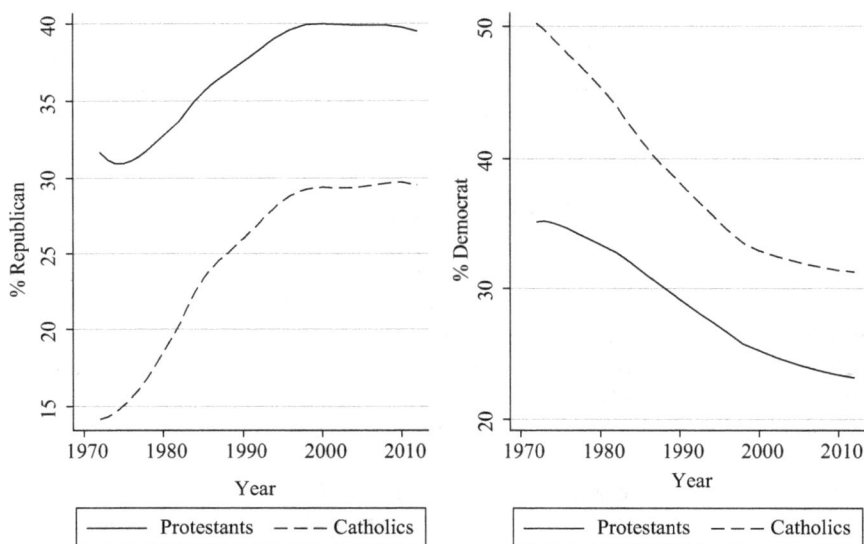

Figure 6.2   Catholic-Protestant Gap in Party Identification

The reason the gap is now smaller is because the slope for Protestants is less steep—while white Protestants also became more Republican and less Democratic during this period, the change was not as dramatic.

We may be able to explain the closing of this gap by the rise of secularism in the United States. As the United States became less overwhelmingly Christian, the schism between different denominations may have become less salient compared to the division between the religious and the secular. It is likely also the case that Catholics and Protestants are motivated by similar issues—both the Catholic Church and most Protestant denominations are officially opposed to abortion, for example.

Part of this gap may be explained by differences in policy preferences, which will be considered in the pages ahead. There may also be an ethnic and regional component to this continuing divide. The regions of the United States with the smallest Catholic presence (the South and the Midwest) are also regions of comparative Republican strength. The regions with the largest number of Catholics (the Northeast and the West) have the largest number of white Democrats[30]—though in the western states, the large Catholic population is probably due primarily to the large Latino presence. There is also an ethnic component. We saw in Chapter 3 that whites who identified with predominantly Catholic ethnicities (those from Ireland and Southern Europe) are more Democratic than whites who identify themselves as English or another Northern European ethnicity.

From this analysis we see that the gap between Protestants and Catholics in party identification, while still substantial, is smaller than it once was, and both groups have been moving toward the Republican Party. This trend is congruent with the many other trends among whites. If we look at the gap between the strongly religious and the less religious or the non-religious, the results may be different.

THE WORSHIP-ATTENDANCE GAP AMONG WHITES

This section examines trends in party identification among those who regularly attend religious services and those who rarely or never attend worship services. It is important to note that this variable is not necessarily a strong indicator of religious *belief*. There are certainly many people who consider themselves devoutly religious but who do not officially belong to a religious congregation and rarely or never attend worship services. Similarly, there are some atheists and agnostics who do attend religious services.[31] The latter are relatively rare, however, and the frequency with which Americans attend religious services can generally serve as a measure of the degree to which they take their religion seriously.

Figure 6.3 shows trends in party identification among white Americans according to the frequency with which they attend worship services, based again on the cumulative GSS survey. Those who attend services at least once a week were categorized as "frequently attending religious services," and those who attend services, at most, a few times a year were categorized as "rarely attending religious services." The trend line for those who attend religious services with some frequency (at least once a month, but less than once a week) was not included in this figure in the interests of simplicity, but that trend falls in between the other two lines.

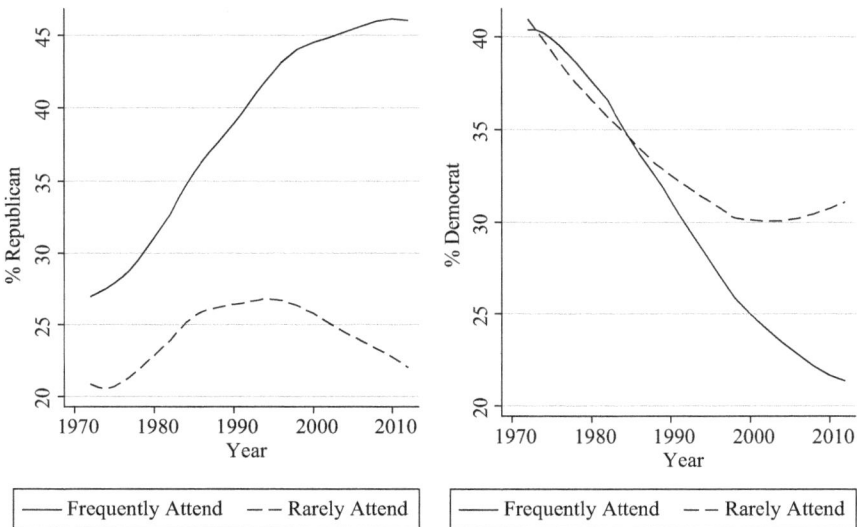

Figure 6.3 Worship-Attendance Gap in Party Identification

Here we see a huge gap between these two groups of whites, and in this case the gap has grown wider over time. We see that Republican identification among those whites who frequently attend a religious service has always been higher than among those who infrequently or never attend services. Throughout the 1970s and 1980s, Republican identification grew for both groups. This began to change in the 1990s, as the Republicans stopped making inroads among the less religious and the trend among this group actually reversed. The worship-attendance gap in Republican identification among whites is now higher than it has ever been since the GSS was first conducted. It is important to note that the size of this gap is due less to the decline in Republican identification among the less religious (those who infrequently attend services are still more Republican today than they were in the 1970s) than to the explosive growth in Republican identification among those who regularly attend services.

We see a similarly gaping divide when we examine trends in Democratic identification. In the early 1970s, those who frequently attended worship services and those who did so infrequently identified with the Democratic Party at equal rates. Both groups experienced a similar major decline in Democratic identification throughout the 1970s and 1980s. There were even brief periods in which those who regularly attended services were *more* Democratic than those who did not. The gap in Democratic identification between these groups did not really open up until the mid-1990s. At that time, the decline in Democratic identification among the less religiously active came to an end and even reversed, whereas the percentage of whites who frequently went to services who identified as Democrats continued to decline through the years of the Bush presidency.

It is interesting to note the insignificance of the political-religious divide among whites in the 1970s, despite the degree to which American politics exhibited characteristics of a "culture war" during this period—recall that the 1972 Democratic presidential candidate, George McGovern, was labeled the candidate for "abortion, amnesty [for those who evaded the draft], and acid."[32] While matters related to religion and culture were politically salient during this period, there was an apparent delay in how these debates translated into changes in party identification.

POLICY PREFERENCES AMONG DIFFERENT RELIGIOUS CATEGORIES

Trends in party identification tell us much about the relationship between religion and politics among whites. This section will further consider the most recent data on religion and party identification. However, it is also important to consider the roots of this relationship. Do the religious and the secular differ substantially on actual public policies, even when it comes to policies unrelated to religious concerns? This section considers the points on which secular and religious whites agree and on which they differ. It looks at differences between Catholics, Protestants, and "nones." It further disaggregates Protestants between those who describe themselves as "born again" and those who do not. It also looks at how policy preferences differ according to the frequency with which they attend religious services. The 2012 ANES provides a useful starting point for considering this question. The full table can be found in Appendix 6.1.

This table indicates that the different party identification rates of different groups in the white electorate are the result of different policy preferences. For most policy issues, the different groups can be ordered according to their conservatism as follows: born again Protestants were the most conservative, followed by Protestants who do not describe themselves as born again, followed by Catholics, and the non-religious were the least conservative.

This ordering of conservatism was not true in every case, however. There were some cases in which born again Protestants were less conservative than other Protestants. For example, born again Protestants were slightly more in favor of greater spending on the poor than other Protestants. Born again white Protestants were also slightly less favorable toward the death penalty. While born again Protestants were more conservative than Catholics on all issues, there were some cases where Catholics were more conservative than other Protestants. A slightly smaller percentage of Catholics favored increased federal spending on public schools and higher taxes on the wealthy compared to non-born again Protestants. The difference was small in both cases.

Not surprisingly, we see the largest religion gaps on social issues. Whereas more than 20 percent of born again Protestants wanted abortion to be illegal in all cases, only 12.4 percent of Catholics, 5.1 percent of non-born again Protestants, and 5.3 percent of secular Americans felt this way. Similarly, whereas 63.8 percent of non-religious whites, 47.8 percent of non-born again Protestants, and 42.6 percent of Catholics favored no restrictions on abortion, only 19.3 percent of born again Protestants believed abortion should be legal in all cases. We also see large gaps when it comes to gay rights, but it is important to note that large majorities of all groups favored protections for homosexuals against discrimination.

It is somewhat surprising that there are large gaps on some issues that do not apparently have any direct relationship with religion. Whereas only about 27 percent of born again Protestants believe it should be more difficult to purchase a gun, for all other religious categories this number was greater than 40 percent.

For non-social issues, the gap was usually rather modest. There were few cases in which there were opposing majorities on policy issues—if a majority of one religious category of whites favored or opposed a particular policy, it was likely that a majority of all other religious groups were in agreement. The one instance in which there was an opposing majority, and the gap was sizable, was on the question of increased government spending on science and technology. Whereas a majority or near-majority of all other religious groups favored more of this kind of spending, only 37 percent of born again Protestants wanted to see more money spent on science and technology.

While the size and importance of these policy differences should not be downplayed, given the relatively small size of so many of these gaps it is perhaps surprising that there was such a substantial gap in party identification. The percentage of born again Protestants who identified as Republicans or leaned toward the Republican Party was more than double the percentage of secular whites who identified as Republican or leaned toward the Republicans. There was a similarly large gap when it comes to Democratic identification.

There are reasons to be concerned that the apparent relationship between party identification and religious affiliation and practices is spurious. That is, some of these differences may be driven by other characteristics. For example, there is a relationship between income and religiosity—though this relationship is not linear[33] and it seems to vary by state.[34] This may also be driven by a generation gap if young white Americans are both more secular and more liberal than older generations. For this reason, a multivariate logit model for vote choice in the 2012 presidential election may provide some important insights. Appendix 6.2 provides a model of Republican identification that includes multiple religious variables, as well as a number of other individual characteristics that may be correlated with religiosity.

This model demonstrates that religion had a direct influence on vote choice in 2012. All of the included religious categories were more likely to vote for Romney than those whites who identified with a different religion or no religion at all. However, the size of this difference varied greatly by religious group. After controlling for all other variables, Catholics who infrequently attended religious services were only 1.33 times as likely to vote for Romney compared to those with no religious affiliation. The coefficient for this variable furthermore did not achieve statistical significance, so we cannot say with any confidence that these two groups were actually different. The group that exhibited the most substantively significant difference compared to non-affiliated white Americans was born again Protestants who attended services at least once a week. These whites were more than four times as likely to vote for the Republican candidate compared to non-affiliated whites.

We also see that, when these additional variables are included in the model, other variables that were once statistically and substantively significantly significant no longer seem to play a role in vote choice. Once we control for these different religious categories, education, with the exception of advanced degrees, ceases to be a statistically significant variable. All age categories also cease to exhibit statistical significance after including these additional controls.

CONCLUSION

Scholars have long known that religion plays an important role in vote choice in the United States. This analysis demonstrates that religion is a particularly important determinant of white vote choice. However, the religious dividing line among whites has changed significantly in recent decades. The gap between Catholics and Protestants has declined, while the gap between the religiously devoted and the secular has grown dramatically.

As was the case with other gaps examined in this volume, the growth of the worship-attendance gap was due primarily to one group abandoning the Democratic Party at a greater rate than another. Democratic support among religiously observant whites fell precipitously over the last three decades and now appears to be approaching a floor. Democratic identification among less observant whites also declined, but not nearly as much and has increased slightly in recent years. Similarly, while the number of less observant who are Republican is greater than it was in the 1970s, this growth was small, and it presently appears to be declining.

The decline in Democratic identification among religious whites represented a major challenge to the party in recent years. However, it is important to note that trends in religious practice and identification among whites are clearly beneficial to the Democratic Party. Although the Democrats have not experienced a major surge in support from secular whites, the size of the secular white community has grown. If religion remains a major political fault line among whites, and the white population continues to become less religiously observant, it will be difficult for the Republican Party to make further gains in the white electorate.

NOTES

1. There is an important caveat to this, as will be noted later in this chapter. This trend is not universal for all racial and ethnic groups. African Americans remain one of the most religious demographic groups in the United States, but this has not undermined their high levels of support for the Democratic Party.
2. Michael Crowley, "James Dobson: The Religious Right's New Kingmaker," *Slate*, November 12, 2004, accessed October 8, 2013, www.slate.com/articles/news_and_politics/assessment/2004/11/james_dobson.html.
3. David D. Kirkpatrick, "Evangelical Leader Threatens to Use His Political Muscle Against Some Democrats," *New York Times*, January 1, 2005, accessed October 8, 2013, www.nytimes.com/2005/01/01/politics/01dobson.html.
4. Kevin Philips, *American Theocracy: The Peril and Politics of Radical Religion, Oil, and Borrowed Money in the 21st Century* (New York: Penguin Books, 2007).
5. Rich Karlgaard, *Life 2.0: How People Across America Are Transforming Their Lives by Finding the Where of Their Happiness* (New York: Crown Publishing, 2004), 5.
6. Robert D. Putnam and David E. Campbell, *American Grace: How Religion Divides and Unites Us* (New York: Simon and Schuster, 2010), 17.
7. Ibid, 122–123.
8. Michael Hout and Claude S. Fischer, "Why More Americans Have No Religious Preference: Politics and Generations," *American Sociological Review* 67(2002), 165.

9. Ronald Inglehart and Wayne E. Baker, "Modernization, Cultural Change, and the Persistence of Cultural Values," *American Sociological Review* 65(2000), 49–50.

10. Hout and Fischer, "Why Americans Have No Religious Preference," 188–189.

11. Jacob Weisberg. "The Erring Republican Majority: Kevin Phillips Is Wrong About Everything. Why Is He Taken So Seriously?" *Slate,* March 29, 2006, accessed October 8, 2013, www.slate.com/articles/news_and_politics/the_big_idea/2006/03/the_erring_republican_authority.html.

12. Michael Kazin, "The End of the Religious Right," *The New Republic,* January 17, 2012, accessed October 8, 2013, www.newrepublic.com/article/politics/99679/whose-afraid-the-christian-right-the-precipitous-political-decline-con servati.

13. Paul Waldman, "The Continued Decline of the Religious Right," *The American Prospect,* December 8, 2011, www.newrepublic.com/article/politics/99679/whose-afraid-the-christian-right-the-precipitous-political-decline-conservati October 8, 2013, http://prospect.org/article/continued-decline-religious-right.

14. Laurie Goodstein, "Obama Made Gains Among Younger Evangelical Voters, Data Show," *New York Times,* November 6, 2008, www.newrepublic.com/article/politics/99679/whose-afraid-the-christian-right-the-precipitous-polit ical-decline-conservati October 8, 2013, www.nytimes.com/2008/11/07/us/politics/07religion.html.

15. Corwin Smidt, Kevin den Dulk, Bryan Froehle, James Penning, Stephen Monsma, and Douglas Koopman, *The Disappearing God Gap?: Religion in the 2008 Presidential Election* (New York: Oxford University Press, 2010), 6.

16. Mark A. Noll. "Religion and the American Founding," in *The Oxford Handbook of Religion in American Politics*, eds. Conwin E. Schmidt, Lyman A. Kellstedt, and James L. Guth (New York: Oxford University Press), 43–68.

17. Robert P. Swierenga, "Religion and American Voting Behavior, 1830s to 1930s." in *The Oxford Handbook of Religion in American Politics*, eds. Conwin E. Schmidt, Lyman A. Kellstedt, and James L. Guth (New York: Oxford University Press), 69–94.

18. Joseph R. Gusfield, *Symbolic Crusade: Status Politics and the American Temperance Movement* (Urbana, IL: University of Illinois Press), 56–57.

19. Laura R. Olson and John C. Green, "The Worship-Attendance Gap," in *Beyond Rest State, Blue State: Electoral Gaps in the Twenty-First Century American Electorate*, eds. Laura R. Olson and John C. Green (Upper Saddle River, NJ: Pearson Prentice-Hall), 41.

20. Ibid, 44–45.

21. Ibid, 47.

22. Putnam and Campbell, *American Grace,* 384–388.

23. Ibid, 472.

24. James L. Guth, Lyman A. Kellstedt, Corwin E. Smidt and John C. Green, "Religious Influences in the 2004 Presidential Election," *Presidential Studies Quarterly* 36(2004): 223–242.

25. Andrew R. Lewis and Dana Huyser de Bernardo, "Belonging Without Belonging: Utilizing Evangelical Self-Identification to Analyze Political Attitudes and Preferences," *Journal for the Scientific Study of Religion* 49(2010), 112–126.

26. Barney Warf and Morton Winsberg, "Geographies of Mega Churches in the United States," *Journal of Cultural Geography* 27(2010), 40.

27. Jeremy Ben-Ami, "America's Jewish Vote," *New York Times*, November 12, 2012, accessed October 11, 2013, www.nytimes.com/2012/11/13/opinion/americas-jewish-vote.html?_r=0.

28. Putnam and Campbell, *American Grace,* 26.
29. David L. Leal, Matt A. Barreto, Jonho Lee, and Rodolfo O. de la Garza, "The Latino Vote in the 2004 Election," *PS: Political Science and Politics* 38(2005): 46.
30. Clifford A. Grammich, "Catholics in the Religious Census: An Overview," *Glenmary Research Center*, November 11, 2012, accessed October 10, 2013, http://rcms2010.org/images/CatholicOverview2012.pdf.
31. Elaine Howard Ecklund and Kristen Schultz Lee. "Atheists and Agnostics Negotiate Religion and Family," *Journal for the Scientific Study of Religion* 50(2011): 728–743.
32. Robert D. Novak, *The Prince of Darkness: 50 Years Reporting in Washington* (New York: Three Rivers Publishing), 225.
33. According to Putnam and Campbell, the most religious are those at the very bottom of the income distribution and those in the very middle. Those in the highest income distribution are the least religious, and those in the lower middle and upper middle portion of the distribution are slightly less religious than those in the very center. Putnam and Campbell, *American Grace,* 25.
34. Gelman et al., *Red State, Blue State, Rich State, Poor State*, 20–23.

Appendix 6.1 The Religion Gaps in Party Identification, Ideology, and Policy Preferences

	Catholic	Protestant "Born Again"	Protestant Not "Born Again"	Not Religious	Frequently Attend Services	Rarely or Never Attend Services
% Republican	30.6	49.3	37.2	22.0	49.3	27.4
% Democrat	29.5	16.1	23.9	33.4	16.1	31.3
% Republican with Leaners	47.5	69.1	50.7	34.3	68.9	39.7
% Democrat with Leaners	40.8	23.3	34.8	49.1	21.1	45.3
Conservatism Scale (0–6)	3.4	4.1	3.4	2.8	4.1	3.1
% Favor Greater Corporate Taxes	57.8	50.6	56.6	62.0	48.8	61.3
% Favor Greater Tax on Millionaires	78.7	68.9	81.1	77.4	68.1	79.9
% Favor Increased Spending in Social Security	48.3	41.3	45.6	45.0	39.2	46.6
% Favor Increased Spending on Public Schools	56.7	52.6	58.4	64.6	49.8	62.1
% Favor Increased Spending on Science and Technology	52.4	37.0	47.1	51.4	36.8	50.6
% Favor Increased Spending on Crime	48.1	52.5	49.7	45.2	46.9	47.8
% Favor Increased Spending on Welfare	9.2	6.9	8.9	12.7	5.5	10.7
% Favor Increased Spending on Childcare	28.7	24.0	26.8	34.0	22.6	30.2
% Favor Increased Spending on the Poor	28.0	27.4	24.1	36.3	22.6	32.2
% Favor Increased Spending on the Environment	37.1	27.4	35.0	45.3	26.9	40.4
% Favor No Restrictions on Abortion	42.6	19.3	47.8	63.8	11.9	59.3
% Favor Complete Abortion Prohibition	12.4	21.4	5.1	5.3	29.1	4.6
% Favor Making it More Difficult to Purchase a Gun	47.4	26.8	43.8	46.5	34.7	44.8
% Favor the Death Penalty	71.3	81.7	84.7	74.9	74.1	79.3
% Favor Civil Right Protections for Gays	81.6	64.9	77.0	80.3	64.1	80.2
% Favor Affirmative Action	9.4	6.7	8.8	17.2	9.8	11.8

Source: 2012 ANES

Appendix 6.2 Logit Model for Voting for Romney in 2012—Religious Characteristics

In this following model, again generated using data from the ANES, vote choice in the 2012 election was the dependent variable—a vote for Romney was classified a 1, and all other votes were classified as 0. The baseline religious category was whites who did not identify with a particular religion.

	Odds Ratio	Std. Err.
Catholic—Weekly Attendance	2.80	(0.63)*
Catholic—Less than Weekly	1.33	(0.20)
Born Again Protestant—Weekly Attendance	4.27	(0.78)*
Born Again Protestant—Less than Weekly	2.85	(0.48)*
Other Protestant—Weekly Attendance	3.39	(1.05)*
Other Protestant—Less than Weekly	2.29	(0.33)*
Income Quartile 2	1.53	(0.26)*
Income Quartile 3	1.97	(0.33)*
Income Quartile 4	1.74	(0.32)*
Income Unknown	1.47	(0.39)
High School Diploma	1.03	(0.25)
Some College	0.96	(0.23)
College Graduate	0.92	(0.23)
Advanced Degree	0.57	(0.15)*
Female	0.81	(0.08)*
Married	1.56	(0.17)*
Age 30–44	1.17	(0.24)
Age 45–64	1.27	(0.24)
Age 65 Plus	1.45	(0.29)
Constant	0.23	(0.07)*
Observations	2790	

* p < 0.05
Parentheses are standard errors

7   White Voters
and Demographic Change

INTRODUCTION

Demographic developments in the United States have justifiably received much attention recently. We regularly pass new demographic milestones as the United States transitions into a nation without a single racial or ethnic majority—be it a new state that joins the majority-minority club, or a year in which white births as a percentage of all births reach a new all-time low. This transition will have many important social implications, but the political implications are the source of much discourse, and for good reason.

The contemporary discussion on race and demographic change in the United States largely focuses on how the increasing numbers of non-whites will make the American electorate, on average, more Democratic. Many of these discussions apparently assume that the white vote will remain relatively stable in the decades ahead. This may be a problematic assumption.[1] Indeed, there is a strong literature indicating that changing demographic contexts will lead to changes in political behavior within the soon-to-be former majority.

Unfortunately, the research on these topics is often contradictory, and there are multiple plausible theories that can be applied to white political behavior during a period of rapid demographic change. As the white share of the electorate, as well as the white share of the total U.S. population, continues to shrink, will whites respond by coalescing into a single defensive voting bloc? Or, in an era where there is no racial majority, will the issue of race begin to fade away? Is a new, post-racial era in American politics just around the corner? At present, this may be the single most important question for scholars of American political behavior to consider.

One of the challenges of understanding how demographic context shapes the white vote arises from the fact that whites living in similar contexts often behave in dramatically different ways. For example, if we could expect local demography to be a primary determinant of white political behavior, then we should anticipate similar political behavior among whites in Texas and California, or in West Virginia and Vermont. But this is not what we see. This lack of an obvious relationship between a state's racial and ethnic makeup and its aggregate white vote choice might lead one to infer that demographic context actually has little or no impact on the white vote. This is also almost surely incorrect.

This chapter will attempt to shed additional light on the question of how diversity influences the politics of white Americans. It will also provide an overview on the literature on this topic. While no study of contemporary opinion data can be used to predict future political behaviors with great accuracy, this chapter will demonstrate that some predictions about future white voter behavior are more plausible than others.

THE CHANGING AMERICAN ELECTORATE:
THE ORIGINS OF CURRENT TRENDS

Before moving on to what the political science literature tells us about demographic context and political behavior, it is worth briefly discussing how current demographic trends came about. While the United States has always been multiracial in the aggregate—this of course varied from state to state and community to community—a huge majority of the electorate was white for most of American history. This was both because many states were overwhelmingly white and because many of the states with large African American populations effectively barred minorities from taking part in the political process—first through slavery and then via Jim Crow era legislation. Latinos and Asians were only a small percentage of the total U.S. population throughout this entire period. While a number of western states, such as California, had a sizable Chinese population in the mid-19th century, few were eligible to vote. The Chinese Exclusion Act of 1882 ended the wave of Chinese immigration.

All of this began to change in the 1960s. The struggle for black civil rights is a well-chronicled story, and one of the most important results of this movement was the passage of the Voting Rights Act of 1965. Prior to this legislation, Southern states were particularly aggressive in implementing policies that effectively barred blacks from taking part in the electoral process. The 15th Amendment to the U.S. Constitution, ratified in 1870, prohibited racial discrimination in voting. However, the selective enforcement of poll taxes, literacy tests, grandfather clauses, white primaries,[2] residency requirements, and other roadblocks to voting ensured white dominance of the political system. The Voting Rights Act outlawed all of these forms of voter discrimination. It additionally required the U.S. Department of Justice to "preclear" any effort to change voter requirements in covered jurisdictions.[3]

This change, of course, had enormous political consequences. For one, it eventually led to a proliferation of majority-minority districts in the House of Representatives and in state legislatures. These districts, whether dominated by Latinos or African Americans, generally provide overwhelming victories to Democratic candidates. Indeed, in such districts the Democratic primary may be more competitive and important than the general election.

Although the extension of the franchise to African Americans, on its face, should have been a boon to the Democratic Party, the civil rights movement and the legislation that resulted also led to an exodus of many white Southerners from the Democratic Party. This was not an unanticipated result, as white opposition to this movement in the South was well known. But the changing voting patterns of white Southerners had important political consequences.[4]

Prior to the civil rights movement, the South had been strongly Democratic since the Civil War, even during periods of Republican dominance of the American political system. From 1880 to 1924, Democratic presidential candidates won every state of the former Confederacy in every presidential election with just a single exception (Tennessee voted Republican in 1920). While Herbert Hoover did well in some Southern states in 1928, the Democratic Party won every Southern state in the presidential elections of the 1930s and early 1940s. When four Southern states defected from the Democratic Party in 1948, it was to support the segregationist candidate Strom Thurmond, not the Republican.

Republican fortunes in the South began to change in the 1960s, and as was noted previously, we have now reached the point where the white vote in some Southern states, such as Alabama and Mississippi, is almost nine-to-one Republican. In 1972, every Southern state provided its electoral votes to Richard Nixon. George W. Bush similarly won every Southern state in both 2000 and 2004. Mitt Romney won every Southern state but Florida and Virginia—two Southern states that have experienced substantial in-migration from both Northern states and other countries.

This is not to say that the Voting Rights Act was, on the whole, a bad thing for the Democratic Party politically. This and related legislation are part of the reason why about 90 percent of African American voters support the Democratic Party in presidential elections. However, it is surely not a coincidence that 1964 was the last time a Democratic presidential candidate won a majority of the white vote.

When thinking about how the American electorate has changed since the 1960s and how it is continuing to change, the Immigration and Nationality Act of 1965 may have been the single most important piece of legislation in the last 50 years. More than any other act of the federal government, this legislation helped assure that the United States would one day become a nation without a single ethnic/racial majority.

While the idea that the United States is a "nation of immigrants" is a foundation of the American historical narrative, it is useful to remember that immigration to the United States has not been consistently high throughout the nation's history. In the 1960s, the United States was at the end of a 40-year period of minimal immigration. Although immigration rates were high during the late 19th and early 20th centuries, Congress passed a series of restrictive immigration laws in the 1920s that effectively ended large-scale immigration to the United States. The Immigration Restriction Act of 1921, also known as the Emergency Quota Act, set strict limits on the number of immigrants that could be admitted from any given country, with a strong bias in favor of Northern European countries. This act was followed by the even more restrictive Immigration Act of 1924, also known as the National Origins Act. Southern and Eastern Europeans, who represented the main source of new immigrants in the years leading up to these acts, were the primary targets of this legislation.

As a result of this legislation, immigration slowed to a trickle for the next several decades.[5] While the primary interest of this and other legislation during the period was designed to stem the flow of immigrants from Eastern and Southern Europe and Asia, concerns about immigration from Latin America would spur additional restrictive measures. Other important immigration-related policies during this period included the Mexican repatriation efforts that took place during the 1930s and "Operation Wetback,"[6] which was a program implemented in 1954 to deport Mexicans who had entered the country illegally.

Prior to 1965, there was some legislation that allowed greater numbers of Latin Americans to enter the country. The most well known was the Bracero Program.[7] It was the result of a series of agreements between the United States and Mexico that allowed for the temporary importation of laborers. Although the initial agreement expired in 1947, the program continued until its formal end in 1964. Given that these workers were always expected to be temporary, however, there was never any expectation that they would play any substantive role in American politics.

The Immigration and Nationality Act of 1965 had a number of important provisions. Notably, it removed the National Origins Formula that had been in place since the 1920s. This ended the bias in favor of Northern European immigrants and ultimately opened the door to large-scale immigration from Latin America, Asia, and Africa. From this point on, the foreign-born population in the United States steadily grew. Comparatively few of these new immigrants were non-Hispanic whites. It is interesting that, although in hindsight the demographic consequences of this legislation now seem rather obvious, this was not apparently the case when it was passed. Senator Edward Kennedy of Massachusetts, a proponent of the law, declared prior to its passage that "this bill is not concerned with increasing immigration to this country, nor will it lower any of the high standards we apply in the selection of immigrants."[8] Kennedy also stated that "the ethnic mix of this country will not be upset" and "our cities will not be flooded with a million immigrants annually."[9]

It was not just legal immigration that led to a substantial increase in the non-white population in the United States. The increasing undocumented immigration to the country has similarly played an important role in this trend. Undocumented immigrants are overwhelmingly from Latin America, predominantly from Mexico.

Although the Bracero Program came to an end, American agriculture and other industries continued to have a demand for unskilled labor. Given the long (nearly 2,000 miles) and relatively porous border between the United States and Mexico, large numbers of migrant workers from Latin America came to the United States to fill that demand. In spite of economic arguments in favor of the free movement of labor, undocumented immigration has long been highly unpopular among native-born Americans.[10]

As the undocumented immigrant population grew, numerous policies attempting to reduce the number of migrants entering the country illegally were considered or implemented, to little effect. In 1986, Congress passed the Immigration Reform and Control Act (IRCA). This bill both provided amnesty to a portion of the undocumented population in the United States and included provisions designed to punish employers who hire undocumented workers. At the time, it was argued that this bill would provide the ultimate solution to the contentious issue of undocumented immigration. However, while the amnesty was applied, the employer enforcement provisions were not. As a result, IRCA did little to stem the number of undocumented immigrants entering the United States.[11]

Although the Constitution clearly specifies that immigration is a federal issue, several states have attempted to implement their own immigration enforcement laws. Some of the most famous such attempts took place in California in the 1990s, where voters passed restrictive ballot initiatives (Propositions 187 and 209). However, the most restrictive aspects of these initiatives were struck down by the Supreme Court. Similarly, the most restrictive elements of a recent controversial Arizona law concerning immigration (Arizona S.B. 1070) were also deemed unconstitutional and therefore not enforced.

One of the few successes of the immigration restrictionist movement was the erection of a border fence in part of Southern California. This certainly did reduce the flow of immigrants into cities such as San Diego, but it had unintended consequences. Douglas Massey argued that increased border security actually *increased* the number of undocumented immigrants in the United States.[12] While border fences effectively discourage border crossings where they are in place, migrants continue to cross elsewhere. However, the new routes followed by undocumented immigrants tend to be in much more difficult and dangerous areas—such as the Arizona desert. Whereas many migrant workers once preferred to enter the United States for a single season and then return home to Mexico for the remainder of the year, the difficulties and dangers associated with crossing the U.S.-Mexico border now discourage them from making repeated trips. Now, according to this theory, migrants are more likely to make the journey only once, to remain in the United States, and to bring their families. While there is no way to precisely determine the number of undocumented immigrants in the United States, demographers usually estimate the total at somewhere around 12 million.[13]

Further increasing the degree to which immigration is causing rapid demographic changes in the United States is the 14th Amendment to the Constitution. This amendment, which was one of the Reconstruction amendments, was written and ratified to ensure the fair treatment of former slaves and their descendants in the aftermath of the Civil War. The amendment includes the following text, "All persons born or naturalized in the United States, and subject to the jurisdiction thereof, are citizens of the United States and of the State wherein they reside." As a result of this wording in the Constitution, all children born in the United States, even if their parents are undocumented immigrants, are themselves citizens of the United States. This is not the case in most other developed countries. As of 2010, only 30 of the 194 recognized nations in the world granted birthright citizenship, and only one other nation with an advanced economy has a similar policy (Canada).[14]

One demographic trend in the United States that is relatively recent is the spread of new immigrants to areas that have not traditionally been known as major immigrant destinations. Whereas new immigrants once tended to cluster in a small number of states (such as New York, California, New Jersey, Florida, and Illinois) and in certain cities (Los Angeles, New York City, Miami, Chicago, and Houston), this is no longer the case.[15] New immigrants are increasingly dispersing into regions of the United States with no recent history of large-scale immigration: states such as Alabama, North Carolina, and Georgia.

All of these developments have played a role in transforming the American electorate from being predominantly white to being quite diverse, and within a few decades no racial or ethnic group will have a clear majority. There is no doubt that the increasing non-white population votes overwhelmingly for the Democratic Party.[16] In terms of how the white population has responded to this diversity, the one thing we know for certain is that Southern whites abandoned the Democratic Party largely because of the civil rights movement. Beyond that, it is not clear how the changing demographic profile of the United States is influencing white voting behavior. There remain a number of plausible theories, each with supporting evidence.

THE WHITE RESPONSE TO A CHANGING NATION: WHAT THE LITERATURE SUGGESTS

In terms of racial attitudes, there are two primary hypotheses regarding how whites will react to greater diversity: that they will respond by becoming less tolerant, or they will respond by becoming more tolerant. This is obviously a gross simplification, and a concept like tolerance is not easily defined and is even more difficult to measure. It is also not obvious how greater or lesser levels of racial tolerance will influence the political attitudes and behaviors of whites—party identification cannot always be inferred from a white person's level of racial tolerance, though this chapter will note that there is a correlation between these two characteristics.

For political scientists, no scholar has been a more influential proponent of the idea that racial diversity can result in racial hostility than V. O. Key. In his work, *Southern Politics in State and Nation*, published in 1949 before the major upheavals of the civil rights era, Key argued that African Americans were the primary explanation for the Solid South—that is, the dominance of the Democratic Party in the former Confederacy. He furthermore found that racial conservatism among Southern whites was strongest in those areas with a large black population: "The hard core of the political South—and the backbone of southern political unity—is made up of those counties and sections of the southern states in which Negroes constitute a substantial proportion of the population."[17] Key further found that areas where whites were most likely to deviate politically from Southern norms were those more homogeneously white regions of the South.

Scholars soon began to argue that Key's intuitions could be generalized to other contexts. That is, the relationship Key demonstrated between the size of the local non-white population and white attitudes toward non-whites may not be unique to the South. Group threat theory suggests that, because of the real or perceived scarcity of political and economic resources in a community, members of different groups will exhibit greater hostility toward each other if they live in close proximity.[18] They do so because they perceive that members of these other groups represent a threat to their access to resources. On the other hand, those living in a relatively homogeneous community may have relatively benign attitudes toward demographic groups with whom they have little direct contact and could not reasonably view as a source of any kind of meaningful competition.

Of course, "threat" is not necessarily an easily defined term. It is usually argued that out-groups represent a cultural or an economic threat[19]—though the present author has argued elsewhere that groups may view each other as political threats as well.[20] For this reason scholars have attempted to discern whether circumstances beyond the local tally of different racial groups shape attitudes toward racial and ethnic issues such as immigration. For example, high unemployment rates may lead to greater hostility toward immigrants, as this increases the likelihood that immigrants will be viewed as an economic threat.[21]

The group contact theory is the primary alternative hypothesis to the group threat theory. This theory suggests that, rather than leading to greater hostility, contact between members of different groups can actually serve as a catalyst for greater tolerance and understanding—though the degree to which this occurs is highly dependent on the type of contact and the context in which it occurs. This theory was first and most famously formulated by

Gordon Allport in 1954,[22] though Rothbart and John provided an excellent summary of it in 1993:

> The contact hypothesis itself has a number of variants, but the basic idea is that antagonistic groups generate unrealistically negative expectations of one another and simultaneously avoid contact. To the extent that contact occurs, the unrealistically negative perceptions of the group members are modified by experience. In other words, hostility is reduced as a result of increasingly favorable attitudes toward individual group members, which then generalize to the group as a whole.[23]

Not all contact is equally likely to lessen group tensions, and Allport acknowledged this from the beginning. In order to actually improve group relations, contacts between groups should meet the following conditions: Contact should be between social equals, the different groups should be pursuing congruent goals, and the laws, customs, and local social atmosphere should encourage this group contact.[24]

Because both the group contact and the group threat theory provide falsifiable hypotheses, they have both been put to the test multiple times in recent decades. Different studies have yielded different conclusions. Whereas initial studies concerning group threat and group contact theory primarily focused on the black vs. white racial divide, they have also been extended to other groups such as Latinos and Asian Americans. These hypotheses have been similarly tested in Western Europe, which is also experiencing greater levels of diversity due to large-scale immigration.

Revisiting Key's hypotheses decades later, James Glaser found in a 1994 study that racial context in the South continued to influence the racial-political attitudes of white Southerners.[25] Studies looking at non-black minorities have provided less consistent results. Group threat theory has been found to be less applicable to white attitudes toward Latinos than to their attitudes toward African Americans.[26] Hood and Morris found that high levels of contact with legal immigrants caused Anglos to be more supportive of progressive immigration policies, but high levels of contact with illegal immigrants made them less supportive.[27]

It is quite difficult to discern precisely how a change in a community's demographics influences attitudes toward racial issues and other political opinions. For one, there is a self-selection issue when it comes to where people live. If we do not find a correlation between white racial attitudes and the local levels of diversity, it may be because whites with racist attitudes will not settle in a diverse community or will move far away if too many racial minorities move in. There are also problems in terms of which unit of analysis one uses to measure local levels of diversity. States, and even counties, may appear racially diverse in the aggregate, but most individuals in those geographic units may nonetheless continue to live in racially and ethnically homogeneous neighborhoods. Experiments in a lab setting can provide useful leverage on these questions, but such experiments are always open to questions regarding their external validity.

One recent study employed a novel approach to discern how even a small demographic change might affect the political attitudes of whites in a once homogeneous community. Over a period of several weeks, Ryan Enos employed young, Spanish-speaking Latinos and had them ride trains in the Boston area every day. Enos surveyed a random sample of train passengers both before the start of the experiment and afterward. He found that even this tiny increase in the number of Latinos these subjects encountered throughout their day had a substantive impact on the train passengers' attitudes on immigration, moving them in a more exclusionary direction—they were more likely to say immigration should be decreased, less likely to say that children of undocumented immigrants should be allowed to stay in the country, and more likely to say that English should be the official language of the United States.[28]

One of the key questions of the 21st century is whether or not whites will become more or less prejudiced in their attitudes as the nation becomes increasingly diverse. A secondary question is how racial prejudice, or a lack of racial prejudice, will manifest politically.

POLITICAL CONSEQUENCES OF RACIAL ATTITUDES

While demographic context may play a role in white peoples' levels of tolerance toward other groups, the degree to which a white person holds egalitarian rather than anti-egalitarian views does not necessarily determine vote choice or other political attributes. There are plenty of racists and racial egalitarians in both parties, and plenty of non-racial issues are important determinants of vote choice. That being said, there is a correlation between racial attitudes and vote choice and party identification, as we saw in Chapter 2 in this volume. A far greater percentage of white Republicans exhibited high levels of racial resentment compared to white Democrats. Other scholars have demonstrated a relationship between white racial attitudes and vote choice. For example, Anthony Greenwald and his colleagues demonstrated that white racial attitudes were useful predictors of vote choice in the 2008 presidential election.[29]

Attitudes toward explicitly racial policies, such as Affirmative Action, are clearly determined at least in part by racial attitudes. Although Chapter 1 demonstrated that very few whites are enthusiastic supporters of this policy, other research has indicated that whites with less egalitarian racial attitudes are particularly unlikely to support Affirmative Action.[30] Racial attitudes also help predict white views on the death penalty,[31] a policy that has a racial angle given that African Americans represent a disproportionate percentage of Death Row inmates.[32]

HAVE WHITE RACIAL ATTITUDES CHANGED
IN RECENT YEARS?

As noted in Chapter 2, assessing the actual attitudes of white Americans on issues of race is extraordinarily difficult. For reasons already mentioned, we may not be able to accept at face value the responses whites provide to pollsters on racial issues. However, although racial hostility has not faded away, the trend has certainly been encouraging for those working toward a more racially egalitarian United States. As Sniderman and Tetlock noted in 1986:

> Racism, [as traditionally] understood, has declined. Repeated surveys of public opinion have shown, for example, that little more than one generation ago only one out of three white Americans believed white and black students should go to the same schools. Nor were they prepared to accept blacks as neighbors—even blacks whose education and income matched their own. . . . Today, on each of these issues, there is considerable consensus in favor of equal treatment for blacks.[33]

Although we make take this as evidence that white racism has seriously declined, the taboo against open expressions of racism may simply mean that whites with racist attitudes simply choose not to openly express them to pollsters.[34]

Scholars are generally confident in the reliability of measures of racial resentment, however. While this is not a perfect proxy for racism, we have evidence that racial resentment and symbolic racism[35] are correlated with racial prejudice and have political consequences.[36] Racial resentment furthermore has not seriously declined among whites despite the continuing strong social pressures to avoid open expressions of racism. Chapter 2 pointed out that, since the election of Barack Obama, the mean white racial resentment score barely has changed at all. There furthermore is not presently a substantial generation gap among whites when it comes to racial resentment.

We should not overstate the degree to which survey questions that reflect "old-fashioned racism" measure the same thing as what scholars call "new" racism or racial resentment. Virtanen and Huddy found that, while old-fashioned racism and the measures of more modern racism were correlated, they had different effects on white attitudes toward policies such as Affirmative Action.[37] They also found that different forms of racial prejudice have different roots: "Old-fashioned racism" among whites appears to result from early socialization, but the degree to which whites endorse certain value stereotypes appears to be strongly driven by their current employment situation.[38]

While the ANES since 1986 has occasionally asked respondents questions regarding what they view as the source of the racial divide in terms of socioeconomic status, it has not asked the question with sufficient frequency to measure year-by-year changes in these attitudes. Fortunately, the GSS has asked similar questions since the 1980s, and has asked them with greater frequency, allowing us to see how attitudes on this subject among whites have evolved since that time.

The GSS has asked respondents regularly since the 1980s[39] what accounts for the lower socioeconomic status of blacks in the United States. They are asked whether they agree that it is due to inborn differences, a lack of education, or discrimination.[40] The percentage of whites who say that the difference between blacks and whites is due to inborn differences has declined since the question was first asked. This suggests that fewer whites endorse biological explanations for racial differences than was once the case.

White attitudes toward the other possible explanations for racial socioeconomic gaps have also changed, however, and they have not done so in ways that suggest greater support for policies designed to end racial disparities. Along with the decrease in the percentage of whites who ascribe racial economic differences to genetics, there has also been an impressive decrease in the percentage of whites who express the view that racial disparities are due to past and present racism. That is, while whites have become less likely to openly say that blacks possess lower, on average, socioeconomic status because of genetic differences, they are also less likely to say that whites are, or were, themselves responsible for this gap.

Denying that white racism is the cause of gaps between black and white Americans is not itself a sign of racism, as one could think of other possible explanations that are not rooted in theories of racial or cultural superiority. However, whites who reject the hypothesis that white racism and discrimination are the source of the black-white economic gap are undoubtedly less likely to support government efforts to close this gap through Affirmative Action and economic redistribution than those who place the blame squarely on racism. As long as whites feel comfortable blaming African Americans for their own situation, we can plausibly speculate that they will also feel comfortable withholding support for government programs designed to close racial gaps.[41]

While the degree to which whites' beliefs on the explanations for racial economic differences have changed in recent decades is an important question, it is also worth knowing if the political consequences of these attitudes have also changed over time. Figure 7.1 shows two trends (again using LOWESS smoothing): the percentage of white GSS respondents who deny that discrimination is the source of racial differences in the United States, and the correlation coefficient between this attitude and Republican voting.

Figure 7.1 demonstrates that the percentage of whites who ascribe socioeconomic differences between blacks and whites to something other than racial discrimination has steadily increased since the mid-1980s. In fact, in recent years this number has approached 70 percent. Even more interesting is that the correlation between these attitudes and party identification has also steadily increased. Whereas in the 1980s there was virtually no

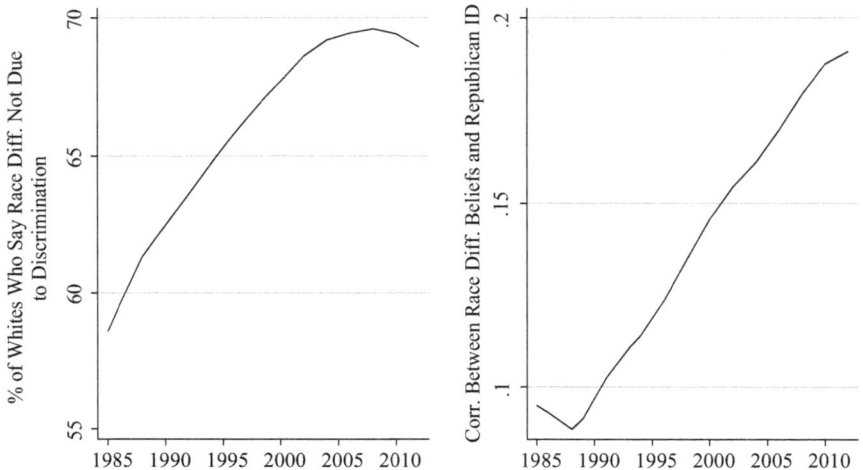

Figure 7.1   Trends in Racial Attitudes and Correlation between Attitudes and Party ID

correlation between white answers to this question and Republican identification, the positive correlation between the two has consistently increased.
Granted, the correlation between the two remains quite small,[42] but it has
more than doubled since the question was asked in 1986 (the Pearson's *r*
was 0.09 in 1986, but 0.2 in 2012).

It is regularly noted that most of the trends in the United States, both
demographic and in terms of public opinion, have not been in the Republican Party's favor in recent years. Here we see one of the few developments
that favors the party, but it is probably not a trend that GOP leadership will
want to publicly acknowledge or appear to be publicly encouraging: The
number of whites who disagree with the statement that discrimination is
the source of lower average economic outcomes for blacks has increased, as
has the probability that such whites will identify with the Republican Party.

LOCAL DEMOGRAPHIC CONTEXT AND WHITE RACIAL
AND POLITICAL ATTITUDES

Looking at aggregate white attitudes on issues related to race can provide
valuable insights, especially when we consider how these opinions have
changed over time. This at least lets us know the direction of the trends.
It is equally important to look at how white attitudes differ according to
the local context. This is useful first because, as previously noted, there is
compelling evidence indicating that local context shapes white attitudes on
racial issues. It is also a useful exercise because, if we want to know what
the future will hold for the white electorate, we should look specifically to

those communities that are already quite diverse. Looking at these communities, do we see that whites in more diverse areas are more or less racially tolerant, or more or less liberal on other issues, compared to whites in less diverse areas? Does diversity drive whites into the arms of the GOP, or do their new non-white neighbors convince whites that the Democratic Party is their best political home?

Before moving forward, it is important to think carefully how to determine the proper geographic unit of analysis when examining the issue of local context. States and even regions may be a useful starting point when considering these issues, but the drawbacks to these enormous geographic units are immediately apparent. Although states may be racially diverse in the aggregate, they all have counties and municipalities that remain overwhelmingly dominated by one racial or ethnic group. Thus, knowing that a white person lives in a particular state does not necessarily tell us the degree to which that white person experiences diversity on a day-to-day basis.

Census tracts, zip codes, or voter tabulation districts have the advantage of being more compact and more likely to correspond to an individual's specific neighborhood, but they are problematic in that few surveys include the zip codes of survey respondents. There is furthermore a dearth of reliable, useful aggregate data for these smallest geographic units. Counties, therefore, represent a useful compromise in that county codes are often available for public opinion survey respondents, and there are a great deal of high-quality, reliable data at the county level covering a great variety of variables. Counties have problems of their own as units of analysis,[43] but they are commonly used in political science to measure contextual effects.

The 2008 National Annenberg Election Survey is a useful starting point for considering how context shapes the political attitudes and behaviors of white voters. This survey has the advantage of including a massive number of respondents who could be coded according to their county.[44] From that point, it is relatively straightforward to generate multilevel regression models in order to discern how context may shape individual attitudes.

The 2008 NAES included a number of questions related to racial attitudes. Among these were a series of statements relating to how the respondents believed black elected officials conducted themselves in office, to which respondents were asked the degree to which they agreed or disagreed. These statements included the following: "Black elected officials are more likely to favor blacks for government jobs over white applicants"; "Black elected officials are more likely to support government spending that favors blacks"; "Black elected officials are more likely to support policies that could cost whites jobs"; and "Black elected officials are more likely to give special favors to the black community." To each question, respondents could "strongly agree," "somewhat agree," "somewhat disagree," and "strongly disagree." The author then coded these scores onto a four-point scale (between 0 and 3) in which higher scores represented a greater suspicion of black favoritism among black officials.

Unsurprisingly, the answers to these questions among respondents were highly correlated, making it possible to make a scale representing the degree to which a white person feared black favoritism among black elected officials. The scale ranged between 0 (never giving any indication that the respondent suspected black favoritism) and 12 (always strongly agreeing that black officials engage in favoritism). The mean score on this scale for white respondents was 4.4.

Following the creation of the scale it was possible to generate a regression model in which the score on this scale from white respondents was the dependent variable. Any number of other characteristics besides the local distribution of various racial and ethnic categories might predict white attitudes toward black government officials—individual characteristics being the most obvious likely predictors. For this reason a large number of additional variables, both individual and contextual, were necessary. At the individual level, the model included the usual demographic controls, along with religious observance and party identification. It also included dichotomous variables indicating whether the respondent lived in an urban, suburban, or rural neighborhood (with rural serving as the base category). At the county level, the model controlled for the percentage of the county population that is black, Latino, and Asian. In case the relative affluence of a community might be contributing to a respondent's overall level of cynicism toward government (whether the elected officials are black or white), various measures of economic success were included: the county-level unemployment rate, the county-level median income, and the county-level median value for single-family homes.[45]

It was also important to include a variable indicating whether or not the respondent lived in the South. While Chapter 3 demonstrated that the North versus South categorization is not the only logical means to geographically divide the nation when performing this type of analysis, there are strong reasons to expect that Southern whites remain clearly distinct from other whites on questions relating to race. Valentino and Sears recently demonstrated that Southern whites remain unambiguously dissimilar compared to whites living elsewhere in the United States when it comes to racial attitudes. In the South there were different political consequences resulting from those racial attitudes: The relationship between racial attitudes and vote choice is stronger in the South than elsewhere. They also demonstrated that the gap in racial conservatism between Southern whites and other whites has not been closing.[46] Kuklinski, Cobb, and Gilens reached similar conclusions in their study of white racial attitudes in the South.[47]

The full model can be found in Appendix 7.1. The model demonstrates that a number of individual characteristics predicted that whites would have a generally negative view of black elected officials. On average, compared to lower income whites, higher income whites were less likely to believe that black elected officials were inordinately concerned with the interests of blacks to the detriment of whites. The same was true of whites with higher levels of education. Higher levels of conservatism were associated with a higher score on this scale, though the coefficient for being a Republican was not statistically significant. In other words, after controlling for all other variables, white Republicans were not more likely to score high on this scale than white Independents.

Once again we see weak evidence for an age gap when it comes to white attitudes on race. Whites in the youngest age cohort were not statistically discernible from whites in the middle two cohorts—though they did, on average, score lower on this scale than the very oldest whites, meaning that they were less suspicious that black officials engaged in racial favoritism. It is worth noting that this survey was conducted in 2008, when the political age gap in voting was at a recent peak. If a similar survey had been conducted more recently, the age gap may have been even more modest. This provides further evidence that younger whites are not actually considerably more progressive on questions of race than older whites.

Turning to the contextual variables, we see that only two variables proved statistically significant: the size of the local black population and whether or not the respondent lived in the South. Both were positively associated with a higher score for whites on the scale measuring the degree to which they believed black officials engaged in racial favoritism. It is important to note that the coefficient for the size of the black population remained statistically significant even after controlling for whether the respondent was a white Southerner—this means that this correlation is not simply due to white Southerners having higher levels of racial hostility and being more likely to live in communities with a large number of African Americans.[48]

Figure 7.2 visually demonstrates the strong linear relationship between the size of the local black population and the degree to which whites suspected black officials of racial favoritism. This is an indication that greater diversity does not lead whites to become more trusting of black officials. There unfortunately were not similar questions about minority officials of other race and ethnicities.[49]

What about a specific public policy? Taxation has been one of the key platform points of the GOP for decades. Might there be a relationship between the local demography and the degree to which a white person is willing to pay higher taxes? We could reasonably hypothesize that whites become more opposed to new taxes when in a more diverse context because they, rightly or wrongly, infer that a greater share of their taxes is being spent on racial and ethnic minorities.[50] If this is the case, then the higher levels of diversity throughout the United States may be nudging more whites into the arms of the GOP. We can consider this possibility again using the 2008 NAES. This survey asked respondents whether or not they favored new tax cuts, which allowed the creation of a multilevel logit model (not provided) in which support for new tax cuts was the dependent variable.

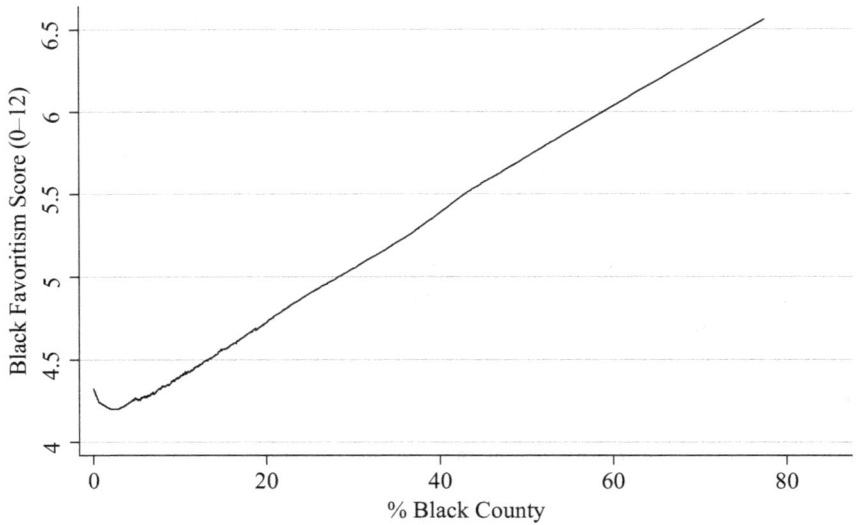

Figure 7.2   Black Favoritism Score by Size of the Local Black Population

This model did not provide any indication that whites were any more or less likely to support tax cuts based on the local racial context.

Respondents were also asked about their feelings on health care. Specifically, they were asked whether they supported government health insurance, the current system (as of 2008), or neither. This allowed the creation of a model in which support for government health insurance was the dependent variable. This model indicates that, as the local Latino population grew, white respondents became *less* likely to support government health insurance, even after controlling for many additional individual and contextual variables. The substantive effect was very small, however. See Appendix 7.2 for the full model.

Some policies mentioned in the NAES were directly related to issues of race and ethnicity. For example, we should expect there to be some relationship between a community's racial and ethnic composition and how whites in that community feel about immigration policy. However, after controlling for other individual-level attributes, the county-level demography did not apparently influence white attitudes toward a pathway to citizenship for undocumented immigrants.[51]

What about some of the most important political characteristics an American may possess: party identification and ideology? Is greater diversity, after controlling for other individual and contextual characteristics, associated with whites becoming more or less Republican or Democratic, or with no change at all? This is exceptionally useful information to have as we attempt to predict future electoral trends in the United States. Other scholars have also considered this question. In a study of Louisiana, Giles and Hertz found that a greater concentration of blacks in a community was associated with greater Republican voting among whites.[52]

Similarly, although ideology is not the same thing as party identification, it is strongly correlated with it—now, more than ever, conservatives are likely to vote for Republicans and liberals are likely to vote for Democrats.[53] It is important to know whether or not whites are becoming, on average, more or less conservative as their communities diversify.

When it comes to both party identification and ideology, local demographic context apparently matters: Higher levels of diversity were associated with a greater average conservatism score and a greater probability of identifying as a Republican. Appendixes 7.3 and 7.4 provide the multilevel models of ideology and party identification, respectively. We see that the size of different racial and ethnic groups has different effects on whites. For example, the size of the local Latino population was positively associated with conservatism among whites. This effect was small. A two-standard deviation increase in the county percentage that identified as Latino population was associated, on average with a 0.03 increase in a white person's conservatism score, controlling for all other variables. This is not a particularly substantive difference. The sizes of the local black and the local Asian American population were not statistically significant. In fact, the coefficient for the Asian American variable was signed in the opposite direction—suggesting that a larger Asian population was associated with greater liberalism among whites.

We see similar results in the multilevel logit model for Republican identification. Once again, the size of the African American population was not statistically significant, but the size of the Latino population was. In this case, we see evidence that a larger Latino population in a county was associated with higher levels of Republican Party identification among whites in that county, after controlling for all other variables. The difference was once again small, however.

Other contextual variables proved significant in both models. Higher median home values and greater population density were both associated with lower levels of conservatism, as was living at an urban address. On the other hand, higher median incomes and living in the South were associated with greater conservatism. Looking at Republican identification, we again see that Southerners were more likely to be Republican, as were those in counties with lower population densities and higher median incomes.

While these tables provide evidence that local context plays a role in white ideology and party identification, the important thing to note is that all contextual variables are dwarfed in terms of substantive significance by most individual-level variables. In other words, knowing an individual's personal characteristics (whether he or she is married, poor, or wealthy, etc.) still conveys far more useful information about a person's likely political leanings than the racial makeup of that person's community.

DIVERSITY AND AGGREGATE WHITE VOTER
BEHAVIOR: WHY IS THE RELATIONSHIP INCONSISTENT?

If we were to look at a map of aggregate voting behavior and state-level demographics that was strictly limited to those states that made up the original 13 American colonies that eventually formed the United States, we would be able to develop a plausible theory of the relationship between state demographics and white voting behavior. Those New England states that were predominantly white were also overwhelming Democratic in the 2012 presidential elections. As we move farther south on this abridged map, we see that states become both more non-white and whites become more Republican, on average. From this we could reasonably infer that, when whites are in a diverse environment, they respond by becoming more supportive of the political party that is comparatively conservative on racial issues.

As plausible and parsimonious as this theory is, however, it becomes increasingly tenuous as we expand our map under consideration. As look farther east we begin to see anomalies. West Virginia, for example, is one of the whitest states in the nation, yet it has been a reliable Republican state in presidential elections for many cycles. Moving farther west this theory seems to fall apart entirely. The demographics of Texas and California are relatively similar (in both states, whites are no longer a majority of the population), yet white Texans are some of the most reliably Republican voters in the United States. On the other hand, Obama won among white Californians in 2008 and lost by only a small margin among whites to Romney in 2012. It turns out that the correlation between the racial makeup of a state and white voting patterns within that state is not particularly strong. The lack of an obvious or consistent relationship between white voter behavior and diversity makes it challenging to predict how whites will continue to evolve politically as the nation continues to diversify.

One way to consider this issue is to compare states with relatively similar demographic trends, but with substantially different voting patterns among whites. As suggested earlier, California and Texas are two such states. However, given that Texas is a Southern state—though culturally distinct from other regions of the South—it may not be appropriate to compare it to a Western state. Another Western border state that is demographically similar, comparatively speaking, to California is Arizona. While white Arizonans are not as strongly Republican as white Texans, 66 percent of white Arizona voters supported Romney in 2012 compared to 53 percent of white Californians. However, both states are in the top ten in terms of the foreign-born population and in the top five when it comes to percent of the population that identifies as Latino (35.9 percent of Californians and 29.2 percent of Arizonans). Both states were won by George H. W. Bush in 1988, though in 1988 the Republican margin of victory was about eight percentage points higher in Arizona. Both states experienced a substantial housing boom and bust in the first decade of the 2000s. Returning to Woodard's classifications, both Arizona and California are a mix of El Norte and the Far West—though California's central and northwestern coastline are classified as part of the Left Coast. Both states also produced important conservative leaders at roughly the same time—Barry Goldwater was a senator from Arizona and Ronald Reagan served as the governor of California.

Given that, superficially, both Arizona and California have a great deal in common, why are Arizona whites so much more Republican, on average, than California whites? Table 7.1[54] demonstrates how whites in California and Arizona differ on a number of politically relevant attributes beyond aggregate vote choice.

One thing we see right away is that white Californians have a higher average level of educational attainment than white Arizonans. We should not expect this to make a tremendous difference, given the relatively modest

Table 7.1 Differences in White Characteristics in Arizona and California

	Arizona	California
% Whites for Obama	32	45
% Whites for Romney	66	53
% of State Latino	29.2	35.9
% of State African American	3	6.2
% of State Asian	2.2	12.1
% of Whites with No High School Diploma	6.8	6.6
% of Whites with Only High School Diploma	24.0	20.0
% of Whites with Some College	37.6	34.6
% of Whites with College Degree	31.6	38.8
Median Age of Whites	44.6	44.6
% of Whites in Owner Occupied Housing Units	73.1	67.3
% of Whites Now Married	53.1	49.7
% of Whites Never Married	21.4	25.3
% of White Women (Ages 15–50) who Gave Birth in Past Year	4.8	4.5
% of State Belonging to Union	6.5	18.4
% of Whites Below Poverty Level	9.19	8.29
Median White Household Income	$54,048	$69,224
% of White Workers Employed by Government	15.2	16.4
% of White Workers Privately Employed	78.2	72.9
Median Home Value of Homes Owned by Whites (2010)	$213,300	$444,000
% of Whites that are Veterans	14.6	11.3

relationship between education and vote choice among whites. However, there is a greater rate of home ownership among Arizona whites, as well as less expensive homes, higher marriage rates, and higher fertility rates among white women. All of these characteristics are associated with higher rates of Republican voting. Union membership, which was one of the more powerful economic predictors of white voter behavior, also differs dramatically in Arizona and Californian. Whereas 6.5 percent of all employed Arizonans were represented by unions in 2012, 18.4 percent of employed Californians belonged to a union.[55] California whites were also slightly more likely to be employed by the government, and polls indicated that Obama had a significant advantage over Romney among government workers.[56] While the median income for whites was higher in California, and higher incomes are generally associated with higher rates of Republican voting, we should keep in mind that the cost of living is considerably higher in California—the median value of homes occupied by whites in California was more than twice the value of white-owned homes in Arizona.

The important thing to note from this table is that whites in these two states differ on a large number of variables. While California is slightly more diverse than Arizona, and previous evidence indicated that more diversity (particularly a larger Latino population) is associated with more Republican voting, on virtually every other characteristic Arizona whites were more likely to possess attributes associated with Republican voting.

The fact that there is not an obvious, linear relationship between levels of diversity within a state and white voting behavior at the state level does not indicate that white political behavior is not at all influenced by demographic context. It simply means that there are many other variables driving white political behavior, and these other variables often have much greater substantive significance than local demographic context.

CONCLUSION

This is not the first study to demonstrate that racial context influences white political attitudes, and the subject will continue to be examined in the years ahead. However, at least in the data examined here, demographic context does not apparently have a strong substantive impact on white political attitudes—though social scientists should refrain from saying one variable is any more or less "important" than another. There was little evidence indicating that local demography strongly influences preferences on important policies. Where we do see statistically significant effects, the substantive effects are often small—for example, there was modest evidence indicating that a larger Latino population decreased support for government health insurance. White Americans also apparently respond differently to different forms of diversity. In no model presented here was there evidence that the size of the local Asian population substantially influenced political or policy attitudes. Of the racial/ethnic contextual variables, only the size of the Latino population apparently influenced the party identification and ideology of whites. The only time the variable measuring the size of the African American variable proved statistically significant was when the dependent variable was specifically related to African American government officials— the more African Americans who lived in a county, the more likely whites were to suspect black government officials of exhibiting racial favoritism.

The general conclusion we can draw from the preceding results is that greater racial and ethnic diversity is associated with higher levels of conservatism and Republican voting. But, for the most part, individual characteristics matter more than contextual characteristics when it comes to political attitudes and even attitudes about race—though, again, we consistently saw that whites in the South differed from whites elsewhere. The average white liberal is not going to become a conservative because one additional Latino family moved in down the street, nor is the average white Republican going to renounce the GOP after her African American neighbor packs a moving van. If there was a powerful relationship between greater diversity and conservatism and Republican voting among whites, then California whites would not be as evenly divided politically as they are. Instead, California whites remain comparatively Democratic, largely because California whites also, on average, exhibit a large number of additional characteristics associated with Democratic voting.

These results suggest that greater diversity will lead to a more conservative and more Republican white electorate. However, it is not clear just how much the white electorate will shift. Evidence from the GSS suggests that whites are increasingly unwilling to ascribe racial disparities to discrimination. These same data indicated that the correlation between these white racial attitudes and Republican identification is growing. It remains to be seen whether white racial resentment has reached a peak and will slowly recede or whether it will continue to rise. We also do not know if the relationship between white racial attitudes and white vote choice will continue. That may ultimately be determined by political elites. If the Republican Party becomes more aggressive in denouncing racism, for example, openly racist and racially resentful whites may abandon the party. Similarly, if the Democratic Party becomes less committed to policies designed to promote racial equality, it may bring some of these white voters back into the fold. On the other hand, if whites increasingly embrace progressive attitudes on race, the United States will reach a point where racially conservative policies have no constituency.

NOTES

1. It may be equally problematic to assume that non-whites will retain their strong attachment to the Democratic Party in the years ahead. Considering this issue is well beyond the scope of this project, however, I leave it to other scholars to make predictions on this subject.

2. White primaries actually ended prior to the Voting Rights Act of 1965 because they were found to be unconstitutional in 1944 (*Smith v. Allright*).

3. "Covered jurisdictions" are those states, counties, and municipalities that have a known history of discriminatory behavior. The U.S. Department of Justice website explains how this determination was made:

"As enacted in 1965, the first element in the formula was whether, on November 1, 1964, the state or a political subdivision of the state maintained a "test or device" restricting the opportunity to register and vote. The Act's definition of a "test or device" included such requirements as the applicant being able to pass a literacy test, establish that he or she had good moral character, or have another registered voter vouch for his or her qualifications.

"The second element of the formula would be satisfied if the Director of the Census determined that less than 50 percent of persons of voting age were registered to vote on November 1, 1964, or that less than 50 percent of persons of voting age voted in the presidential election of November 1964. This resulted in the following states becoming, in their entirety, "covered jurisdictions": Alabama, Alaska, Georgia, Louisiana, Mississippi, South Carolina, and Virginia. In addition, certain political subdivisions (usually counties) in four other states (Arizona, Hawaii, Idaho, and North Carolina) were covered. In fully covered states, the state itself and all political subdivisions of the state are subject to the special provisions. In "partially covered" states, the special provisions applied only to the identified counties. Voting changes adopted by or to be implemented in covered political subdivisions, including changes applicable to the state as a whole, are subject to review under Section 5." Accessed July 14, 2013, www.justice.gov/crt/about/vot/misc/sec_4.php#formula

There was a recent change to the Voting Rights Act: In June 2013 the U.S. Supreme Court in the case *Shelby County v. Holder* struck down parts of Section 4(b) that dealt with the coverage formula. The majority argued in its decision that because the formula was based on facts more than 40 years old, it did not have a sufficient connection to the present day to be constitutional.

4. There is also evidence that the deliberate creation of new majority-minority districts actually helped Republican fortunes in the South. By packing large numbers of African Americans into particular districts, neighboring districts actually became more Republican. For a thorough discussion of this possibility see Kevin A. Hill, "Does the Creation of Majority Black Districts Aid Republicans? An Analysis of the 1992 Congressional Elections in Eight Southern States," *Journal of Politics* 57(1995): 384–401.

5. While this legislation was surely the primary determinant of this low level of immigration, we should not discount the effect that America's Great Depression and World War II had on immigration. Even in the absence of these restrictionist laws, immigration may have been quite low in the 1930s and 1940s.

6. Daniel J. Tichenor, *Dividing Lines: The Politics of Immigration Control in America* (Princeton, NJ: Princeton University Press, 2002), 224–225.

7. Ibid, 173–174.

8. This quote from Kennedy comes from Vernon Briggs, *Mass Migration and the National Interest* (Armonk, NY: M. E. Sharp, 1992), 130.

9. Ibid.

10. Peter H. Schuck, "The Disconnect Between Public Attitudes and Policy Outcomes in Immigration," in *Debating Immigration*, ed. Carol Swain (New York: Cambridge University Press, 2007), 17–31.

11. Pia M. Orrenius and Madeline Zavodny, "Do Amnesty Programs Reduce Undocumented Immigration? Evidence from IRCA," *Demography* 40 (2003): 437–450.

12. Douglas S. Massey, "Borderline Madness: America's Counterproductive Immigration Policy," in *Debating Immigration*, ed. Carol Swain (New York: Cambridge University Press, 2007), 129–138.

13. Jeffrey S. Passes, "The Size and Characteristics of the Unauthorized Migrant Population in the U.S.: Estimates Based on the March 2005 Current Population Survey," Pew Hispanic Center, March 7, 2006, accessed July 17, 2013, http://pewhispanic.org/files/reports/61.pdf.
14. Jon Feere, "Birthright Citizenship in the United States: A Global Comparison," *Center for Immigration Studies, Backgrounder*, August 2010, accessed October 22, 2013, www.cis.org/birthright-citizenship.
15. Douglas S. Massey and Chiara Capoferro, "The Geographic Diversification of American Immigration," in *New Faces in New Places: The Changing Geography of American Immigration*, ed. Douglas Massey (New York: Russell Sage Foundation, 2010), 25–50.
16. James Gimpel, "Immigration, Political Realignment, and the Demise of Republican Political Prospects," *Backgrounder* (Washington, DC: Center for Immigration Studies, 2010), accessed July 16, 2013, www.cis.org/republican-demise.
17. V. O. Key, *Southern Politics in State and Nation* (Knoxville, TN: University of Tennessee Press), 5.
18. For the reader interested in the important studies working within this framework, the following would be good places to start: Hubert M. Blalock, *Towards a Theory of Minority Group Relations* (New York: Wiley, 1967); Herbert Blumer, "Race Prejudice as a Sense of Group Position," *Pacific Sociological Review* 1(1958): 3–7.
19. Walter G. Stephan, Oscar Ybarra, and Guy Bachman, "Prejudice Toward Immigrants," *Journal of Applied Social Psychology* 29(1999): 2221–2237.
20. George Hawley, "Political Threat and Immigration: Party Identification, Demographic Context, and Immigration Policy Preference," *Social Science Quarterly* 92(2011): 404–422.
21. Lincoln Quilian, "Prejudice as a Response to Perceived Group Threat: Population Composition and Anti-Immigrant and Racial Prejudice in Europe," *American Sociological Review* 60(1995): 586–611.
22. Gordon W. Allport, *The Nature of Prejudice* (New York: Doubleday, 1954).
23. Myron Rothbart and Oliver P. John, "Intergroup Relations and Stereotype Change: A Social-Cognitive Analysis and Some Longitudinal Findings," in *Prejudice, Politics, and the American Dilemma*, eds. Paul M. Sniderman, Philip E. Tetlock, and Edward G. Carmines (Stanford, CA: Stanford University Press, 1993), 42.
24. Allport, *The Nature of Prejudice*, ch. 16.
25. James M. Glaser, "Back to the Black Belt: Racial Environment and White Racial Attitudes in the South," *Journal of Politics* 56(1994): 21–41.
26. Jeffrey C. Dixon and Michael S. Rosenbaum, "Nice to Know You? Testing Contact, Cultural, and Group Threat Theories of Anti-Black and Anti-Hispanic Stereotypes," *Social Science Quarterly* 85(2004), 257–280; Marylee C. Taylor, "How White Attitudes Vary with the Racial Composition of Local Populations: Numbers Count," *American Sociological Review* 63(1998): 512–535.
27. M. V. Hood and Irwin L. Morris, "Give Us Your Poor, . . . But Make Sure They Have a Green Card," *Political Behavior* 20(1998): 1–15.
28. Ryan D. Enos, "The Causal Effect of Prolonged Intergroup Contact on Exclusionary Attitudes: A Test Using Public Transportation in Homogeneous Communities." Working paper, Harvard University, 2013.
29. Anthony G. Greenwald, Colin Tucker Smith, N. Sriram, Yoav Bar-Anan, and Brian A. Nosek, "Implicit Race Attitudes Predicted Vote in the 2008 U.S. Presidential Election," *Analyses of Social Issues and Public Policy* 9(2009): 241–253.
30. David R. Williams, James S. Jackson, Tony N. Brown, Myriam Torres, Tyrone A. Forman, and Kendrick Brown, "Traditional and Contemporary Prejudice and Urban Whites' Support for Affirmative Action and Government Help," *Social Problems* 46(1999), 503–527.

31. James D. Unnever and Francis T. Cullen, "The Racial Divide in Support for the Death Penalty: Does White Racism Matter?" *Social Forces* 85(2007): 1281–1301.
32. For a breakdown of past and current racial breakdowns of executions in the United States, see www.deathpenaltyinfo.org/race-death-row-inmates-exe cuted-1976, accessed July 26, 2013.
33. Paul M. Sniderman and Philip E. Tetlock, "Symbolic Racism: Problems of Motive Attribution in Political Analysis," *Journal of Social Issues* 42(1986): 130.
34. Ibid.
35. Symbolic racism is based on the "moral feeling that blacks violate such traditional American values as individualism, the work ethic, obedience, and discipline." Donald Kinder and David Sears, "Prejudice and Politics: Symbolic Racism Versus Racial Threats to the Good Life," *Journal of Personality and Social Psychology* 40(1981): 416.
36. Stanley Feldman and Leonie Huddy, "Racial Resentment and White Opposition to Race-Conscious Programs: Principles or Prejudice?" *American Journal of Political Science* 49(2005), 168–183; P. J. Henry and David O. Sears, "The Symbolic Racism 2000 Scale," *Political Psychology* 23(2002): 253–283.
37. Simo V. Virtanen and Leonie Huddy, "Old-Fashioned Racism and New Forms of Racial Prejudice," *Journal of Politics* 60(1998): 311–332.
38. Ibid, 329.
39. These questions were also asked in 1977, but because they were not asked again until 1985, 1977 is not included in the trend lines.
40. Specifically, the questions begin with, "On the average (Negroes/Blacks/African Americans) have worse jobs, income, and housing than white people. Do you think these differences are . . ." Respondents are then asked if they agree or disagree whether they are due to educational differences, inborn differences, or due to discrimination. Respondents may agree with more than one of these explanations or with none of them.
41. James Kluegel examined similar data in the 1990s and discovered findings similar to those presented here. He also argued that these trends have political consequences: "Judging by the findings of this research and by the current political climate surrounding policies to improve the economic status of black Americans, we seem to have reached an era of stable, comfortable acceptance by whites of the black-white economic gap. As long as white Americans blame blacks for their economic condition, they have reason to oppose such policies, or to withhold support for them in their private actions." James Kluegel, "Trends in Whites' Explanations of the Black-White Gap in Socioeconomic Status, 1977–1989," *American Sociological Review* 55(1990), 524.
42. A general rule of thumb when interpreting correlation coefficients is that an *r* between –0.2 and 0.2 indicates a negligible relationship or no relationship.
43. See Hawley, *Voting and Migration Patterns in the U.S.*, 16–19 for a discussion on the relative merits of counties as units of analysis.
44. The publicly available version of the 2008 NAES does not include county FIPS codes for respondents, and accessing these data requires permission from both the Annenberg Public Policy Center and a scholar's own university's IRB.
45. To ease interpretation of these latter two coefficients, these values were each divided by 10,000 before being entered into the model. This means that a one-unit increase in either variable corresponds to a $10,000 increase.
46. Nicholas A. Valentino and David O. Sears, "Old Times There Are Not Forgotten: Race and Partisan Realignment in the Contemporary South," *American Journal of Political Science* 49(2005): 672–688.
47. James H. Kuklinski, Michael D. Cobb, and Martin Gilens, "Racial Attitudes and the 'New South,'" *Journal of Politics* 59 (1997): 323–334.

48. It would have been ideal to include a variable indicating whether the respondents lived in a county in which African Americans had attained a major political office, such as county commissioner or mayor of a major city. Unfortunately, a lack of reliable data made such an inclusion impossible.

49. It would have obviously been ideal to code respondents according to whether they actually lived in a county or a municipality in which there were African Americans elected to prominent elected office. Unfortunately, the author is not aware of a high-quality and reliable dataset that could be easily merged with the NAES based on FIPS codes.

50. Alesina and his colleagues found, for example, that higher levels of diversity were associated with lower levels of spending on public goods. Alberto Alesina, Reza Baqir, and William Easterly, "Public Goods and Ethnic Divisions," *Quarterly Journal of Economics* 114 (1999): 1243–1284.

51. This may seem incongruous with some of the present author's previous work on immigration using 2004 data (Hawley, "Political Threat and Immigration," 404–422). However, in those earlier models the local context was interacted with individual partisanship, which was not the case in the models considered in this chapter. The dependent variable was also different in that article.

52. Michael W. Giles and Kaenen Hertz, "Racial Threat and Partisan Identification," *American Political Science Review* 88(1994): 317–326.

53. The demise of liberal Republicans and conservative Democrats in Congress is one of the more important political developments in the United States in recent decades. Of equal importance, though less frequently remarked on in popular discourse, is the decline of liberal Republicans and conservative Democrats in the *electorate*. In this author's opinion, the best book on the latter subject is Matthew Levendusky's *The Partisan Sort* (Chicago: University of Chicago Press, 2009).

54. With the exception of the percentage of the state belonging to unions, all of these data come from the U.S. Census Bureau's American FactFinder website (http://factfinder2.census.gov/faces/nav/jsf/pages/index.xhtml). All results were based on 2010 data.

55. See the Bureau of Labor Statistics for more information on trends in union membership: www.bls.gov/opub/ted/2013/ted_20130124.htm (accessed July 25, 2013).

56. Kellie Lunnie, "Poll: Obama Leads Romney Among Government Workers," *Government Executive*, August 21, 2012, accessed July 25, 2013, www.govexec.com/pay-benefits/2012/08/poll-obama-leads-romney-among-government-workers/57563/.

57. Marco R. Steenbergen and Bradford S. Jones, "Modeling Multilevel Data Structures," *American Journal of Political Science* 46(2002), 218–237.

Appendix 7.1 Multilevel Regression Model of Black Favoritism by Black Officials Scale

The models in this chapter include both individual and contextual variables. The contextual-level variables were gathered at the county level and include the percent of the county that was black, the percent Hispanic, and the unemployment rate. Because these models include both individual- and contextual-level variables, multilevel models are appropriate. Although the relationship between these independent variables and individual views toward the local community can be examined using a straightforward OLS or logit model, this is problematic given that the forthcoming models use both individual and contextual independent variables. Failing to deal with this hierarchical structure could therefore lead to the estimation of incorrect standard errors.[57]

	Coef.	Std. Err.
Conservatism (0–6)	0.51	(0.05)*
Republican	0.07	(0.17)
Democrat	−0.45	(0.17)*
Female	−0.41	(0.10)*
Married	−0.17	(0.12)
College Degree	−0.28	(0.11)*
Income Quartile 2	−0.64	(0.15)*
Income Quartile 3	−0.76	(0.16)*
Income Quartile 4	−0.88	(0.19)*
Income Unknown	−0.55	(0.19)*
Age 30–44	−0.25	(0.23)
Age 45–64	0.26	(0.22)
Age 65 Plus	0.89	(0.22)*
Frequently Attend Religious Services	−0.05	(0.10)
County % Black	0.02	(0.01)*
County % Hispanic	0.00	(0.00)

	Coef.	Std. Err.
County % Asian	0.00	(0.02)
County % Unemployed	0.02	(0.04)
County Median Income (Divided by $10,000)	0.05	(0.06)
County Median Home Value (Divided by $10,000)	−0.01	(0.01)
County Log of Population Density per Square Mile	0.08	(0.06)
Urban	−0.33	(0.23)
Suburban	−0.25	(0.22)
South	0.57	(0.14)*
Constant	3.23	(0.57)*
Observations	4468	
Number of Counties	731	
Log Restricted Likelihood	−11558.319	

* $p < 0.05$

Appendix 7.2 Multilevel Logit Model for Probability That White Respondent Supported Government Health Insurance

	Coef.	Std. Err.	Odds Ratio	Std. Err.
Democrat	0.77	(0.06)*	2.15	(0.13)
Republican	−0.59	(0.06)*	0.55	(0.03)
Conservative	−0.47	(0.02)*	0.63	(0.01)
Female	0.01	(0.04)	1.01	(0.04)
Married	−0.13	(0.04)*	0.88	(0.04)
College Degree	−0.19	(0.04)*	0.82	(0.04)
Income Quartile 2	−0.27	(0.06)*	0.76	(0.04)
Income Quartile 3	−0.54	(0.06)*	0.58	(0.04)
Income Quartile 4	−0.77	(0.08)*	0.46	(0.04)
Income Unknown	−0.56	(0.07)*	0.57	(0.04)
Age 30–44	−0.08	(0.09)	0.92	(0.08)
Age 45–64	−0.11	(0.08)	0.89	(0.07)
Age 65 Plus	−0.41	(0.08)*	0.66	(0.05)
Frequently Attend Religious Services	−0.12	(0.04)*	0.89	(0.04)
County % Black	0.00	(0.00)	1.00	(0.00)
County % Hispanic	−0.01	(0.00)*	0.99	(0.00)
County % Asian	−0.01	(0.01)	0.99	(0.01)
County % Unemployed	0.03	(0.02)*	1.03	(0.02)
County Median Income (Divided by $10,000)	−0.04	(0.02)	0.96	(0.02)
County Median Home Value (Divided by $10,000)	0.01	(0.00)*	1.01	(0.00)
County Log of Population Density per Square Mile	0.04	(0.02)	1.04	(0.02)
Urban	−0.24	(0.09)*	0.79	(0.07)
Suburban	−0.23	(0.09)*	0.79	(0.07)

	Coef.	Std. Err.	Odds Ratio	Std. Err.
South	0.01	(0.05)	1.01	(0.05)
Constant	1.42	(0.22)*		
Observations	15,200			
Number of Counties	777			
Log Likelihood	−8566.76			

* p < 0.05

Appendix 7.3 Multilevel Regression Model for Conservatism (0–6 Scale)

	Coef.	Std. Err.
Female	−0.248	(0.012)*
Married	0.215	(0.014)*
College Degree	−0.002	(0.013)
Income Quartile 2	0.017	(0.018)
Income Quartile 3	−0.005	(0.019)
Income Quartile 4	0.000	(0.023)
Income Unknown	0.111	(0.022)*
Age 30–44	0.072	(0.027)*
Age 45–64	0.085	(0.026)*
Age 65 Plus	0.156	(0.026)*
Frequently Attend Religious Services	0.567	(0.012)*
County % Black	0.001	(0.001)
County % Hispanic	0.002	(0.001)*
County % Asian	−0.003	(0.003)
County % Unemployed	0.007	(0.006)
County Median Income (Divided by $10,000)	0.037	(0.010)*
County Median Home Value (Divided by $10,000)	−0.009	(0.001)*
County Log of Population Density per Square Mile	−0.043	(0.009)*
Urban	−0.080	(0.032)*
Suburban	0.020	(0.031)
South	0.142	(0.022)*
Constant	2.000	(0.081)*
Observations	33425	
Number of Counties	779	
Log Likelihood	−49309.910	

* $p < 0.05$

Appendix 7.4 Multilevel Logit Model for Republican Self-Identification

	Coef.	Std. Err.	Odds Ratio	Std. Err.
Conservative	1.30	(0.02)*	3.67	(0.06)
Female	−0.17	(0.03)*	0.85	(0.02)
Married	0.20	(0.03)*	1.22	(0.04)
College Degree	0.25	(0.03)*	1.28	(0.04)
Income Quartile 2	0.39	(0.04)*	1.47	(0.06)
Income Quartile 3	0.62	(0.05)*	1.86	(0.09)
Income Quartile 4	0.84	(0.06)*	2.31	(0.13)
Income Unknown	0.32	(0.05)*	1.37	(0.07)
Age 30–44	−0.25	(0.07)*	0.78	(0.05)
Age 45–64	−0.46	(0.06)*	0.63	(0.04)
Age 65 Plus	−0.46	(0.06)*	0.63	(0.04)
Frequently Attend Religious Services	0.34	(0.03)*	1.41	(0.04)
County % Black	0.00	(0.00)	1.00	(0.00)
County % Hispanic	0.01	(0.00)*	1.01	(0.00)
County % Asian	−0.02	(0.01)*	0.98	(0.01)
County % Unemployed	0.00	(0.01)	1.00	(0.01)
County Median Income (Divided by $10,000)	0.07	(0.02)*	1.07	(0.02)
County Median Home Value (Divided by $10,000)	0.00	(0.00)	1.00	(0.00)
County Log of Population Density per Square Mile	−0.04	(0.03)	0.96	(0.03)
Urban	0.02	(0.07)	1.02	(0.07)
Suburban	0.05	(0.07)	1.05	(0.07)
South	0.30	(0.05)*	1.35	(0.06)
Constant	−3.26	(0.33)*	0.04	(0.01)
Observations	33425			
Number of Counties	779			
Log Likelihood	−16713.80			

* $p < 0.05$

8 Conclusion

This book was written to help shed light on political trends within what remains the single largest demographic group within the American electorate: non-Hispanic whites. The political behavior of this group in the coming years will largely determine the political future of the United States. This is not to say that whites are any more or less "important" than other groups within the electorate; in a close presidential election, small swings in vote choice within any sizable racial or ethnic group can determine the winner. However, all present evidence indicates that the Democratic Party is going to maintain its sizable advantage among non-whites for the foreseeable future. Given that minorities, on average, have more progressive policy preferences than whites, this is perfectly rational on their part. How whites will behave in the years ahead may be less easy to predict. Is 59 percent of the white vote the most a Republican presidential candidate can ever expect, or is there a possibility for further Republican growth among whites? While no study of this type can reliably predict what will happen in the decades ahead, the preceding analysis revealed a number of useful findings.

To begin with, we see that whites remain highly heterogeneous politically. Their voting behavior differs according to region, ethnicity, social class, marital status, and other characteristics. This is true of all racial and ethnic groups in the United States, but on key political variables such as vote choice and party identification, whites are more evenly divided, on average, than African Americans, Latinos, or Asians. While there are some states where whites are overwhelmingly Democratic and others in which the Republican Party enjoys a massive advantage, the same cannot be said for any of the other largest racial and ethnic groups in the United States.

Looking to the future, one might rightly be concerned that whites, feeling threatened by the greater racial diversity in the United States, will coalesce into a single voting bloc, leading to a racially polarized electorate. However, the degree to which whites remain highly heterogeneous suggests that such a development remains, at the very least, a great distance away. In fact, if we look to California, which presently looks demographically similar to what the United States as a whole will look like in several decades, that day may never arrive.

Making it further unlikely that whites will soon coalesce into a unified voting bloc is the fact that there are relatively few major policy issues on which whites are in near total agreement. While there are a few issues on which large majorities of whites share the same opinion, it is questionable that any of them are issues that determine vote choice. Further, on some of these issues whites are almost all united on the conservative side of the debate and on others they are almost all in agreement with the liberal perspective. Affirmative Action is hugely unpopular among whites. Whites also oppose increases in welfare spending, and a large majority does not wish to see immigration increased. There is also widespread agreement among whites that homosexuals should be allowed to serve openly in the military (a policy that has already been implemented), that there should be laws protecting homosexuals from discrimination, that Americans with the highest incomes should be taxed at a higher rate, and that more government money should be spent on education.

Although whites are not unified on many policy issues, the preceding analysis indicates that most categories of whites are, on average, becoming more conservative and Republican—this includes California whites, who actually gave the Republican presidential candidate a greater percentage of their votes in 2012 than they did in 1996 (53 percent compared to 46 percent). Certain gaps within the white vote are closing, and closing in a direction favorable to Republicans. White Americans descended from Southern and Eastern Europeans, for example, are no longer dramatically more Democratic than traditional WASPs; the gap between young whites and older whites in vote choice has narrowed dramatically in just the last four years. Traditional economic cleavages are also waning, as poorer whites are becoming less likely to identify with the Democratic Party. At this stage in American history, the political opinions of the wealthiest and the poorest white Americans do not differ radically, even though their interests clearly diverge.

The one economic cleavage among whites that remains strong is the union versus non-union divide. Members of unions were considerably more likely to support the Democratic Party—though they were not particularly different from other whites in terms of actual policy preferences. However, this cleavage is becoming less important given that union membership in the United States continues to wane.

While all of these developments are positive for the GOP, the party's steady growth among whites is not occurring quickly enough for the party to compensate for other demographic changes that are more beneficial for the Democratic Party. Furthermore, the GOP will have to win an ever greater share of the white vote each election cycle going forward if it is to remain competitive—assuming that the Democratic Party is able to maintain its lopsided advantage among non-white voters. We also see that the GOP's growth among whites, at least in terms of party identification, has stalled in recent years. The most explosive growth in Republican support from whites occurred in the 1980s and 1990s, but it has held relatively steady in the last decade. There was no evidence of an increase in Republican identification among whites between 2008 and 2012, for example—though Romney did win a greater percentage of the white vote than McCain.

The trends among whites are not all beneficial for the Republican Party. While the relatively recent and growing correlation between marriage and Republican voting certainly helps the GOP, it is problematic for the party that marriage is on a serious decline among whites, just as it is for other racial and ethnic groups in the United States. While most groups within the white electorate have become more Republican in recent years, this is not true of single white women, who have been trending toward the Democratic Party. For the Republican Party, policies that encourage marriage, and at an earlier age, would certainly be good politics—though it is not entirely clear what a successful pro-marriage policy would entail.

While this book was more focused on white political behavior than on white racial prejudice per se, this analysis would have been woefully incomplete without at least a brief consideration of the subject. It is abundantly clear that open and explicit expressions of white supremacy have declined markedly within living memory. The Ku Klux Klan has all but vanished; Aryan Nations was sued into irrelevance in the early 2000s; the National Alliance, once one of the nation's leading white supremacist organizations, no longer exists at all. Explicitly racist comments by politicians are far more politically deleterious than beneficial. While groups like the Southern Poverty Law Center regularly announce that white hate groups are on the rise,[1] these groups are apparently all but invisible to those not explicitly looking for them, and their activities seem to be predominantly restricted to the internet.

That being said, it is difficult to prove that these developments in reported white feelings on race are primarily due to actual changes in attitudes. It could be that white survey respondents are now hesitant to give racist answers to public opinion survey questions, even if those answers accurately reflect their feelings. Whites may also avoid open affiliation with blatantly racist organizations because they fear such affiliations will lead to their social ostracism and perhaps even threaten their livelihood. This is not to say that the most dangerous and intense forms of white racism have not declined in the past several decades—they surely have—but one should be cautious about inferring that we are approaching the end of white racism.

Although openly racist remarks by whites have declined, other forms of racial resentment, which can generally be expressed to pollsters without fear of crossing the line into open racism, remain strong within the white electorate. There has been relatively little movement among whites over time when it comes to racial resentment. While a high racial resentment score is not necessarily an indication of racism, it is indicative of a weaker attachment to egalitarian values and a lower level of support for government efforts to promote racial equality such as Affirmative Action.

There are other indicators we might look for to discern whether white racial prejudice has declined. For example, we could consider whether racial segregation in housing has decreased. Although laws enforcing racial segregation are now illegal, and higher levels of aggregate racial and ethnic diversity presumably make greater integration all but inevitable, across the nation our cities remain highly segregated at the neighborhood and census tract level even when they are highly diverse in the aggregate.[2]

Another indicator that white racial prejudice has precipitously declined would be a significantly higher rate of interracial marriage. Despite the declaration in *Loving v. Virginia* that anti-miscegenation laws are unconstitutional, and the fact that the current president of the United States was born to an interracial couple, interracial marriages remain relatively uncommon in the United States—far more uncommon than one would expect if people were equally likely to marry individuals of all races living within their communities. In 2010, fewer than 10 percent of all white newlyweds married outside of their racial group.[3]

A 2013 poll commissioned by NBC News and the *Wall Street Journal* asked Americans their views on race relations in the United States. According to this poll, 58 percent of African Americans and 45 percent of whites believed race relations were very bad or fairly bad. This is a significant increase from 2009, when only 30 percent of blacks and 20 percent of whites had such unfavorable views.[4]

The public's reaction to the George Zimmerman murder trial in 2013, which ended in Zimmerman's acquittal, demonstrated the degree to which Americans are deeply divided by race. Although not all whites supported George Zimmerman, and not all African Americans believed he was guilty of murder, the correlation between race and feelings toward this case was impossible to ignore. A poll commissioned by the *Washington Post* and ABC News indicated that, while 86 percent of African Americans disapproved of the not-guilty verdict, only 31 percent of white Americans disagreed with it.[5] If we compare reactions to this case to those of older racially charged cases such as the O.J. Simpson trial,[6] it would be difficult to argue that America has become any less racially polarized than it was in the 1990s.

Those looking forward to a day when evidence of white prejudice has disappeared from public opinion data will find little to comfort them in this book. Levels of racial resentment, at least as measured by the ANES, do not seem to have declined much in recent years. Perhaps even more importantly, the generation gap among whites when it comes to racial resentment is miniscule. This indicates that young whites—who have never known officially sanctioned policies of white separatism or supremacy—nonetheless are almost as likely to exhibit feelings of racial resentment as older white Americans. When we looked at GSS data over time, an increasingly small percentage of whites now ascribe economic racial discrepancies to racism and discrimination—though the percentage that blames these social differences on biological differences is also quite small.

This study had little to say about the future of explicitly racial politics among whites. There are good reasons for this. At present, there is little evidence that white nationalism or any other form of explicitly racial politics has much support or potential support from whites, even if they exhibit relatively high levels of racial resentment and other forms of prejudice. As noted before, it is possible that the dearth of evidence suggesting whites are becoming more racist over time is due more to a change in social norms and what whites feel they can safely express publicly, rather than an actual change in opinion on racial issues. That being said, even if whites become increasingly racist in the coming years, there is not presently an effective vehicle to channel that racism in a productive political direction.

While charges that the Republican Party and the conservative movement engage in dog-whistle racism[7] and other, more subtle forms of activating racial animosity among whites (such as the famous Willie Horton advertisement during the 1988 presidential election), there can be no doubt that the party's leading voices carefully avoid explicitly racist comments, and the party's expansion of its support among non-whites has been a perennial goal. Since David Duke's unsuccessful senate bid in the early 1990s, no major Republican candidate for statewide or national office has run on an explicitly racist platform. GOP politicians are now even careful to avoid employing staffers with histories of racially insensitive remarks—or, at the very least, are willing to jettison these staffers after such remarks are made public. Just months before this writing, Jack Hunter, an aide to Senator Rand Paul, resigned from his position after it was revealed that, during his previous career as a radio host, he had praised John Wilkes Booth and expressed sympathy for the Confederacy.[8] His resignation was deemed necessary despite the fact that he explicitly renounced his previous views. More recently, a GOP precinct chair in North Carolina was forced to resign his position after making racist remarks while discussing voter ID laws during a television interview.[9]

The increasing willingness to drive open racists from their ranks now appears to extend beyond the Republican Party to the leading organizations of the conservative movement. In recent years, there were a number of high-profile resignations from leading conservative institutions due to racist remarks. In 2012, *National Review* fired[10] one of its prominent columnists, John Derbyshire, for making racially inflammatory comments in a different online venue.[11] At about the same time it also dismissed Robert Weissberg as a columnist when it was uncovered that he had previously given a speech at a conference sponsored by American Renaissance[12]—an organization described by the Southern Poverty Law Center as white nationalist. The Heritage Foundation, one of the premier conservative think tanks, more recently dismissed Jason Richwine, a policy analyst. Richwine resigned his position when it came to public attention that his doctoral dissertation at Harvard argued that people from countries with comparatively low IQs should be discouraged from immigrating to the United States.[13]

None of the above should be taken as evidence that the Republican Party—both in government and in the electorate—and the conservative movement more broadly do not contain a large number of white racists. Indeed, much of the evidence presented here indicates that whites with less progressive attitudes on race are more likely to support the Republican Party. However, at this point there is no evidence that the GOP or the major mainstream conservative institutions have any interest in serving as vehicles for white nationalism or open white supremacy.

This brings up an additional question: If whites become more hostile to non-whites in the decades ahead—which is a possibility, although the preceding analysis does not indicate that it is inevitable—and the GOP and the mainstream conservative movement choose to pursue an anti-racist (or at least non-racist) platform, will these whites remain within the Republican fold? At present, there are no signs indicating a mass defection of whites, racist or otherwise, from the GOP. In a number of states, there was an openly racist political party running a presidential candidate: In 2012, Merlin Miller ran for president as the candidate for the American Third Position Party.[14] He won fewer than 3,000 votes nationwide.[15] There clearly is not a high demand for explicitly racial white politics in the United States at this time.

While it makes sense to speculate whether the Republican Party can survive as the "white party"—and a number of journalists have considered this question in recent months—it is also worth asking whether the GOP can remain the white party without eventually becoming more explicitly pro-white. That is, will whites remain loyal to a Republican Party that officially espouses color-blind policies rather than policies explicitly designed to benefit whites? A recent study indicates that white Americans not only believe anti-black bias has declined significantly, but an increasing number of them perceive anti-white bias as a greater societal problem than anti-black bias.[16] Will whites become frustrated with a party that concludes, after every loss, that it needs to engage in greater minority outreach? While it is unlikely that any white voter who is dissatisfied with the GOP because it was insufficiently pro-white will become a Democrat, it would not be a surprise if such people simply stayed home on Election Day. The low turnout among whites with high levels of racial resentment in 2012 may indicate that this is already happening.

On the other hand, the GOP's popularity among whites may paradoxically limit its appeal to many whites, and perhaps the Republican Party has already hit a ceiling in white support. Alex Roarty argued in the *National Journal* that an effort to reach out to whites, at the expense of outreach efforts to other groups, will harm the Republican Party among some white voters, particularly Millennials:

> But if the GOP determines that its future lies with an all-out pursuit of whites, it might find an unwanted surprise. Some white voters, particularly young ones, won't align themselves with a party that can't attract

support from Hispanics, African Americans, and Asians. To attract more white voters, the GOP, ironically, might first need to attract more minorities.[17]

Looking at demographic and political trends, there are four possible scenarios for the future of American politics. One possibility is that the United States could finally begin approaching a post-racial period in politics, in which larger numbers of non-whites support the Republican Party and the Democratic Party regains some ground among whites. In this scenario both parties remain competitive and racial polarization is minimized. This would be a first step in moving the United States in a direction in which race and ethnicity truly cease to matter, at least politically, and knowing whether a voter is non-Hispanic white, African American, Latino, Native American, or Asian American conveys no useful information when it comes to vote choice.

It could be the case that the Democratic Party's loss of support among whites has reached a floor, and support may even increase in the years ahead, but the Republican Party will be unable to break new ground among non-whites. In this scenario, the Republican Party continues its slide toward permanent minority status as changing demographics tip an increasing number of states into the solid Blue State category. While the GOP has a shot at securing the presidency one or two more times, once Texas tips into the permanent Democratic majority category, the Republican Party will be effectively locked out of the White House indefinitely. While political progressives may welcome such a scenario, the permanent, total marginalization of one party in a two-party system raises questions of the legitimacy of American democracy—even if the failed party can blame no one but its own leadership.

On the other hand, the Democratic Party's declining support among whites may have just begun, and white Americans nationwide may become as loyal to the Republican Party as African Americans are, on average, to the Democratic Party. A complete collapse of white support for the party would be devastating for the Democrats, despite the demographic winds at its back. A big increase in support for Republicans from whites nationwide would bring almost the entire Midwest into the Red State camp, which would bring in enough electoral votes to offset losses in the Southwest. With enough GOP support from whites, even California could once again give its electoral votes to a Republican. While such a scenario may be good for the Republican Party, it would also be problematic as it would indicate that American politics has become completely polarized along racial lines. The long-term stability of the nation is particularly questionable in this scenario, as Balkanization and even secession movements would perhaps represent genuine concerns.

Finally, the GOP may continue its slow but steady growth among white voters. In this scenario, the Democratic Party's advantage in national elections is probably maintained, but the Republicans remain a viable national party for many years to come, capable of winning congressional majorities and even the presidency when the conditions are favorable. While the growing non-white populations in states such as Arizona and Colorado represent a major challenge for Republican candidates, growing Republican strength among whites would be equally problematic for the Democratic Party in Minnesota, Michigan, Pennsylvania, and Ohio. In this scenario, we may see a realignment in which the Democratic Party comes to dominate the western portion of the "Sun Belt," but the Republicans successfully recapture much of the "Rust Belt."

While it is impossible to know how American politics will be reshaped by changing demographics in the decades ahead, the preceding study, as well as the literature on which it builds, allows us to make some informed speculation. The first scenario seems unlikely at present. The Republican Party's dismal performance among minority voters in presidential elections suggests that race will continue to be a major dividing line within the American electorate for many years to come. We should not overstate this, however. New Jersey Governor Chris Christie's impressive performance among minority voters in his recent reelection campaign indicates that a strong Republican candidate can capture a sizable percentage of the minority vote[18]—though it is too soon to infer that Republicans overall are improving their image among non-white voters.

The second scenario, in which the Democratic Party has already reached a floor among whites, may also be unlikely. President Obama's approval rating among whites, particularly whites without college degrees, dropped substantially between November 2012 and July 2013—according to a recent Pew Poll, only 22 percent of white men without college degrees approved of President Obama's job performance as of mid-2013.[19] The next Democratic presidential candidate may have a great deal of difficulty bringing these voters back into the party's coalition, and the United States has not yet reached the point where Democrats can win the presidency without substantial support from the white working class.

It is also unlikely that the millions of remaining white Democrats are going to switch their party affiliation en masse at any point in the near future. Barring any major exogenous shocks, party identification is quite stable for most people in most conditions. While Republican strength among whites in presidential voting and party affiliation has grown steadily since the 1970s, there is little evidence indicating that the party is on the verge of a huge breakthrough among the remaining white Democrats. The Democratic Party can probably feel secure that California will remain a Blue State in 2016, for example.

The fourth scenario is perhaps the most likely of those presented. Growing minority populations apparently encourage whites to identify with the Republican Party, though individual characteristics remain a more powerful determinant of party identification than contextual characteristics. The decline in union identification among whites will likely also continue, further bolstering Republican fortunes. This scenario maintains relative parity between the parties for many election cycles to come. It is important to note that there are reasons to be skeptical of this scenario as well. If the trend toward secularization and the decline of marriage continues, the Republican Party may find it difficult to achieve additional electoral gains among whites.

This book is primarily concerned with long-term trends, rather than ephemeral political or policy debates. Given that party identification is consistent over time for most people and not usually determined by any single political battle, this is not unreasonable. However, the future of aggregate vote choice in America will also be largely determined by the choices made by politicians. Even if it is conceivable that one of the two major parties could make massive new inroads among a racial or ethnic group, doing so will require considerable political skill. At present, the Democratic Party clearly seems to have an advantage in this regard. Shortly before this writing, the Republicans in Congress struck a major blow to their own image in a ham-handed government shutdown intended to block the implementation of the Affordable Care Act. According to the *Washington Post*, the public image of the GOP reached an all-time low in October of 2013.[20] Whereas it once appeared that the Republican Party had a strong chance of retaking the U.S. Senate in 2014, this seems less likely as of this writing—though any number of political developments may reverse Republican fortunes between now and then.

It is important to remember that current trends in vote choice and party identification, among individuals or major demographic groups, can only be used to make informed speculations about what the future holds. The choices made by parties and candidates are no less important to the outcome of an election than the findings of the most recent U.S. Census.

NOTES

1. A list of hate groups identified by the Southern Poverty Law Center can be found at the following URL: www.splcenter.org/get-informed/hate-map (accessed July 26, 2013).
2. Richard Wright and Mark Ellis, "The Racially Fragmented City? Neighborhood Racial Segregation and Diversity Jointly Considered," *The Professional Geographer* 64(2012): 63–82.
3. Wendy Wang, "The Rise of Interracial Marriage: Rates, Characteristics Vary by Race and Gender," *Pew Research Social and Demographic Trends*, February 16, 2012, accessed July 24, 2013, www.pewsocialtrends.org/2012/02/16/the-rise-of-intermarriage/.
4. Neil Munro, "Race Relations Have Plummeted Since Obama Took Office, According to Poll," *The Daily Caller*, July 25, 2013, accessed July 25, 2013, http://dailycaller.com/2013/07/25/race-relations-have-plummeted-since-obama-took-office-according-to-poll/.

5. Daniel Distant, "George Zimmerman Trial Poll: Disagreement on Verdict Split Down Racial and Party Lines," *Christian Post*, July 24, 2005, accessed July 25, 2013, http://global.christianpost.com/news/george-zimmerman-trial-poll-disagreement-on-verdict-split-down-racial-and-party-lines-100761/.
6. Polls taken at the end of the Simpson trial were similarly polarized along racial lines. According to an ABC News poll near the end of the trial, 77 percent of whites thought Simpson was guilty and 72 percent of blacks said he was innocent. William R. Macklin, "Guilty? Innocent? A Racial Divide on the O.J. Simpson Trial," *Philadelphia Inquirer*, October 1, 1995, accessed July 25, 2013, http://articles.philly.com/1995–10–01/news/25697504_1_simpson-trial-whites-nicole-brown-simpson.
7. In politics, a "dog whistle" is a message that seems generally innocuous to most people, but is meant to signal a different message to a particular group. Usually this refers to comments that will energize white racists in favor of a candidate, while allowing the candidate to maintain the ability to plausibly deny that there was a racial element to his or her comments.
8. W. James Antle III, "Southern Avenger No More: Rand Paul Aide Jack Hunter Leaves Staff, Returns to Punditry," *The Daily Caller*, July 21, 2013, accessed July 25, 2013, http://dailycaller.com/2013/07/21/controversial-rand-paul-aide-leaves-staff-returns-to-punditry/.
9. Igor Bobic, "NC GOPer Resigns After Criticizing 'Lazy Black People,'" *Talking Points Memo*, October 24, 2013, accessed November 8, 2013, http://talkingpointsmemo.com/livewire/nc-goper-fired-for-making-racist-comments-on-daily-show-video.
10. Rich Lowry, "Parting Ways," *National Review Online,* April 7, 2012, accessed July 25, 2013, www.nationalreview.com/corner/295514/parting-ways-rich-lowry.
11. John Derbyshire, "The Talk: The Non-Black Version," *Taki's Magazine,* April 5, 2012, accessed July 25, 2013, http://takimag.com/article/the_talk_nonblack_version_john_derbyshire#axzz1rJPlABLB.
12. Rich Lowry, "Regard Robert Weissberg," *National Review Online*, April 10, 2012, accessed July 25, 2013, www.nationalreview.com/phi-beta-cons/295729/regarding-robert-weissberg-rich-lowry.
13. Aaron Blake, "Jason Richwine Resigns from Heritage," *Washington Post*, May 10, 2013, accessed July 26, 2013, www.washingtonpost.com/blogs/post-politics/wp/2013/05/10/jason-richwine-resigns-from-heritage-foundation/.
14. This is now known as the American Freedom Party.
15. This estimate comes from David Leip's U.S. Election Atlas, accessed July 30, 2013, http://uselectionatlas.org/RESULTS/national.php?year=2012&minper=0&f=1&off=0&elect=0.
16. Michael I. Norton and Samuel Sommers, "Whites See Racism as a Zero Sum Game That They Are Losing," *Perspectives on Psychological Science* 6(2011): 215–218.
17. Alex Roarty, "Why White Voters Will Flee a White-Only Party," *National Journal*, August 1, 2013, accessed August 7, 2013, www.nationaljournal.com/magazine/why-white-voters-will-flee-a-white-only-party-20130801.
18. Mark Hugo Lopez, "Republican Chris Christie Captures About Half of Latino Vote," *Pew Research Center*, November 6, 2013, accessed December 12, 2013, www.pewresearch.org/fact-tank/2013/11/06/a-republican-captures-the-latino-vote/.
19. Nate Cohn, "Obama is Losing the White Working Class," *New Republic*, July 23, 2013, accessed July 30, 2013, www.newrepublic.com/article/114002/obama-approval-rating-polls-white-working-class#.

20. Dan Balz and Scott Clement, "Poll: Major Damage to GOP after Shutdown, and Broad Dissatisfaction with Government," *The Washington Post*, October 21, 2013, retrieved October 24, 2013, http://www.washingtonpost.com/politics/poll-major-damage-to-gop-after-shutdown-and-broad-dissatisfaction-with-government/2013/10/21/dae5c062-3a84-11e3-b7ba-503fb5822c3e_story.html.

Index

For Product Safety Concerns and Information please contact our EU
representative GPSR@taylorandfrancis.com
Taylor & Francis Verlag GmbH, Kaufingerstraße 24, 80331 München, Germany

www.ingramcontent.com/pod-product-compliance
Lightning Source LLC
Chambersburg PA
CBHW062022270326
41929CB00014B/2287